The State

KU-605-860

The idea of 'the state' has been at the centre of historical and political debates in recent years in Britain, Europe and the USA. *The State*, edited by Richard English and Charles Townshend, tackles the problems of defining and studying the state and the role the nation state has played as the basic political unit in Europe and throughout the world.

Featuring original contributions from a variety of disciplinary backgrounds, including history, sociology and politics, this collection concentrates on states in Britain and Ireland (within a European setting) and examines multi-nationalism within the state. It also includes thematic studies of nationalism, sovereignty, religion and identity.

The State offers a comprehensive survey of the whole process of state-building over the last two centuries and considers the contemporary state as well as supra-states (such as the European Union). Drawing on the current debates on secessions within the United Kingdom, this book analyses the British state today and its place in the future.

Richard English is Reader in Politics at Queen's University, Belfast. **Charles Townshend** is Professor of International History at Keele University.

The State

Historical and political dimensions

Edited by Richard English and Charles Townshend

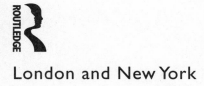

London and New York

First published 1999
by Routledge
11 New Fetter Lane, London EC4P 4EE

Simultaneously published in the USA and Canada
by Routledge
29 West 35th Street, New York, NY 10001

© 1999 Selection and editorial matter, Richard English and Charles
Townshend; individual chapters, the contributors

Typeset in Baskerville by Routledge
Printed and bound in Great Britain by Biddles Ltd,
Guildford and King's Lynn

All rights reserved. No part of this book may be reprinted or
reproduced or utilized in any form or by any electronic,
mechanical, or other means, now known or hereafter
invented, including photocopying and recording, or in any
information storage or retrieval system, without permission in
writing from the publishers.

British Library Cataloguing in Publication Data
A catalogue record for this book is available from the British Library

Library of Congress Cataloging in Publication Data
The State: Historical and political dimensions / edited by
Richard English and Charles Townshend.
Includes bibliographical references and index.
1. State, The. 2. Political science – Great Britain – History.
3. Great Britain – Politics and government – 1945–
I. English, Richard, 1963– . II. Townshend, Charles.
JC11.S758 1999 98-29174
320.1'0941–dc21 CIP

ISBN 0–415–15477–4

Contents

Contributors

D. George Boyce gained his BA and PhD degrees at Queen's University, Belfast. He was appointed graduate assistant in the Bodleian Library, Oxford, in 1968 and lecturer in the Department of Politics, University of Wales, Swansea, in 1971. He is currently professor in that department. He is the author of various books on Irish political history and Anglo-Irish relations, including *Nationalism in Ireland* (3rd edition 1996), *The Irish Question and British Politics, 1868–1996* (revised 1996) and co-editor (with Alan O'Day) of *Parnell in Perspective* (1991).

Steve Bruce has been professor of Sociology at the University of Aberdeen since 1991. He was previously lecturer, reader and professor at Queen's University, Belfast. He is the author of *God Save Ulster: the Religion and Politics of Paisleyism* (1986), *The Rise and Fall of the New Christian Right: Conservative Protestant Politics in America, 1978–1988* (1988), *Pray TV: Televangelism in America* (1990), *The Red Hand: Loyalist Paramilitaries in Northern Ireland* (1992), *The Edge of the Union: the Ulster Loyalist Political Vision* (1994), *Religion in the Modern World: From Cathedrals to Cults* (1996).

Bernard Crick is emeritus professor of Politics, University of London, and honorary fellow of Birkbeck College. He holds honorary doctorates from Queen's University, Belfast, Sheffield University, the University of East London and Kingston University. His many books include *In Defence of Politics* (1962), *George Orwell: a Life* (1980), *Political Thoughts and Polemics* (1990) and *National Identities* (1991).

Mary E. Daly is associate professor of Modern Irish History at University College Dublin. Her recent publications include *The Buffer State: the Historical Roots of the Department of the Environment* (1997), *Women and Work in Ireland* (1997) and *The Spirit of Earnest Inquiry: the Statistical and Social Inquiry Society of Ireland, 1847–1997* (1997).

David Eastwood is professor of Social History and dean of the Faculty of Arts and Social Studies at the University of Wales, Swansea. His recent publications include *Governing Rural England: Tradition and Transformation in Local Government, 1780–1840* (1994), *Government and Community in the English Provinces, 1700–1870* (1997) and (with Laurence Brockliss) *A Union of Multiple Identities: the British Isles, 1750–1850* (1997). He has published numerous articles on the development of the state and public policy in modern Britain, and is currently literary director of the Royal Historical Society.

Richard English is reader in Politics at Queen's University, Belfast. He is the author of *Radicals and the Republic: Socialist Republicanism in the Irish Free State, 1925–1937* (1994) and *Ernie O'Malley: IRA Intellectual* (1998). He is co-editor of *Unionism in Modern Ireland: New Perspectives on Politics and Culture* (1996) and *Rethinking British Decline* (1999).

Ernest Gellner joined the teaching staff at the London School of Economics in 1949, where he remained until 1984, becoming, successively, professor of Philosophy and professor of Sociology. In 1984 he became William Wyse Professor of Social Anthropology at the University of Cambridge. His many books include *Words and Things* (1959), *Thought and Change* (1964), *Muslim Society* (1981), *Nations and Nationalism* (1983), *Postmodernism, Reason and Religion* (1992) and *Conditions of Liberty* (1994).

Christopher Harvie is professor of British Studies at the University of Tübingen. He is the author of *The Lights of Liberalism: University Liberals and the Challenge of Democracy, 1860–1886* (1976), *The Centre of Things: Political Fiction in Britain from Disraeli to the Present* (1991), *Fool's Gold: the Story of North Sea Oil* (1994) and *Scotland and Nationalism* (1994).

Elizabeth Meehan is professor of Politics and Jean Monnet Professor of European Social Policy at Queen's University,

Belfast. Her main publications cover women's rights at work in the USA, UK and EU, citizenship in the EU and UK, and Northern Ireland and the EU. She is the author of *Citizenship and the European Community* (1993). Her forthcoming research is on British–Irish relations in the context of the EU.

Charles Townshend is professor of International History at the University of Keele. He is the author of *The British Campaign in Ireland, 1919–1921: the Development of Political and Military Policies* (1975), *Political Violence in Ireland: Government and Resistance Since 1848* (1983), *Britain's Civil Wars: Counterinsurgency in the Twentieth Century* (1986) and *Making the Peace: Public Order and Public Security in Modern Britain* (1993).

Acknowledgements

The editors are grateful to the following for their assistance with the book: Lorna Goldstrom and Ruth Dilly at Queen's University, Belfast, for invaluable technical help with the manuscript; professor Bob Eccleshall and the Centre for Irish Politics, also at Queen's, for holding the series of lectures in which the book has its origins; and Gillian Kay and Heather McCallum at Routledge, for their patience and expert help throughout the project.

Introduction

Richard English and Charles Townshend

The state is making a comeback in Britain. For many years it was barely visible in public thinking and talking about politics. It was noticeably absent from most academic studies of the British political system, and an authoritative account of the European state tradition published in 1980 held that in Britain, 'Little or no attention is paid to [the] state as a political concept which identifies the nation in its corporate and collectivist capacity', or indeed as a legal institution or as an expression of 'a new, unique form of associative bond'.[1] But just about that time, historians were waking up to the odd neglect of this concept, and there was, in the USA, an attempt to 'bring the state back in' to political science.[2] In 1995 James Meadowcroft showed that around the turn of the twentieth century 'the state' was a far more salient concept in British political thought than has been widely assumed.[3] It remains an odd fact that for two generations afterwards, and especially from the beginning of the Second World War through to the 1970s, it was almost lost to sight.[4] The apparent revival of intellectual interest in this concept during the 1980s[5] has been followed by significant calls for a redefinition of focus. The recent plea of one scholar that 'British history ... ought properly to refer to the whole process of state-building in the archipelago'[6] points in a direction which many modern historians have followed: towards a precise understanding of the interconnectedness of the islands of Britain and Ireland, and of the complicated relations between the various cultures found therein. In relation to the state, this is surely a vital development. The United Kingdom is a multi-national state, and one from which independent Ireland's secession is a comparatively recent phenomenon. Such reflections provide, in part, the rationale for this book. The volume examines English, Welsh, Scottish and Irish experiences of the state, within a European setting, and with attention also to key thematic questions concerning public order, political violence, religion, nationalism, sovereignty and identity.

Despite the differences made by supra-state units such as the European Union, the nation state remains the basic political unit in Europe, with states' ultimate priorities operating at the national rather than a higher level. Changes have occurred, and continue to occur, in relation to traditional notions of sovereignty. But these tend to increase rather than diminish the importance of defining and scrutinizing the state in its different contexts. Similarly, changing dynamics within Britain itself point to the significance of regional particularity, and therefore further underline the need to be precise about the state. The early modern period saw the south-east of England establish control over what were – when viewed, at least, from the south-east – the remote parts of Britain and Ireland. During that period the influence of Englishness over neighbouring cultures was more powerful than was the reverse process.[7] But it is important to appreciate also the nuanced redefinitions of our understanding of the state implied by varied local experience,[8] and in this sense the trend during the late-1990s towards regional devolution of power within the UK renders consideration of the state more rather than less crucial.

This Introduction will discuss definitions of the state, precision here being essential to clear-sighted analysis. It will then consider the distinctive approach and arguments offered by this book.

I

The battle over the definition and study of the state has been fought under diverse ideological banners.[9] The difficulty of definition has been so marked that it has led some to argue that the term is not in fact viable, its meaning too elusive for it to be of operational value. Certainly, defining the state involves the boxing in of an ambiguous phenomenon. But it also involves scrutiny of what is arguably the most important concept in modern political theory, and as such the endeavour remains vitally important.

Attempts to segregate definitions of the state as between the structural and the functional are likely, in the end, to prove rather forced. Any serious analysis of what the state is, in terms of its institutional structures, will necessarily involve reflection on the perceived, intended or actual functions of the various bodies concerned; and the reverse is also true. The state must therefore be defined with simultaneous sensitivity to what it is and what it does. With emphasis on the latter, one might suggest that the maintenance of order within a given territory be proposed as the state's most significant responsibility or function. This leads to the question of force. Certainly the state's activities relate to the maintenance of order within a particular community, and definitions of the state have long and often focused on force. In doing so they have frequently echoed Weber (the state successfully claiming a monopoly of legitimate force within a given territory), and it is undeniable that, externally as well as internally, force has been crucial in the development and definition of the modern state. On occasions, those defining the state have paid aggressively distinctive attention to the role of force. In Lenin's view, for example, 'The state is a special organization of force: it is an organization of violence for the suppression of some class' (that class being the proletariat under the bourgeois state, and the bourgeoisie under the proletarian). According to such a view, the battle over attitudes to the state was crucial to the struggle for freedom: the state was a product of the irreconcilability of class antagonisms, 'an organ of the rule of a definite class which *cannot* be reconciled with its antipode'; 'under capitalism we have the state in the proper sense of the word, that is, a special machine for the suppression of one class by another, and, what is more, of the majority by the minority'. The bourgeois state – which, whatever its form, represented the dictatorship of the bourgeoisie – was to be abolished through revolution. Under ensuing proletarian rule, class distinctions and antagonisms would disappear and the state would consequently wither away: 'only communism makes the state absolutely unnecessary, for there is *nobody* to be suppressed – "nobody" in the sense of a *class*, of a systematic struggle against a definite section of the population'.[10]

But even viewed from less ideologically determined perspectives, force has frequently been considered central to a conception of the state. The importance of the military in the formation and growth of modern states has often been commented upon.[11] Not only is the state an organization which controls the main (and the sole legitimate) means of coercion within a given territory, but the very origins of European states owed much to violent conflict. War required that rulers build armed forces and that they acquire revenue from their population for the prosecution of the conflict. The modernization of war, sometimes called the 'military revolution', powered systemic developments which were vital to the formation of modern states; war helped, at least, to make the states which were then able to wage it. Modern European states might rely largely on implied rather than actual force; but if the state is taken to be the guarantor of law within its territory, then the Weberian emphasis does identify one significant and distinctive strand of the state's identity.

Whether through force, persuasion or some other mechanism, the business of government is undeniably central to state activity. So clear is it that the state has to do with governance that the terms 'government' and 'state' are sometimes used interchangeably. This tendency should be resisted, certainly to the extent of distinguishing between '*the* state' and '*the* government', which are not coextensive. Rather, the latter is one component of the former, performing its executive function (while other bodies deal, for example, with its military, legislative, administrative or judicial work). A society without a state can, in principle at least, be a society with a government: humans governed themselves for centuries prior to the emergence of states, and certainly the nation state is a comparatively recent feature of human experience. But the modern state has been the framework for the autonomous governance of a given community, and the control of a population within clearly defined territorial boundaries. The logic by which these boundaries have become fixed may seem erratic – accidents of history and dynastic quirks jostle with geographical and ethnic pressures in the fixing process – but the units produced share one vital characteristic. The authority they exert has shifted from a personal to an impersonal structure of governance, which continues beyond those who hold its offices or those over whom it governs.[12] It has involved a set of institutions separate from the rest of society, enabling one to demarcate public and private spheres. And those who administer or manage the state tend to be recruited, trained and worked in a bureaucratic manner, specialized expertise forming a notable feature of the phenomenon. Rule-governed and public, state power has in many ways been bound by the constraints of publicly acknowledged procedure. Its continuous institutions of regulated rule have been regularized, bureaucratized and distinctively centralized. The state's relatively centralized institutions have been characterized by internal co-ordination, and by a necessary differentiation from other institutions within the relevant territorial unit. Thus the state has been marked both by a differentiation from non-governmental organizations and by the impersonal quality of its offices. Thus, while it is not only members of the government who hold power within the state, it is also true that the state's powerful elite does prioritize the process of governance. Institutions or agents of the state (judiciary, police, civil servants, military, parliamentary assemblies, as well as central and sub-central government) in various ways govern.

Another defining feature of the state is the impermeability of its territorial boundaries. At its simplest, it might be suggested, a state is merely a political unit whose institutions are acknowledged as legitimate by the people within a sharply delimited territory. For the term 'state' clearly relates not only to the institutions within a given territory, but also to the distinct political societies among which such institutions operate. From the perspective of international relations, indeed, it is this outward-facing dimension which is crucial to state definition. On this view, what matters are the external actions of a state in the international system rather than a state's domestic arrangements. In particular, the degree of independence which a state possesses in its outward action is plainly a key issue.

Such independence involves the issue of sovereignty; and external as well as internal aspects of state sovereignty are centrally important. Although the notion of sovereignty long predates the modern state, it is a key point that the modern state possesses sovereignty over a given territory, and that the state's institutions defend such sovereignty against both internal and external threats. The modern concept of sovereignty couples supreme legal jurisdiction with collective legitimation. In Britain, political power is derived, either explicitly or inferentially, from popular sovereignty, hence the importance of electoral mandates. The Western state has been notably marked by such questions of political representation, and they carry weighty implications for the issue of state legitimacy. As noted in relation to Weber's force-centred definition of the state, legitimacy is crucial. In modern states government has involved the definition, provision and administration of law, and the latter has both underwritten and limited political power. The state must be considered legal, with the strength and constraints which this implies. Supreme, exclusive authority and jurisdiction have been claimed by the state, and the support or acquiescence of people within the relevant territory have been underpinned by the notion of state legitimacy. The administrative and coercive aspects of the state are arguably the key ones, but legitimacy in the eyes of internal (and, on occasions, external) actors has been of vital significance in relation to both. For while law is ultimately guaranteed by a monopoly of force, such force is unlikely to be lastingly effective without consent – the popular endorsement of the state's legitimacy. This should involve not merely compliance through routinization or apathy, but rather an obedience which arises from the state being considered right and good. Something approaching *gesellschaft* (even *gemeinschaft*) – shared within the territory, and embodied through the institutions, of the state – is desirable. Thus, thinking about the state calls for thinking about communal meaning. If the state is to be able to legitimize and defend itself, then it requires both close identification with the law and also popular endorsement of what that law represents. Constitutions provide the framework for such legality and law-making, but the construction of public symbolism is a complex process. Emblems, traditions and institutions will be imbued with meanings essential to the state's satisfactory functioning, and the reconciliation of bureaucracy with implicit meaning is one of the key tasks facing the modern state.

The state, therefore, carries the following attributes: an independent political society (within a system of other such societies), recognized as exercising sovereignty over a given territory, and vindicating that sovereignty in the face of external and internal challenges; a political entity with the power to regulate individuals and organizations within its territory, successfully claiming a monopoly on legitimate force and recognized by its population as legitimate; an organization (or co-ordinated and relatively centralized set of organizations) with military, legislative, administrative, judicial and governmental functions; and a political entity relating fundamentally to the maintenance of order within its territory and to the business of government, with the latter role involving institutions marked by their public and impersonal quality.

Another approach to the question of definition might be to consider important phenomena to which the state is related, but from which it must in some way be distinguished. Four of these suggest themselves: the nation, civil society, the individual and the economy.

Questions of the state frequently focus attention on the nation and on nationalism. John Breuilly's argument is significant here: that nationalism should be read as political behaviour which makes sense in some of the contexts established by the modern state and modern state system.[13] Definitions of the nation and of nationalism are themselves notoriously difficult, and a considerable literature has emerged to dispute such questions.[14] But key points may be established at this stage. First, one of the central paradoxes of the nation – that of simultaneous universality and particularity – is echoed in the case of the state. Almost the whole planet is divided into states, and the state is therefore a practically universal norm; yet the essential quality of states (as the following essays demonstrate) is their individual distinctiveness and particularity. Second, while the dominant political form of the modern period has been the nation state, there are few entities which deserve this as a literal title. Few (if any) states have a population whose national identity is homogeneous, and which forms one homogeneous ethnic group. Nation states are rarely, in fact, just that. Indeed, one of the reasons why the British and Irish experiences are considered particularly instructive is that the advantages and problems of state and nation, not being coextensive, are especially clear in this historically unfolding case study.

The relationship between state and civil society raises further questions. The state–society relationship (characterized by one author as involving a process by means of which the two 'interact to disappoint and render each other miserable'[15]) can be dissected institutionally, with the bodies of the state (parliaments, governments, armed forces) contrasted with those of civil society (churches, social movements, trade unions). But the issue is more blurred in practice. What are we to make, for example, of an Established Church? Moreover, the dynamics are constantly, often speedily, shifting; and, even having established acceptable boundaries between the two phenomena, it is difficult to be precise about the nature and direction of the influence exerted between them. Organized interests bring to bear great influence on the state, and much has been written about the cumulative effects of this in liberal democracies.[16] But precisely how autonomous is the state from its ambient civil society? To what extent does the state serve its own ends? How significantly has the state–society divide been eroded by a reconfiguration or a dispersion of state power under the pressure of such developments as marketization and privatization?

In the nineteenth-century English liberal conception the state would act as a neutral referee between individuals pursuing their own interests. In the late twentieth century, the reconciliation of order maintenance with the protection of individual liberty has become an acute problem, and one which states have found difficult to resolve. Within the UK, such difficulties have been most conspicuous in relation to Ireland. In the Irish Troubles of 1916–22, and also during the post-1960s Northern Irish version, attempts to guarantee levels of individual safety have involved the state in actions which have seriously threatened personal liberty; these actions have also had the paradoxical result, on occasions, of giving sustenance to those anti-state forces against which they were directed. But it is not only in Ireland that the UK state has had difficulties in reconciling public order with individual freedom. During the 1980s, a series of perceived threats – by no means all Irish – was held to justify the acceleration of a shift away from public rights and towards concern with public order.[17]

The state ultimately relies upon the economy to fund its actions, and the enhancement of economic performance has become a distinctive expectation for the twentieth-century state.[18] As with the state–society divide, however, it is difficult to trace the interface between state and economy, or to be precise about the direction(s) in which influence is moving. The emergence of states owed much to the need of their rulers to raise revenue, and continued reliance on various forms of taxation directs us to crucial questions concerning the changing dynamics of the modern state. The state remains the largest and most powerful single economic actor; but has its role (in the UK, for example) diminished in recent years? The redistributive effects of taxation represent one of the state's major impacts, but how far is it the economy which in fact shapes the state, even in relation to such issues as the nature and scale of redistribution?

II

The contributors to this book come from diverse disciplinary backgrounds, each of which has riches to offer in exploring and explaining the state. We need not be deterred by the wonderful candour of one sociologist of the state, who observed that he found anthropology boring, did not understand economics, and found that political scientists had either tried to forget the state or in approaching it had frequently deployed an unappealing Marxism.[19] Twenty years on from those remarks, it seems clear that the disciplines of anthropology, economics, political science, sociology and history all need to be enrolled in furthering the study of the state.

There have been signs, as at least one outstanding historian has observed, of a rapprochement during the twentieth century between history and the social sciences.[20] But despite the mutual influence which this has involved, disciplinary frontiers remain; and it is the historical approach which predominates in this book. In part, this surely focuses on the notion of historical particularity, according to which historical events necessitate explanation in their own (arguably unique) terms, rather than in terms of general patterns. Such an emphasis offers a challenge to more general theorizing about the emergence or development of states. Indeed, consideration of historical peculiarity leads one to consider just how systematic one can be about the state while remaining accurate in regard to specific cases. This book concerns states primarily in Britain and Ireland; but there are no necessary generalizations from the experience of these islands. The suggestion, for example, that British state formation represents a deviation from the European norm[21] implies perhaps that there is more of a generalized 'state experience' than is in fact the case.

In particular, it is important to exercise caution in deploying general laws for predictive purposes. One does not have to endorse the entire philosophy of Geoffrey Elton[22] to argue that historians make their principal contribution to our understanding by their preference for particularizing, nuanced, contextually sensitive studies. These latter may permit maturely cautious judgment on wider, related matters, but they are not routinely presented as possessing predictive powers. Close scrutiny suggests that historical events offer an unreliable basis for establishing predictive patterns; 'While many people, especially politicians, try to learn lessons from history, history itself shows that in retrospect very few of these lessons have been the right ones. Time and again, history has proved a very bad predictor of future events ... history cannot create laws with predictive power.'[23] Indeed, it might be suggested that the kind of historically and geographically precise focus reflected in this book can allow one to reinspect wider hypotheses and supposed laws in a critical spirit. Attention to arresting theories – however illuminating they may appear – should not distract us from the importance of empirical enquiry and verification, or from specific historical experiences.

The historical approach will tend to be attentive to detail: chronological, regional, individual. The state will be disaggregated for examination. States are not always unitary actors, and their different sections frequently pursue dissimilar (sometimes contradictory) goals. To understand the state it is necessary that it be divided and differentiated: functionally, regionally and hierarchically it is a complex phenomenon, one divided into many layers and parts.

To the 'specificity' of causation, historians would add 'multiplicity': indeed, the complexity of the latter is what lies behind the former. With the state, as with many phenomena, multicausality is fundamental. It is not one but many things which 'cause' specific events, and it is in the unique interaction of forces that the key to persuasive explanations of historical developments is to be found. Grasping that events have multiple causes underlines the uncontrollability, by any particular actor, of historical outcomes. Recognition of this reinforces an hostility to inevitabilism and teleology which is reflected throughout this book.

III

How do the chapters of this book relate to the lines of approach to the definition of the state, identified above, and to the approach adopted towards it by historians? It has been suggested that disaggregation rather than generalization is helpful, and sensitivity to regional difference is crucial here. From what follows it becomes clear that the state in Ireland differed from that in Britain even prior to 1922. Moreover, diversity among regions within (as well as between) the nations of the UK state is important and has very long roots: the current fashioning of devolved government in the UK need not – indeed, cannot – be seen as entirely innovatory. Parallels can be illuminating (Ernest Gellner, for example, looking at Bohemia and Algeria with a readiness to hear Irish echoes); but they are as often helpful for what they demonstrate about difference as about similarity, and elucidation of very local detail is profoundly helpful in itself. This is ably demonstrated by David Eastwood's essay, in which he considers the question of whether English state formation was in fact characterized, as is often assumed, by early centralization, and by subsequent evolution rather than revolution. Eastwood argues that from the eighteenth century onwards the construction of the subject/citizen in England was (in contrast with Continental European experience) political rather than legal: 'the characteristic mode of discourse in eighteenth-century England was one in which rights, liberties and entitlements were bestowed on subjects by parliament'. At the start of the twentieth century in England, the basis of political orthodoxy was the doctrine of the sufficiency of parliament. But was parliamentary legislation an adequate basis on which to build citizens' freedom? Was there to emerge, in fact, a 'representative deficit' in English parliamentary structures? Certainly, as Eastwood points out, nineteenth-century public opinion was 'at best an imperfect check upon parliament's political primacy'.

As he demonstrates, the question of long-standing English centralization also requires qualification. He points to the profound dispersal of English power to the localities: local government and local political association were crucial parts of the story of English state development, and much policy was made in the localities rather than at the centre. There was, according to this innovative argument, a complicated division of labour, in the pre-modern English state, between local and central government. Yet when centralization occurred, in the profound changes of the second quarter of the nineteenth century, there emerged a language which failed adequately to reflect local dimensions, 'a distinctively English language of political representation, a language rich in parliamentary resonance but strikingly impoverished of any very potent discourse on the rights of localities, communities, regions, and sub-cultures. As the representative principle triumphed in parliament it entombed local liberties.' The theoretical impoverishment of the English state helped produce a strikingly limited conception of citizenship within modern Britain.

But might complacency and theoretical poverty be challenged in the context of the European Union and the process of UK devolution? Might the impact of the European Union on states and their definition be more extensive still? Are states being undermined, their power and role eroded, by global forces, or by supra-state developments such as those which characterize the European Union? Significantly, Elizabeth Meehan does not argue that the EU is a state-in-the-making, but offers the very different thesis that 'changes are taking place which alter conventional assumptions, have an impact on inter-state relations, and give greater international standing to sub-state regions than has been customary – all of which may have a dynamic potential to result in unforeseeable outcomes'. Unforeseeable – arguably uncontrollable? – changes are in prospect. The definition and the central activities of the state are changing, and the development of the European Union reflects these uncertainties.

As noted, the question of force is central to definitions of the state. Central to this book are case studies relating to Ireland, and the prominence of Ireland in a book on the state might be thought justifiable not least because that island has been the site of such fierce contestation of the legitimacy of state (and other) force. This has some ironic aspects to it. As Steve Bruce points out, for example, illegal pro-state loyalist violence in Northern Ireland rests upon the paradox that the state 'has an obligation to maintain its monopoly of coercion and thus to protect its citizens from the political violence of others'. Loyalist paramilitaries feel the state to have failed in this respect. But it is arguable both that the maintenance of public order has been the state's most pressing aim in Northern Ireland for much of the post-1969 period, and also that it is one which has been fulfilled more successfully than might have been feared.

The state must be related also to questions of communal meaning, and the contributors to this book offer telling reflections on one area in particular within which such meaning might be found: religion. Again, Ireland provides valuable material for consideration. Why was Catholic Ireland, unlike Scotland, Wales and Protestant Ireland, unable to find accommodation within the British state? Certainly, Mary Daly's essay demonstrates the profound influence of Catholicism and of the Catholic Church in the Irish state after 1922. But in different ways religion helped to mould the distinctive shape of the state elsewhere in these islands too. The salience of religion in Northern Ireland, so commonly regarded as entirely alien to British experience and attitude, is perhaps less distant than might be thought. Religion was crucial in the definition of 'Britishness' and has remained important to the state in certain ways, however often these might be ignored. Few Europeans would now argue the Zwinglian case that those most fitted to govern are Christians, or that prince as well as preacher should be a servant of God; but it would be wrong to forget the persistent role of religion in the development of modern European states, including those in Britain and Ireland. As George Boyce observes of late-nineteenth-century Wales: 'Welsh national feeling was closely associated with Nonconformity; and Nonconformity wanted the British state to deliver certain reforms, especially educational policies which did not discriminate against Nonconformists in the interests of Anglicans, and the disestablishment of the Church of Wales.' In a very different setting, and deliberately chosen for its illuminating contrasts, Ernest Gellner's Algerian case study demonstrates the profound significance of another kind of religion for the state.

If Gellner considers states and religions, then he examines also a third related phenomenon: that of nations. Other chapters explore this question in varying contexts. George Boyce reflects on the degree of compatibility between Welsh nationalism and membership of the British state. Indeed, could the vibrancy of the Welsh nation be better preserved within that state? Twentieth-century changes have meant that 'in institutional terms, Wales acquired more recognition as a special nation in the United Kingdom than at any time in her previous history'. Moreover, gaining power in one's own independent state need not lead to the achievement of all that one anticipates. Mary Daly suggests that Irish nationalists, some of whom did in fact obtain their own state in 1922, frequently evinced excessive confidence in the power of the state to achieve their desired goals. She argues also that the history of the independent Irish state is characterized by tensions and contradictions: change competed with continuity; British-inherited liberalism struggled against a more prescriptive Roman Catholicism; all-island aspiration fought against the 26-county political reality; and there was further tension 'between the naive faith that the state could determine a country's economic destiny and the practical constraints applying to a small country on the periphery of Europe'.

If such arguments reflect the complexity of states, their inherent tensions and the distinctiveness of each state's experience, then they also point towards the importance of economic choice for the development of states. Subordinating economic development to cultural, social and political objectives is hardly likely to encourage competitiveness, as the case of independent Ireland demonstrates. And the pace and nature of economic development are likely to help determine the relationship between nation and state. This has been true of nationalist and unionist Ireland, while the industrialization of south Wales had profound implications for the British Labour Party's strength there, and consequently for the degree of Welsh integration within the British state. Long Scottish, Welsh and Irish experience of forming part of the UK state – whether such experience was liked or loathed – has crucially conditioned those places, as it has England, too. To take but one example, independent Ireland inherited from Britain an administrative apparatus and a political culture which greatly influenced the Irish state's development after 1922. But what of the state as a unit? Bernard Crick argues 'that the United Kingdom has been from its origins in 1707 a multi-national state pretending, for the sake of internal peace, to be a unitary state'. He comments: 'Perhaps the theory of national sovereignty in its strong historical sense has had its day in the British Isles as elsewhere in Europe'.

By the 1970s a significant body of opinion had come to consider that there were deep problems in the British welfare state, that its costs were too high and that the benevolence of both its aims and its results was questionable. The moral authority of the British state has perhaps declined since the Second World War; and the dramatic extension of the state's powers is likely to find few advocates at present. All of this points to a reduction in the state's range and influence, and suggests that its commitments will decrease in number and/or weight. The cost of the state is surely the practical motor for movement here. To the problem of funding a constantly growing welfare budget might be added the difficulties concerning the rigidities or inflexibilities of the welfare state structures themselves. The neo-liberal charge that the state has exceeded its proper role – its overactivity leading to inefficient and undesirable outcomes – might be seen to have had its practical outworking in the process of privatization. The selling-off of public utilities in the UK was striking, but to what extent was it a sign of genuine retreat on the part of the state? It is arguable, with regard at least to the economy, that the state has been restructuring as much as retreating.[24] But are other forces threatening the state? To what degree does the multi-faceted process of globalization threaten its autonomy? How far does disaffection, in its various guises, demand something beyond the state; or does it seek in various forms a statist response? The latter might be considered more plausible in that part of the UK – Northern Ireland – in which disaffection from the state is most acute (and, as Steve Bruce's essay demonstrates, not merely among Catholics).

But there has undeniably emerged in recent decades considerable disenchantment with states' performance. And there are also long roots to the view that states will eventually disappear. Marx and Engels famously took the view that future communist society would be stateless in character and there are currently those who – in very different ways – also look beyond the state.[25] But just as Marxist states did not, in practice, wither away at all, so too it might be suggested that other kinds of post-statal order are difficult to foresee, in practice. More persuasive, perhaps, are the more modest suggestions that the nation state will find its dominance qualified.[26] And to the question of desirability (are the putative alternatives to the state more desirable in practice?) should be added the issue of how far the state is actually being superseded in the changes which are currently unfolding. UK devolution presents telling evidence. Does devolution in Scotland and Wales represent the building of new (and strengthening?) dimensions to the British state, or rather its demise? Christopher Harvie argues here that, from 1979 onwards, the gradual dissolution of the British state has led to a much more explicit nationalism on both sides of the border between Scotland and England. Will Scottish nationalism develop in the direction of independent statehood, with consequences clearly threatening to the British state? George Boyce observes in relation to Wales:

> The stage is set for a battle, not between nationalism and unionism in Wales, not for some last great struggle – or even little struggle – between Wales and England, but between those who see devolution as one way of strengthening the institutions of the British state, and those who see it as a way of weakening the state, which can best be preserved by injecting new life into existing institutions of the union.

We are perhaps dealing not with the death of the state but with a recasting of its contours. The demise of the state may be a long way away, but its relayering, refocusing and redefinition are already with us.

Notes

1 K. H. F. Dyson, *The State Tradition in Western Europe: a Study of an Idea and Institution* (Oxford: Martin Robertson, 1980), p. 43.
2 See P. B. Evans, D. Rueschemeyer and T. Skocpol (eds) *Bringing the State Back In* (Cambridge: Cambridge University Press, 1985).
3 J. Meadowcroft, *Conceptualizing the State: Innovation and Dispute in British Political Thought, 1880–1914* (Oxford: Oxford University Press, 1995).
4 J. Harris, 'Political Thought and the State', in S. J. D. Green and R. C. Whiting (eds) *The Boundaries of the State in Modern Britain* (Cambridge: Cambridge University Press, 1996), p. 15.
5 Intellectual debates here had wider political linkages. By 1984 one leading authority could claim that the question of the state had

become 'the principal point of contention in British politics, and in other liberal democracies'. See S. Hall, 'The State in Question', in G. McLennan, D. Held and S. Hall (eds) *The Idea of the Modern State* (Milton Keynes: Open University Press, 1984), p. 14.

6   S. G. Ellis, 'The Concept of British History', in S. G. Ellis and S. Barber (eds) *Conquest and Union: Fashioning a British State, 1485–1725* (London: Longman, 1995), p. 4.

7   S. Barber, 'A State of Britishness?', in ibid.

8   For sensitive treatment of the relations between governed and government in England, offering innovative attention to the nature of the state in the localities, see D. Eastwood, *Government and Community in the English Provinces, 1700–1870* (Basingstoke: Macmillan, 1997).

9   For a valuable survey, see P. Dunleavy and B. O'Leary, *Theories of the State: the Politics of Liberal Democracy* (Basingstoke: Macmillan, 1987).

10   V. I. Lenin, *The State and Revolution: the Marxist Theory of the State and the Tasks of the Proletariat in the Revolution* (Moscow: Progress, 1977 [1918]), pp. 8, 10–11, 19–21, 24, 26, 30, 36, 86.

11   See, for example, T. R. Gurr, 'War, Revolution and the Growth of the Coercive State', in J. Caporaso (ed.) *The Elusive State* (London: Sage, 1989).

12   For a precise consideration of the emergence of a recognizably modern concept of the state during the Renaissance, see Q. Skinner, 'The State', in T. Ball, J. Farr and R. L. Hanson (eds) *Political Innovation and Conceptual Change* (Cambridge: Cambridge University Press, 1989).

13   J. Breuilly, *Nationalism and the State* (Manchester: Manchester University Press, 1993 [1982]).

14   See, for example, E. Gellner, *Nations and Nationalism* (Oxford: Blackwell, 1983); E. J. Hobsbawm, *Nations and Nationalism since 1780: Programme, Myth, Reality* (Cambridge: Cambridge University Press, 1990); L. Greenfeld, *Nationalism: Five Roads to Modernity* (Cambridge, MA: Harvard University Press, 1992); A. D. Smith, *Theories of Nationalism* (London: Duckworth, 1971); A. D. Smith, *The Ethnic Origins of Nations* (Oxford: Blackwell, 1986); E. Kedourie, *Nationalism* (Oxford: Blackwell, 1993 [1960]); B. Anderson, *Imagined Communities: Reflections on the Origin and Spread of Nationalism* (London: Verso, 1983).

15   A. de Jasay, *The State* (Oxford: Blackwell, 1985), p. vii.

16   M. Olson, *The Rise and Decline of Nations: Economic Growth, Stagflation and Social Rigidities* (New Haven, CT: Yale University Press, 1982).

17   C. Townshend, *Making the Peace: Public Order and Public Security in Modern Britain* (Oxford: Oxford University Press, 1993).

18   P. Clavin, 'Economism', in A. Danchev (ed.) *Fin de Siècle: the Meaning of the Twentieth Century* (London: I. B. Taurus, 1995), p. 111.

19   G. Poggi, *The Development of the Modern State: a Sociological Introduction* (London: Hutchinson, 1978), p. xiii.

20   E. Hobsbawm, 'Has History Made Progress?', in E. Hobsbawm, *On History* (London: Weidenfeld & Nicolson, 1997), p. 63.

21 P. Allum, *State and Society in Western Europe* (Cambridge: Polity Press, 1995), p. 97.

22 Pugnaciously articulated, for example, in G. R. Elton, *Return to Essentials: Some Reflections on the Present State of Historical Study* (Cambridge: Cambridge University Press, 1991). Grounds for scepticism about parts of Elton's approach are outlined in Q. Skinner, 'Sir Geoffrey Elton and the Practice of History', *Transactions of the Royal Historical Society*, 6th series, vol. 7 (1997).

23 R. J. Evans, *In Defence of History* (London: Granta, 1997), pp. 59, 61.

24 C. Pierson, *The Modern State* (London: Routledge, 1996), p. 126.

25 John Hoffman, for example, has recently argued that in order to avoid possible extinction, to counter threats such as those of nuclear or environmental disaster, and to pursue true democracy, states must acquiesce in their own eclipse; he looks for a post-statal order based on common interests shared in an international society, and for increasingly stateless government founded on supra-statist institutions. See J. Hoffman, *Beyond the State: an Introductory Critique* (Cambridge: Polity Press, 1995).

26 See, for example, David Beetham's argument that nation state supremacy was based on the satisfaction of economic, military and cultural needs, but that it is precisely the nation state's increasing incapacity to deliver as effectively in these three areas which will cause the partial erosion of its dominance as a political formation. See D. Beetham, 'The Future of the Nation State', in McLennan, Held and Hall (eds) *The Idea of the Modern State*.

Chapter 1

The state we were in

Parliament, centralization and English state formation[1]

David Eastwood

It is currently a commonplace of politico-historical discourse to characterize the English state as a 'long-formed state'.[2] Viewing English state development from across the Channel, the great French historian Marc Bloc observed that England 'was a truly unified state much earlier than any continental kingdom'.[3] Gerald Aylmer has written powerfully of the ways in which elements of 'involuntary uniformity' – by which he means principally linguistic unity and the inherent geo-political integrity of a smallish island – contributed to England's precocity in developing unitary political, administrative and legal systems.[4] The present historiographical consensus is that English centralization pre-dated the elaboration of the Anglo-Norman state. James Campbell has recently assured us that by 1066 'England was ... a nation-state. It is highly improbable that any European rulers enjoyed closely organized authority over so wide an area as did its kings ... England had a system of government which was substantially uniform.'[5] England's early centralization and subsequent parliamentary development have been presented as an ideal type of constitutional evolution. In contrast to states which have been forged through processes of revolutionary upheaval, the English state, it has been argued, was the product of a sustained process of historical *evolution*. English government and English political practices have been modernized and developed through peaceful political evolution. This reading of English history has been highly influential within Britain and beyond,[6] though I want to question it a little later. Moreover, this English state presided over the first Industrial Revolution and went on to develop a very considerable imperial capacity. Given the importance of the English state both to theories of political evolution and to the shaping of the modern world, the history of English state formation is of more than parochial interest.

This essay retells the story of English state formation, but does so with a particular accent. The accent is on centralization. Conventional accounts – here perhaps best exemplified by Philip Corrigan's and Derek Sayer's richly suggestive study of English state formation, *The Great Arch* – argue that the English state was formed early and became centralized early.[7] At one level this kind of analysis is persuasive. Certainly, if we regard contemporary continental states as the appropriate comparators, the late-medieval English state was *relatively* centralized. However, in understanding the long-run development of the English state other comparisons may be appropriate, and may even be more illuminating. If we compare the pre-modern English state (by which I mean the state forged in the period from the eleventh to the eighteenth century) with the modern English state (the state constructed in and since the nineteenth century), then it appears that the pre-modern English state decentralized power more systematically and more effectively than has the modern state. This may be a story which deals in relativities rather than absolutes, but the relativities in English state formation are crucial.

The narrative of English state formation works in many different ways, and indeed operates at varying levels of sophistication. At its simplest, the story was one which every schoolboy used to know as a hymn to English liberty: a hymn which might begin by mourning the miseries of unfettered monarchical power, but only as a prelude to celebrating the palladia of Englishmen's liberties – Magna Carta, habeas corpus, the common law, Anglicanism, and the development of parliamentary sovereignty. Thus Lindsey Keir introduced the constitutional history of Britain to generations of students by declaring:

> Continuity has been the dominant characteristic in the development of English government. Its institutions, though unprotected by fundamental laws which safeguard the 'rigid' constitutions of many other states, have preserved the same general appearance throughout their history, and have been regulated in their working by principles which can be regarded as constant. Crown and Parliament, Council and the great offices of state, courts with their judges and magistrates, have all retained, amid varying environments, many of their inherent

attributes....Ancient institutions have been ceaselessly adapted....Neither in its formal and legal, nor in its informal and practical aspect, has English government at any stage of its history violently and permanently repudiated its own tradition.[8]

Like many narratives, this popular narrative of English state formation had an explicitly legitimizing role. From Edmund Burke's *Reflections on the Revolution in France* onwards, this understanding of English state formation embodied a narrative of difference. It constantly hinted at, or openly celebrated, not only the deep continuities but also the profoundly anti-revolutionary character of the history of the English state. If state formation in Continental Europe, after 1789 at least, was characterized by revolutionary discontinuity, English state formation was a process of organic modernization.[9] At the heart of these traditional accounts of English state formation is a central legitimizing concept – a concept I want to call the 'doctrine of the sufficiency of parliament'.

If English parliamentary history is rooted in the *general* conflict between crown and estates in medieval Europe, the outcome of this political and cultural conflict in England was quite different.[10] This difference is perhaps most apparent in the period of the European Enlightenment. By the eighteenth century, first the English and then, from 1707, the British parliaments had established a virtually unassailable constitutional primacy. In the major European states, the power and role of the estates were subverted by the political and administrative capacities of an increasingly capable bureaucratic style of royal absolutism.[11] By contrast, the early-modern period had witnessed a profound increase in the capacity of the English *parliament*. The English Reformation of the sixteenth century had been articulated in the form not of royal edicts but of parliamentary statutes. In the short term, certainly under Henry VIII, we should be careful to distinguish form from substance. The legal form of the English Reformation may have been that of parliamentary statute, but substantial political power continued to reside with the crown.[12] In the longer run, though, form can become substance, and the formal statutory power of parliament constituted the basis from which real political authority was developed. The symbolic and substantive apotheosis of the English parliament's long-run contest with monarchial power came in the Revolution of 1688–90. True, the Restoration monarchy in England possessed neither the fiscal capability nor the administrative resources of the Catholic absolutisms on the Continent, Louis XIV's France most notably. Nevertheless, under Charles II and James II the English crown was attempting to renegotiate the relationship between crown and parliament and to diminish the autonomy of the county gentry and municipal oligarchies. Restoration monarchs envisaged a quite different constitutional settlement from that which emerged in the 1690s, a constitutional settlement whose fulcrum would have been the crown rather than parliament, and whose ideological spirit would have owed much to Robert Filmer and little or nothing to John Locke.[13] In establishing annual parliaments, triennial elections, limited religious toleration, and a restrictive financial settlement, and in twice claiming the right to dispose of the crown (in 1689 and 1701), the revolutionary Settlement foreclosed the early-modern constitutional struggle in parliament's favour.[14] By the eighteenth century the central constitutional question was not whether parliament would succeed in achieving constitutional supremacy but rather the extent to which its authority would be subject to real constraints.[15]

Faced with the realities of royal power, the European Enlightenment developed a political theory which constructed the individual – we might even begin to say the citizen – as a legal as well as a political entity. The weakness of political constraints on royal power was palpable, and the residual political institutions of *ancien régime* states, however much Montesquieu might have wished it otherwise, offered few real constraints on royal absolutism.[16] Hence a theory of individual rights which relied exclusively on political strategies for defining and preserving those rights was simply inappropriate to the royal absolutisms of Continental Europe. Against this background, the European Enlightenment, most notably in Montesquieu, Rousseau, Beccaria, and the German jurists, began to construct the individual and to conceive of liberty in terms of legal rights.[17] The relationship between the individual and the state could thus be mediated, not through political institutions, but through legal forms. State power which was articulated in codified legal forms would be constrained by precisely those same legal forms. Viewed in this way, the eighteenth century constitutes a critical parting of the ways between Continental and English political culture. In England, first the subject and then the citizen have been constructed in wholly political terms, with the relationship between the individual and the state ultimately mediated through parliament. The symbolic acts in the struggle for English liberty had been chapters in a prolonged and ultimately triumphant struggle against royal absolutism. The instruments by which any tendency to absolutism was checked were parliamentary instruments: the Bill of Rights of 1689, the Triennial Act of 1694 and the Act of Settlement of 1701. That peculiarly English fusion, 'the crown in parliament', gave a theoretical dignity to this political victory.[18] Whereas Continental theorists privileged the idea of balanced equilibrium between institutions, notably the beneficial tension which Montesquieu sought to engineer between royal and noble institutions, English political practice sought not to establish checks and balances but to confirm the primacy of parliament. William Blackstone, in his *Commentaries on the Laws of England*, was unambiguous: 'so long ... as the English constitution lasts, we may venture to affirm that the power of parliament is absolute and without control'.[19] Edmund Burke similarly defended the unrestricted authority of parliament.[20] The only legitimate checks on the power of parliament were the self-limiting checks of parliamentary statute.[21] Thus the characteristic mode of discourse in eighteenth-century England was one in which rights, liberties and entitlements were bestowed on subjects by parliament. This was a mode of political discourse which admitted no notion of an individual's fundamental or natural rights that parliament was obliged to respect and by which parliament might thus be constrained.

If the eighteenth century developed the notion of the sufficiency of parliament in the vibrant but restricted language of Blackstone and Burke, the nineteenth century confirmed it in the popular language of parliamentary reform. Through the processes of parliamentary reform in 1830–32, 1867, 1884–5, 1918 and 1928, parliament established itself as the sole legitimate arbiter of its own composition and of subjects' political rights. The slow extension of limited political rights in nineteenth-century Britain was presented as an ideal mode of political modernization. Shortly after the passage of the 1832 Reform Act, Lord Grey told the people that the Act was the authentic expression of British constitutional reformism, 'strengthening and preserving all settled institutions of the State...preserving, and effectually improving, according to the intelligence of the people, and the necessities of the times, the constitution of the country'.[22] The combination of revolutionary upheavals and juridically articulated notions of citizenship might have promoted a more dramatic extension of citizens' public rights on the Continent, but the British alternative was, at least retrospectively, celebrated as organic, safe and successful. The tone of mid-nineteenth-century constitutional discourse can be gauged from the closing sections of W. N. Molesworth's *History of the Reform Bill*. With the passage of the 1832 Reform Act, Molesworth suggested, 'the dangers which menaced the state have passed away. The constitution has acquired a new vigour – tranquillity, contentment, security, and the wealth of the nation have increased enormously, and many excellent measures have been passed, to the great advantage of all classes.'[23] By 1918 the formal machinery of a democratic polity had been elaborated in Britain, but it was unmistakably a *parliamentary* democracy, with no permanent and few political checks on the authority of parliament. Thus Britain entered the twentieth century with the doctrine of the sufficiency of parliament established as the fulcrum of political orthodoxy.

The development of British parliamentary sovereignty has been predicated on a very English understanding of 'constitutionalism'. As Thomas Paine pointed out in *Rights of Man*, British political practice made no distinction between what was constitutional and what parliament actually did. In so far as the English constitution was described in terms of normative political acts – Magna Carta, the Bill of Rights, the Triennial and Septennial Acts, for example – this was a sinister form of sophistry which accorded constitutional authority to mere political or legislative acts. By contrast Paine insisted that 'A constitution is not the act of government, but the act of constituting government.'[24] In his insistence that constitutions are anterior to the establishment of governments and parliaments, Paine sought to constrain parliamentary power in two distinct but related ways. First, a real constitution, in Paine's terms, was the formal mechanism through which the power, and indeed the sphere of activity, of parliament would be constrained. Second, a constitution constructed in Painite terms – and here Paine was very close to the Lockean notion of a constitution – explicitly recognized that 'the people' had rights which were anterior to any rights which parliamentary actions might subsequently construct. In other words constitutions for John Locke and Thomas Paine constructed citizens and potentially other interests within the state – communities, ethnic groups, even property – as entities whose integrity and autonomous rights parliament and government must respect.[25]

In a related but distinct way, Jeremy Bentham challenged the idea of parliament's legitimizing itself by invoking the language of constitutionalism. For Bentham, too, constitutions were instruments through which the rights of the people were articulated and the domain of the legislature determined. But Bentham also embraced Continental traditions of jurisprudence which implicitly rejected the sufficiency of parliament as a guarantor of individual and collective rights. For Bentham the citizen was to be defined legally as well as politically.

> In regard to a government that is *free*, and one that is *despotic*, wherein is it then that the difference consists?...on the *manner* in which the whole mass of power, which taken together, is supreme, is, in a free state, *distributed* among the several ranks of persons that are sharers in it: – on the *source* from whence their titles to it are successively derived: – on the frequent and easy *changes* of condition between govern*ors* and govern*ed*; whereby the interests of the one class are more or less indistinguishably blended with those of the other: – on the *responsibility* of the governors; or the right which a subject has of having publicly assigned and canvassed of every act of power that is exerted over him...[26]

Bentham's central proposition was that citizens could not be said to be genuinely free if they possessed no defined and enduring rights beyond those bestowed from time to time by the legislature. Liberty demanded a guaranteed public space, and that public space could not be constructed through parliamentary legislation alone. To be free, citizens must enjoy constitutional rights of free speech, rights to freedom of assembly and rights to good government.[27]

Viewed from the perspective of the parliamentary tradition, Paine, Bentham and even John Locke emerge as strikingly un-English thinkers.[28] The authentic English discourse on the constitution is better represented by Burke and best represented by Walter Bagehot's *The English Constitution*. Evoking Bagehot rather than Locke, Paine, Bentham or J. S. Mill as the authentic voice of English constitutionalism is doubly revealing. In the first place it says something about the quality of mind of English constitutionalism. Second, it reveals that – to my mind peculiarly English – preoccupation with processes rather than principles. As is well known, Bagehot's account of the English constitution runs something like this: the English constitution looks like a limited monarchy, but it is in fact a disguised republic in which parliament has pre-eminent power; the English constitution looks as if efficient power lies within the chamber and theatre of parliament, but in fact the efficient secret of the English constitution lies in the composition and authority of the Cabinet; and, finally, the English constitution looks as if it delicately balances crown, Commons and Lords, but in reality there are only limited internal checks on the primacy of the House of Commons.[29] Now, as a description of how British government works, Bagehot's essay was and remains remarkably perceptive. Yet what is striking, and deeply revealing, is that he called it *The English Constitution*, but saw no need to discuss abstract constitutional principles. His work celebrated not the nature of the English constitution but its mechanisms. Opening his work with an explicit repudiation of John Stuart Mill's *On Representative Government*, Bagehot suggested that 'an observer who looks at the living reality [of the British constitution] will wonder at the contrasts to the paper description. He will see in the life much which is not in the books; and he will not find in the rough practice many refinements of the literary theory.'[30] Bagehot's frequent comparison of the British constitution with that of the United States never addressed Paine's central concern: the relationship between constitutional intention and political practice. Instead Bagehot frequently asserted that 'experience' – and here his language is authentically that of the English conservative tradition – has demonstrated the superiority of the British over the American constitution.[31] At no point did Bagehot identify very clearly whose experience he regarded as normative, nor did he seriously consider the extent to which citizens' experience of a given political system might differ radically, indeed might be fundamentally dichotomous. The arbitrary nature of Bagehot's construction of citizens' experience of the constitution is revealed in his attribution of such opinions to that other great proxy of conservative thought, the 'man on the Clapham omnibus'.

I have dwelt on Bagehot's analytical mode because it seems to me to have become the dominant mode of English constitutional discourse.[32] It has become the principal mode of British political journalism, and has spawned a class of *soi-disant* political and academic mechanics, solemn and largely self-appointed 'constitutional experts'. These 'constitutional experts' are the academic courtiers of the British constitution, duly explaining to citizens and electors its deep mysteries, its great antiquity and its apparent capacity. To be sure, they often do so late at night on BBC2 when many citizens are asleep, and those who are awake are generally watching movies or sport on other channels. But, as Bagehot might have told us, the great thing is that they are there, assuring us that the English constitution is still working, and solemnly warning the more hot-headed members of the chattering classes against dangerous tampering with its delicate mechanisms. True, many, although by no means all, 'constitutional experts' do see some scope for a very modest refurbishment of the British constitution, a little gentle proportional representation here, a reformed but still genteel second chamber there, devolved but carefully circumscribed assemblies in Celtic Britain, and some will even entertain the possibility of a Bill of Rights. Now, one should not deride all this: some such changes are desirable, and almost certainly would make Britain's political structures more democratically sensitive. But there is nothing here which can be described as in any real sense *radical*. Refurbishment of the constitution was admitted as necessary by Burke, and was reluctantly conceded as inevitable by Bagehot; while parliamentary reform was sponsored or abetted by such authentic conservatives as the Marquis of Blandford in 1830–1, Lord Derby in 1859, Benjamin Disraeli in 1866, Lord Salisbury in 1884–5, and Stanley Baldwin in 1928. Even when articulated in the modern and programmatic form of Charter '88, this language of parliamentary reform is far from being a language of political radicalism. Indeed in so far as these kinds of reformist discourses are committed to parliamentary means and to parliamentary reform, they tend to reaffirm rather than challenge the doctrine of the sufficiency of parliament. Their avowed objective is to render parliament 'more representative', and, in adopting this easiest of democratic clichés, they do not pause to ask the more fundamental, the more constitutionally disturbing, question: to what extent can parliamentary sovereignty be regarded as a sufficient representation of citizens' rights and democratic debate? If we concede that there is a representative deficit in our present parliamentary structures, might we not need to ask rather searching questions about the ways in which power is distributed, and exercised, within the British state?

If we are to explain the centralization of the English state, the doctrine of the sufficiency of parliament is pivotal. The centralization of power has been legitimized in terms of the sovereignty and political capacity of parliament. In so far as Bagehot had a definition of underlying constitutional principles, it was the doctrine of the sufficiency of parliament *toute simple*. 'The English Constitution, in a word, is framed on the principle of choosing a single sovereign authority, and making it good.'[33] Here Bagehot's 'making it good' is a serious – and in some ways sinister – gloss on the pattern of development of the modern English state. From the 1830s onwards, making a single sovereign authority work has consisted in large measure in eliminating traditional checks on the power and political authority of parliament.

This takes us back to the notion of England as 'a long-formed state'. Most narratives of English state formation, even those embodying a high degree of empirical sophistication, construe the story of state formation in terms of a powerfully articulated parliamentarianism. Parliament is accorded a privileged position both as the agent of liberalization and the agent of modernization. The transition from feudal authoritarianism to representative liberty is, *par excellence*, a story about parliament.[34] As we have seen, parliament's apparent ability to reform itself in the nineteenth century made it not only the theatre in which competing representative visions could be contested but actually the agent and symbol of political modernization. After The Great Reform Act of 1832 a confident and self-consciously *reformed* parliament claimed the authority to remodel other public institutions after its own image.[35] The monothematic, one might even say impoverished, language of English constitutionalism offered few grounds upon which the sovereignty of parliament might be challenged, and none from which it might effectively be checked. The Chartists in the late 1830s and early 1840s protested that much of the legislation passed by the reformed parliament in the 1830s was 'unconstitutional', but they protested in vain, not simply because they lacked physical force but also because they were seeking to indict as 'unconstitutional' legislation enacted by a parliament which was utterly convinced of its constitutional legitimacy.[36] The Chartists may have secured over two million signatures to their petition of 1842, but men such as Lord John Russell and Thomas Babington Macaulay, men who had been enthusiasts for parliamentary reform in 1831–2, were equally passionate in their refusal even to consider the Chartist petitioners a decade later.[37] Nothing did more than the Great Reform Act to convince English Whiggism that it was the only authentic language of English constitutionalism. The 1832 Reform Act may have been the consequence of the political victory of English Whiggism in the

House of Commons, but it was presented symbolically as a redefinition of the English political nation. Thus G. M. Trevelyan concluded that 'the Reform Bill ... had asserted the power of the whole nation, enfranchised and unenfranchised, because it had been carried by the popular will'.[38] The Whiggish defence of the English constitution rested on its assumption that, in some deep and real sense, the constitution – at least as mediated through the Whig/Liberal Party – was a popular constitution. This assumption was most frequently articulated in the suggestion that parliament was receptive to public opinion, emphatically expressed. But the advance in the power of public opinion was at best uncertain. For every jubilant member of the Anti-Corn Law League there were three or four disappointed Chartists. For every advocate of civil service reform there were several frustrated and legally disadvantaged trades unionists. And for every elector who celebrated his acquisition of the franchise in 1832 or 1867 there were more who wondered at their continued exclusion from electoral processes. Parliament may have been sensitive to certain strains in public opinion, but it was hardly dominated by them. In short, while public opinion might have influenced parliament, it was at best an imperfect check upon parliament's political primacy. Moreover, by a deep irony, the autonomous power of public opinion could be diminished by the progressive extension of the franchise. The essence of the British parliamentary system lies in its insistence that the will of the electorate, however imperfectly expressed, is the pre-eminent statement of the popular will. From the nineteenth-century notion of the 'mandate' of governments to the twentieth-century politician's cliché that 'the only poll which matters is the General Election', the tendency of parliamentary rhetoric has been to narrow rather than to enhance the formal space for public opinion within the framework of the constitution.[39]

If we examine the distribution of power within the pre-modern English state, we can see a striking paradox. From the Norman Conquest onwards – and arguably even before the middle of the eleventh century – power was formally constructed around and legitimized through the person of the king. Government, justice and policy were formally grounded in the will of the king. Yet from this highly centralized governmental idiom power was systematically dispersed, through sheriffs, justices of the peace and coroners; through the lord-lieutenancies, the incorporation of boroughs and the quarter sessions; and through the devolution of judicial, fiscal and administrative authority. In short, the English crown elaborated an infrastructure which not only governed the localities but did so in a way which gave considerable discretion to individual officials and substantial autonomy to counties, boroughs and parishes. The pattern of government which emerged is best described as 'local government at the king's command', within which patterns of power were to an important extent negotiated between royal authority and local governing elites.[40] Now, it is important that we do not exaggerate the formal stability of this pre-modern distribution of power. What the king gave, the king could take back. There were medieval instruments which attempted to mediate the relationship between king and subjects, between kingly power and the rights of royal agents, but these were weak instruments. Coronation oaths used both legal and rhetorical forms to situate kingly power between divine authority on the one hand and traditional political forms on the other.[41] If coronation oaths offered one formal mechanism for articulating a distribution of power, then custom, practice, and the English common law offered perhaps the more potent means of codifying political and administrative relationships within the English polity.[42]

Although relationships within the later medieval polity were shaped by statute, custom and practicality, they were also contested. Indeed the contestation of authority between king and localities became a *leitmotif* of late-medieval England. The struggle for local rights was prominent in the political contest which culminated in Magna Carta in 1215. Yet even this did not resolve the issue, as Magna Carta was reissued in 1216, 1217, 1225 and 1237 – reissues which testified to a continuing struggle between royal and baronial power and the Carta's utility as an instrument of constitutional arbitration. Moreover, the claims of localities and of locally constructed networks of political power were crucial in the Baronial Rebellion of 1258–65, to the political struggles under Edward II and in the systemic upheavals of the fifteenth century.[43] Civil war may be the most brutal theatre in which power relations can be contested, but it is not necessarily the most conclusive, and in the sixteenth century parliament came to offer a more subtle context in which power could be contested.[44]

In terms of the history of the English state, the outcome of the constitutional and political struggles of the later medieval period is profoundly important and conceptually complex. Perhaps a modern historian should have the humility to withhold comment, but an understanding of long-run historical developments is central to the understanding of English state formation. In terms of the historical evolution of state structures the continuity of the formal structures of power in the localities is crucial. Justices of the peace became increasingly involved in local administration, extending the sphere of their discretionary power, while urban communities used incorporated powers and royal privileges to define an urban political space within which local authorities enjoyed similar discretionary power. Thus local government at the king's command created increasingly elaborate structures of administration which themselves served to disperse rather than concentrate power within the English polity, while simultaneously nurturing habits of local government and powerful forms of local political association. Local elites came to expect to exercise local power. The duty of service to the crown over time led to the development of a tensely contested equilibrium between the authority of the crown and the political ambitions of the landed class.[45] It was out of precisely this dialectic that the English gentry was born.

The English gentry was a ruling class *par excellence*.[46] Not, it is true, a ruling class in the manner of European nobilities, who defined their status initially in terms of political and personal proximity to the king and later in terms of formal legal privilege.[47] The English gentry never enjoyed formal privileges. In law they were commoners, and in practice their status was dependent upon their ownership of modest landed estates (typically perhaps 2,000–5,000 acres). Culturally and economically the world of the gentry was the world of the county. This cultural affinity with the county enabled the gentry to colonize and then monopolize the political institutions of the county: the magistracy, the commission of the peace, the office of sheriff, and the grand juries of presentment. Local landownership, fierce local patriotism and a monopoly on the major offices of local government were mutually reinforcing. Tocqueville captured both the essence and the nuance of the social history of landed political authority: 'Great territorial properties localize, if we may so speak, the influence of wealth; and forcing it to exert itself always in the same place and over the same persons, give it by that means a more intense and a more permanent character.'[48]

Thus the institutions which decentralized power in pre-modern England had their roots in local government at the king's command, but these institutions had become aristocratic rather than royal in character. To this extent Montesquieu's sense of the dynamics of the pre-modern English constitution was right: the crown, and latterly the crown in parliament, focused power; aristocratic institutions and the political culture of the gentry dispersed it.[49]

Expressed in these terms, patterns of decentralization in pre-modern England might appear to have been little more than constitutional curiosities or theoretical abstractions. Here again, though, form and substance are linked; in this case I want to suggest that there is a profound connection between, on the one hand, institutional structures which devolved political power and the political culture which animated them, and, on the other, the day-to-day distribution of power within the English polity. Crucially, the manner in which the crown ceded power to a landed elite demystified power. Land came both to denominate and to legitimize political power. By the eighteenth century both central and local government could legitimize their power in terms of the political prerogatives of land. Locke, Bolingbroke, Blackstone, Burke and Coleridge, and a host of lesser writers in different ways asserted the political primacy of property and accorded a special status to landed property.[50]

Moreover, in crucial areas, policy was made not at the centre but in the localities. In this sense, the devolution was as much of political as of administrative power. Until its remodelling in 1834, responsibility for poor-law policy lay with magistrates and parish vestries, with the parameters of policy being established by magistrates in quarter sessions and day-to-day implementation of policy being in the hands of the vestries and parish overseers. The poor law was, perhaps, the dominant social institution in eighteenth- and early-nineteenth-century England. It defined a huge network of entitlements, and it distinguished between the respectable and the feckless, the deserving and the undeserving, and the independent and the dependent. By 1818 some £8 million was being spent on poor relief – 13 per cent of total public expenditure. The decentralization of power was predicated on a decentralization of fiscal responsibility, and the poor law was funded wholly through local rates. Ratepayers enjoyed rights of local political participation, having the right to attend parish vestry meetings in person and the right to vote for local officials, most notably the overseers of the poor. Rates were voted by ratepayers and collected by the officials they elected. The discretionary power of magistrates over social policy was well exemplified in 1795 when they authorized a system of income supplements via the poor law. In the same year in which parliament threw out Samuel Whitbread's Minimum Wage Bill as an affront to the delicate sensibilities of market mechanisms, the magistrates in southern England agreed on tables of minimum family incomes, and ensured that those falling below these levels, whether in work or unemployed, received income supplements through vastly increased levels of local taxation.[51]

Simultaneously magistrates were embarking on a great penal experiment. If England played its part in Foucault's great confinement, this was, in substantial measure, the result of magistrates' decisions to remodel the penal system and move towards the construction of penitentiaries rather than rely on capital punishment, transportation and corporal punishment. Magistrates rather than ministers developed penal theories based around Enlightenment notions of the reformability of the criminal within a carefully constructed corrective environment. In the period between 1770 and the late 1830s magistrates authorized hugely inflated county rates in order to finance the creation of a national system of county gaols. As a result, annual county rates which had averaged around £225,000 in the early 1790s exceeded £700,000 in the late 1830s. Moreover, when parliamentary committees investigated the state of prisons and punishment, in 1810–11 and in 1819, the leading witnesses and acknowledged experts were not men such as Bentham, peddling his retrospectively celebrated panoptican scheme, but men such as the gloriously named Sir George Onesiphorous Paul, a leading Gloucestershire magistrate and prison reformer. In a similar vein the new prison to serve Manchester was known as the 'New Bayley' after Thomas Butterworth Bayley, the chairman of the Salford quarter sessions, on whose energy and inspiration the whole project had rested.[52]

If we recognize the gentleman magistrate of Hanoverian England as a leading architect of Foucauldian modernity, then we recognize something of crucial importance in England's state formation. The social basis of power within the pre-modern English state, notably the role of landed property as the denominator of power, facilitated a division of labour between central and local government. MPs and JPs were drawn from the same social class, sometimes indeed were the same people, but when acting as justices of the peace they did so as locally resident ruling elites. Nineteenth-century radicals were fond of pointing out that the magistracy was elected by nobody and accountable to nobody.[53] In terms of representation they were indeed both unaccountable and irresponsible. But the language of political legitimation in pre-modern England was not a language of representation but a language of social power. Land defined governing elites. This aristocratic principle of power underpinned an elaborate and capable structure of local, traditional and voluntary institutions through which power was devolved from the centre to the localities. This complex of political and public institutions, animated by an aristocratic political culture, was memorably and accurately characterized by Disraeli as 'the territorial constitution of England'.[54]

To its defenders the aristocratic principle within the English constitution had played a crucial role in inhibiting the disposition to centralization. For men such as Disraeli, the principle of centralization was sinister because it was abstract. It conceived of power and power relations not in real terms – such as the balancing of landed interests – but in ideal terms. From a quite different tradition, Alexis de Tocqueville, travelling in these islands in 1833 and 1835, saw both the compelling power of the centralizing principle and the effectiveness of English aristocratic institutions in impeding the centralizing disposition: his 'lucky obstacles' to centralization in England.[55] Yet even as Tocqueville wrote, the territorial constitution was being forcibly remodelled.

The second quarter of the nineteenth century was a period of massive political and ideological contestation, a period in which the aristocratic principle was decisively repudiated. The language of aristocratic power is a language of custom, of privilege and traditionally articulated status: it is the language of Montesquieu, of Burke, of Coleridge and of English Toryism. The language of reform in nineteenth-century England was a language of efficiency, of economy, of specialization, of expertise, of rationalization: the language of Bentham, of Edwin Chadwick, of the Mills, of the Liberal centralizers, of the *soi-disant* bureaucrat.[56] As the Whig administration embarked on a systematic reform of English public institutions in the wake of the 1832 Reform Act, the rhetoric of the reforming commissions established by the ministry to investigate poor-law administration, municipal corporations, prisons, policing and education, was uniformly hostile to the aristocratic principle. The politics of reform was specifically Whig/Liberal, and was preoccupied with breaking the power of Tory elites in the localities: the discourse of reform was rationalizing, centralizing and modernizing. The discourse of reform is well exemplified in the *Report of the Royal Commission on the Poor Laws* (1834). The commissioners had little hesitation in ascribing what they took to be the chronic failure of English local government to 'the necessary consequence of their [the magistrates'] social position', and went on to conclude: 'A more dangerous instrument cannot be conceived than a public officer, supported and impelled by benevolent sympathies, armed with power from which there is no appeal, and misapprehending the consequences of its exercise.'[57]

During the political upheavals of the 1830s the first pillars of the modern centralized state were put in place. Primary responsibility for poor relief, prisons, and factory inspection were taken away from magistrates and entrusted to central commissions appointed by ministers. In the process the autonomy of parish vestries, the most representative institutions in the pre-modern English constitution, was further eroded. Parochial self-government was not celebrated for its representative role or its function in bringing the governing process close to the governed. Rather it was condemned for its violation of the new axioms of uniformity, bureaucratic efficiency and expertise. The Royal Commissioners on the Poor Laws wrote dismissively of 'the fourteen thousand republics of England', by which they meant the English parishes. In so describing this modest republicanism they repudiated it. The parish, like the county, was to be brought to heel, and to be subordinated to central direction. In short, although local government would retain a functional role it would be deprived of its autonomy. A reformed parliament at the centre had no hesitation in claiming the right to remodel unre-formed institutions in the localities and, in the process, to authorize a substantial transfer of effective power from the localities to the centre.[58]

Disraeli described the process in narrowly political terms, arguing that '[t]he Whigs have ever been opposed to the national institutions, because they [the national institutions] are averse to the establish-ment of an oligarchy. Local institutions, supported by the landed gentry, check them; hence their love of centralization, and their hatred of unpaid magistrates.'[59] This captures the form but not the essence of the process. There was something more profound at stake here than the contingencies of party politics. We see in the middle of the nineteenth century the development of a distinctively English language of political representation, a language rich in parliamen-tary resonance but strikingly impoverished of any very potent discourse on the rights of localities, communities, regions and sub-cultures. As the representative principle triumphed in parliament it entombed local liberties. An extreme formulation of the point I am making is to be seen in the pro-central and anti-federal tendency of the language of representation in England. Certainly the absence of any very rich federalist tendency in modern English political culture is deeply impoverishing. But my counter-factual here is not the suggestion that nineteenth-century Britain might have developed formal federal structures but rather that it might have developed a more complex institutional and cultural infrastructure to disperse power within the polity.

Viewed in this way, the crucial failure in nineteenth-century England was the failure to replace aristocratic local institutions with equally potent representative institutions. In ideological terms, an aristocratic principle of decentralization was replaced by representative centralism. Certainly mid-nineteenth-century liberalism developed a new notion of the public role and representative utility of local institutions, but it was a theory of local governance which strictly subordinated locality to the centre. Thus participation in local government came to be regarded as a form of political apprenticeship which would nurture citizens in their primary responsibility: that of becoming informed parliamentary electors. The sphere of authority of local government would be carefully circumscribed by parliament, and infant citizens could cut their political teeth in voting for the comparatively trivial, while the real rulers of the state could rest assured that no substantive power was being dispersed to the localities. The case was eloquently (and revealingly) argued in John Stuart Mill's *On Representative Government* of 1861: 'these local functions, not being in general sought by the higher ranks, carry down the important political education which they are a means of conferring to a much lower grade in society'. Nevertheless, Mill insisted that even where power could be localized, knowledge must be centralized.[60] This centralization of knowledge has been the most potent motor of the centralization of power in modern Britain. The great Royal Commissions of the mid-nineteenth century created a new kind of political knowledge, 'official knowledge', which gave the central organs of the state – the executive, central commissions, departments of state – an apparently superior status in the business of policy formation. The paternalism of landed power was giving way to the paternalism of bureaucratic expertise. [61]

If we move again from a theoretical to a functional analysis, in other words from Mill to Bagehot, we find a still lower doctrine of the utility of devolving power. The English, Bagehot noted, used to have a striking reverence for local authorities:

> De Tocqueville indeed used to maintain that in this matter the English were not merely historically excusable but likewise politically judicious.... But in a country like England where business is in the air, where we can organize a vigilance committee on every abuse and an executive committee for every remedy ... we need not care how much power is delegated to outlying bodies, and how much is kept for the central body. We have had the instruction municipalities could give us: we have been through all that. Now we are quite grown up, and can put away childish things.[62]

Here again we encounter the fatal constitutional complacency of the English (now we are quite grown up): the impoverished notion of what might comprise the public domain (we need not care how much power is delegated); and an almost wilful theoretical illiteracy (business is in the air). In terms of rethinking the political culture of the English constitution, the programme of Fabian socialism was almost as desiccated as that of Bagehot's Burkean liberalism.[63] For quite different reasons, no doubt, Conservatives and reformers in the twentieth century have seen no reason to challenge the doctrine of the sufficiency of parliament and have displayed little appetite to redistribute power within the polity.[64] Bagehot spoke for many when he suggested that 'now we are quite grown up'.

Where does this story of English state formation leave the modern Britain? Let me attempt an evaluation first in terms of the British citizen. The rights, capacities and modes of expression of citizens in Britain are strikingly limited, and this immiseration of citizenship is a function of the impoverished theories of representation developed by the modern British state. The most pessimistic evaluation might suggest that all we have to show for a century-and-a-half of political reform is the right of a minority to elect a government about every four years. Citizens have other franchises, but these turn out to be deeply unempowering votes. The sphere of authority of local government is steadily eroded; real displays of voter independence in local elections, as with the Greater London Council and the metropolitan authorities in the 1980s, are rewarded with the abolition of that tier of local government. At a quite different level, on 9 February 1994 Mr Justice Laws ruled that

Somerset County Council had exceeded its powers in banning stag-hunting on land owned by the Council. It was, he argued, solely a matter for parliament to determine whether hunting should or should not be banned.[65] Parliament and the executive, ever jealous of their supremacy within the polity, will brook no opposition and will tolerate no serious and sustained check on their power. In this they are still frequently abetted by the judiciary, the onward march of judicial review notwithstanding. Parliament's opposition to the challenge of citizens' participation in a supra-national parliament is legitimized in terms of the still ascendent doctrine of the sufficiency of parliament. A European parliament is thus generally presented, not as potentially enriching citizens' representative rights and amplifying their political voice, but rather as a challenge to the sovereignty of the British parliament. This same doctrine was, at least until 1 May 1997, offered as the ground for continuing to resist European notions of citizenship articulated in and through legal rights.

If the process of centralization has resulted in a strikingly impoverished conception of citizenship, it has also left us with a very limited range of legitimate political concepts through which to order the relationships between regions, localities, cultures and sub-national institutions. There is, for example, a persistent and pervasive propensity among British politicians to present European federalism as centralization. Here the Westminster parliament's tendency to adopt a narrow and indivisible notion of sovereignty retards rather than facilitates the construction of modern political relations within and outside the UK. Moreover in the debates both on European integration and on British devolution it is revealing that parliamentarians tend to think in terms of the impact on the sovereignty of the Westminster parliament. In British constitutional discourse, parliament rather than the people is generally projected as the sovereign authority. The doctrine of the sufficiency of parliament constructs parliament not as the representative but rather as the embodiment of the sovereign.[66]

Finally, the failure to develop a resonant language through which to legitimize the decentralization of power in the modern British polity abetted the apotheosis of English centralization (and I use the term 'English' deliberately) during the Thatcher–Major years. Had Britain developed a language of representative government which embodied a discourse on the relationship between the decentralization of power and the empowerment of the citizen, then the abolition of metropolitan authorities would have been rendered an ideological impossibility. But throughout the 1980s centralization marched ineluctably on. Elected local bodies – health authorities, police authorities, regulatory bodies of diverse kinds – were abolished and replaced by new statutory authorities largely appointed by, and answerable to, ministers. Moreover, the reconfiguration of power is justified on the ground that hand-picked nominees of ministers – businessmen *par excellence* – are the authentic representatives of local communities. With the rise and rise of the businessman and the business ethic in the British polity the wheel has turned full circle. Over the past century-and-a-half, the unaccountable ascendency of a landed aristocracy has been replaced by the unaccountable ascendency of a shopocracy of businessmen. The aristocratic principle has been displaced by the commercial principle, but the representative deficit remains almost as large as ever. Viewed in this context devolution is a bold experiment. Opponents of devolution are right to point out – but wrong to complain – that devolution runs counter to three centuries of parliamentary centralism. If devolution is to work, a new and richer language of citizenship will have to take root. Devolving power within the United Kingdom and sharing power within the European Union will finally subvert the doctrine of the sufficiency of parliament, and English exceptionalism may then have run its course.

Notes

1 Many friends and colleagues have contributed to the making and improvement of this paper. Richard English asked me to write it, invited me to Queen's University Belfast to present it, and often sustained me by his scholarly enthusiasm. I am grateful to audiences at Queen's Belfast, the University of Oxford, the University of Virginia, Cornell University, and the University of Wales, Swansea, for comments on earlier versions of the paper. Anna Gambles and Stephen Whitefield read and commented perceptively on drafts, and Andrew Thompson has been most generous in giving advice and in sharing ideas and references.

2 My emphasis here is on the English state rather than the British state. In so far as the British state was constructed through parliamentary unions, the argument holds, with important qualifications, for much of British state formation; see L. Brockliss and D. Eastwood (eds) *A Union of Multiple Identities: the British Isles, c.1750–c.1850* (Manchester: Manchester University Press, 1997), esp. pp. 1–6, 193–7.

3 M. Bloch, *Feudal Society* (London: Routledge & Kegan Paul, 1967), p. 430.

4 G. Aylmer, 'The Peculiarities of the English State', *Journal of Historical Sociology*, vol. 3 (1990), pp. 91–108.

5 J. Campbell, 'The United Kingdom of England: the Anglo-Saxon Achievement', in A. Grant and K. J. Stringer (eds) *Uniting the Kingdom? The Making of British History* (London and New York: Routledge, 1995), p. 31.

6 The most committed recent statement of this position is G. Elton, *The English* (Oxford: Blackwell, 1992).

7 P. Corrigan and D. Sayer, *The Great Arch: English State Formation as Cultural Revolution* (Oxford: Blackwell, 1991 edn).

8 D. L. Keir, *The Constitutional History of Modern Britain, 1485–1937*, 4th edn (London: A. & C. Black, 1950), pp. 1–2.

9 E. Burke, *Reflections on the Revolution in France*, ed. C. C. O'Brien (Harmondsworth: Penguin, 1968 [1790]), pp. 96–138, and *passim*.

10 The argument here advanced is by no means novel. It was elegantly formulated by Macaulay in 'Hallam's Constitutional History', reprinted in T. B. Macaulay, *Critical and Historical Essays Contributed to the* Edinburgh Review, 3 vols (London, 1878 edn), vol. 1, pp. 113–216, esp. pp. 154–60. See also S. Clark, *States and Status: The Rise of the State and Aristocratic Power in Western Europe* (Cardiff: University of Wales Press, 1995); A. R. Myers, *Parliaments and Estates in Europe to 1789* (London: Thames & Hudson, 1975).

11 The classic statement of this argument, and still in many ways the most subtle, is Alexis de Tocqueville, *The* Ancien Regime *and the French Revolution* (London: Dent, 1988 edn). See also P. Anderson, *Lineages of the Absolutist State* (London: New Left Books, 1974).

12 G. R. Elton, *Policy and Police: the Enforcement of the Reformation in the Age of Thomas Cromwell* (Cambridge: Cambridge University Press, 1972).

13 R. Filmer, *Patriarcha and Other Writings*, ed. J. P. Somerville (Cambridge: Cambridge University Press, 1991); R. Beddard (ed.) *The Revolutions of 1688* (Oxford: Clarendon Press, 1991); R. Beddard (ed.) *A Kingdom without a King: The Journal of the Provisional Government of the Revolution of 1688* (Oxford: Phaidon, 1988).

14 W. C. Costin and J. S. Watson, *The Law and Working of the Constitution: Documents 1660–1914*, 2 vols (London: A. & C. Black, 1952), vol. 1, pp. 63–75, 92–6; W. A. Speck, *Reluctant Revolutionaries. Englishmen and the Revolution of 1688* (Oxford: Oxford University Press, 1988); J. R. Jones, *The Revolution of 1688 in England* (London: Weidenfeld & Nicolson, 1972); J. A. Downie, *To Settle the Succession of the State: Literature and Politics, 1678–1750* (London: Macmillan, 1994), pp. 5–62; J. H. Plumb, *The Growth of Political Stability in England, 1675–1725* (Harmondsworth: Penguin, 1973), pp. 42–74.

15 P. Langford, *Public Life and the Propertied Englishman, 1689–1798* (Oxford: Clarendon Press, 1991), pp. 139–287; H. T. Dickinson, *The Politics of the People in Eighteenth-Century Britain* (London: St Martin's Press, 1995), pp. 13–92; J. Brewer, *Party Ideology and Popular Politics at the Accession of George III* (Cambridge: Cambridge

University Press, 1976), pp. 219–64; B. Kemp, *King and Commons, 1660–1832* (London: Macmillan, 1957).

16 Montesquieu, *The Spirit of the Laws* (Cambridge: Cambridge University Press, 1989 [1748]), pp. 156–66.

17 L. Krieger, *Kings and Philosophers, 1689–1789* (New York: Norton, 1970); M. Raeff, *The Well-Ordered Police State: Social and Institutional Change Through Law in the Germanies and Russia, 1600–1800* (New Haven: Yale University Press, 1984); C. B. A. Behrens, *Society, Government and the Enlightenment: the Experiences of Eighteenth-Century France and Prussia* (London: Thames & Hudson, 1985); T. C. W. Blanning, *Reform and Revolution in Mainz, 1743–1803* (Cambridge: Cambridge University Press, 1974).

18 Kemp, *King and Commons*, pp. 76–112; A. V. Dicey, *Lectures on the Relation between Law and Public Opinion in England*, 2nd edn (London: Macmillan, 1948); G. H. L. Le May, *The Victorian Constitution. Conventions, Usages and Contingencies* (London: Duckworth, 1979), pp. 1–22, 152–88.

19 W. Blackstone, *Commentaries on the Laws of England*, 7th edn, 4 vols (Oxford, 1775), vol. 1, p. 162.

20 Burke, *Reflections*, pp. 193–7.

21 See H. T. Dickinson, *Liberty and Property: Political Ideology in Eighteenth-Century Britain* (London: Methuen, 1977), p. 287; and 'The Eighteenth-Century Debate on the Sovereignty of Parliament', *Transactions, Royal Historical Society*, 5th series, vol. 26 (1976), pp. 189–210.

22 Cited in E. A. Smith, *Lord Grey, 1764–1834* (Oxford: Clarendon Press, 1990), p. 2.

23 W. N. Molesworth, *The History of the Reform Bill of 1832* (London: Chapman and Hall, 1865), pp. 339–40.

24 T. Paine, *Rights of Man*, ed. E. Foner (Harmondsworth: Penguin, 1985 [1791–2]), p. 185. See also D. Eastwood, 'John Reeves and the Contested Idea of the Constitution', *British Journal for Eighteenth-Century Studies*, vol. 16 (1993), pp. 197–212.

25 J. Locke, *Two Treatises of Government*, ed. Peter Laslett, (Cambridge: Cambridge University Press, 1988 [1698]), pp. 330–74, 406–28.

26 J. Bentham, *A Fragment on Government*, reprinted in *A Fragment on Government and an Introduction to the Principles of Morals and Legislation*, ed. Wilfred Harrison (Oxford: Oxford University Press, 1967), pp. 94–5.

27 Ibid., pp. 3–112.

28 Bentham's *Fragment on Government* was a sustained critique of that most English of texts, Blackstone's *Commentaries on the Laws of England*.

29 W. Bagehot, *The English Constitution* (London: Fontana 1963 [1867]); S. Collini, D. Winch and J. Burrow, *That Noble Science of Politics: a Study in Nineteenth-Century Intellectual History* (Cambridge: Cambridge University Press, 1983), pp. 161–81; A. Buchan, *The Spare Chancellor: a Life of Walter Bagehot* (London: Chatto & Windus, 1959), pp. 159–88.

30 Bagehot, *English Constitution*, p. 59.

31 Ibid., pp. 310ff. and *passim*.
32 See e.g. S. B. Chrimes, *English Constitutional History*, 2nd edn (Oxford: Oxford University Press, 1953), esp. pp. 10–11.
33 Bagehot, *English Constitution*, p. 220.
34 W. Stubbs, *Constitutional History of England: in its Origins and Development*, 3rd edn, 3 vols (Oxford, 1880); J. Campbell, *Stubbs and the English State* (Reading: University of Reading Press, 1989).
35 D. Eastwood, *Government and Community in the English Provinces, 1700–1870* (London: Macmillan, 1997), pp. 78–84, 155–67.
36 *The Trial of Feargus O'Connor and Fifty-Eight Others…* (Manchester: Abel Haywood, 1843), pp. v–x; D. Thompson, *The Early Chartists* (London: Macmillan, 1971), pp. 46–9; R. G. Gammage, *History of the Chartist Movement, 1837–1854* (London: Merlin, 1969 [1854]), pp. 87–90; G. Stedman Jones, *Languages of Class. Studies in English Working Class History, 1832–1982* (Cambridge: Cambridge University Press, 1983), pp. 90–178.
37 *Hansard*, 3rd series (1842, vol. 47, cols 1373–1381; vol. 58, cols 13–88).
38 G. M. Trevelyan, *British History in the Nineteenth Century and After* (London: Longmans, Green & Co., 1937 edn), p. 241.
39 Le May, *Victorian Constitution*, pp. 127–88; J. Vernon, *Politics and the People: a Study in English Political Culture, c. 1815–1867* (Cambridge: Cambridge University Press, 1993); J. Vernon (ed.) *Re-Reading the Constitution: New Narratives in the History of England's Long Nineteenth Century* (Cambridge: Cambridge University Press, 1996).
40 This argument is developed more fully in Eastwood, *Government and Community*, pp. 1–19.
41 C. Stephenson and F. G. Marcham, *Sources of English Constitutional History: a Selection of Documents from A.D. 600* (New York: Harper & Row, 1937), pp. 46–9.
42 P. Hyams, *Kings, Lords and Peasants in Medieval England: the Common Law of Villeinage in the Twelfth and Thirteenth Centuries* (Oxford: Clarendon Press, 1980).
43 J. C. Holt, *Magna Carta*, 2nd edn (Cambridge: Cambridge University Press, 1992), pp. 378–405; J. R. Maddicott, 'Magna Carta and the Local Community, 1215–1259', *Past and Present*, vol. 102 (1984), pp. 25–65; K. B. McFarlane, *The Nobility of Later Medieval England* (Oxford: Clarendon Press, 1978).
44 The literature on Tudor parliaments is large and contentious. The outlines of the debate are quickly apparent from G. R. Elton, 'Parliament', in C. Haigh (ed.) *The Reign of Elizabeth I* (London: Macmillan, 1984), pp. 79–100; G. R. Elton, *Studies in Tudor and Stuart Politics and Government*, 3 vols (Cambridge: Cambridge University Press, 1974–83), vol. 3, pp. 3–20; J. Loach, 'Parliament: a "New Air"?', in C. Coleman and D. Starkey (eds) *Revolution Reassessed* (Oxford: Clarendon Press, 1986), pp. 117–34; P. Williams, *The Tudor Regime* (Oxford: Clarendon Press, 1979), pp. 21–54, 394–406.
45 For an elegant discussion see Frederic Maitland's Introduction to O. Gierke, *Political Theories of the Middle Ages* (Boston: Beacon Press, 1958), pp. xxxvi–vii.

46 For a rich and perceptive study see F. Heal and C. Holmes, *The Gentry in England and Wales, 1500–1700* (London: Macmillan, 1994); also P. Jenkins, *The Making of a Ruling Class: the Glamorgan Gentry, 1640–1790* (Cambridge: Cambridge University Press, 1983); D. W. Howell, *Patriarchs and Parasites. The Gentry of South-West Wales in the Eighteenth Century* (Cardiff: University of Wales Press, 1986); Eastwood, *Government and Community*, pp. 94–104.

47 Important comparative perspectives emerge in G. Chaussinand-Nogaret, *The French Nobility in the Eighteenth Century: from Feudalism to Enlightenment* (Cambridge: Cambridge University Press, 1984); J. Blum, *The End of the Old Order in Rural Europe* (Princeton: Princeton University Press, 1978); D. Spring (ed.) *European Landed Elites in the Nineteenth Century* (Baltimore: Johns Hopkins University Press, 1977); Clark, *States and Status*.

48 Quoted in D. Spring, 'Alexis de Tocqueville on Aristocratic Politics and Society in Nineteenth-Century Britain', *Albion*, vol. 12 (1988), pp. 122–31; cf. S. Drescher, *Tocqueville on England* (Cambridge, MA: Harvard University Press, 1964), pp. 40–5.

49 Montesquieu, *Spirit of the Laws*, pp. 159–61 and *passim*.

50 D. Eastwood, *Governing Rural England: Tradition and Transformation in Local Government, 1780–1840* (Oxford: Clarendon Press, 1994), pp. 11–23.

51 P. Dunkley, *The Crisis of the Old Poor Law in England, 1795–1834* (New York and London: Garland, 1982); P. Dunkley, 'Paternalism, the Magistracy, and Poor Relief in England, 1795–1834', *International Review of Social History*, vol. 22 (1979), pp. 371–97; M. Neuman, *The Speenhamland County, Poverty and the Poor Laws in Berkshire, 1782–1834* (New York and London: Garland, 1982); Eastwood, *Governing Rural England*, pp. 99–187.

52 Anon., *Biographical Memoirs of Thomas Butterworth Bayley* (Manchester, 1802); M. de Lacy, *Prison Reform in Lancashire, 1700–1850: a Study in Local Administration* (Manchester: Chetham Society, 1986), vol. 33; Eastwood, *Government and Community*, pp. 134–47.

53 J. S. Mill, *Representative Government*, in Mill, *Utilitarianism, On Liberty and Considerations on Representative Government*, ed. H. B. Acton (London: Dent, 1972 [1861]), pp. 346–59.

54 B. Disraeli, *Sybil; or, The Two Nations* (Harmondsworth: Penguin edn [1845]), p. 330.

55 A. de Tocqueville, *Journeys to England and Ireland*, ed. J. P. Mayer (London: Faber & Faber, 1958), p. 109.

56 D. Eastwood, ' "Amplifying the Province of the Legislature". The Flow of Information and the English State in the Early Nineteenth Century', *Historical Research*, vol. 62 (1989), pp. 276–94.

57 *The Poor Law Report of 1834*, ed. S. G. and E. O. A. Checkland (Harmondsworth: Penguin, 1974), pp. 240–1.

58 E. Chadwick, *County Government* (London, 1879); W. J. Forsythe, 'Centralization and Local Autonomy: the Experience of English Prisons, 1820–1877', *Journal of Historical Sociology*, vol. 4 (1991), pp. 317–45; W. Apfel and P. Dunkley, 'English Rural Society and the New

Poor Law: Bedfordshire, 1834–1847', *Social History*, vol. 10 (1985), pp. 37–68; J. Prest, *Liberty and Locality. Parliament, Permissive Legislation and Ratepayers' Democracies in the Mid-Nineteenth Century* (Oxford: Clarendon Press, 1990).

59 [B. Disraeli], *The Letters of Runnymede* (London: John Macrone, 1836), p. 184.
60 Mill, *Representative Government*, pp. 348–57, at p. 348.
61 A. Ashforth, 'Reckoning Schemes of Legitimation: on Commissions of Inquiry as Power/Knowledge Forms', *Journal of Historical Sociology*, vol. 3 (1990), pp. 1–22; Eastwood, ' "Amplifying the Province of the Legislature" '.
62 Bagehot, *The English Constitution*, pp. 264–5.
63 A. M. McBriar, *Fabian Socialism and English Politics, 1884–1918* (Cambridge: Cambridge University Press, 1962).
64 A. Gamble, *Britain in Decline: Economic Policy, Political Strategy and the British State*, 4th edn (London: Macmillan, 1994), pp. 87–95.
65 *Guardian*, 10 February 1994, p. 7.
66 R. Barker, *Politics, Peoples and Government: Themes in British Political Thought since the Nineteenth Century* (London: Macmillan, 1994), pp. 116–37.

Chapter 2

Wales and the British state

'The outer form of subjugation'[1]

D. George Boyce

In his comparison of Welsh and Irish nationality, J. Vyrnwy Morgan declared in 1912 that 'history shows how the Welsh have suffered through too loose a government from within, and how they have prospered under a resolute government from without'.[2] Whether or not this is a justifiable claim, there is no doubt about Wales's long experience of 'government from without'. The acts of parliament relating to Wales, passed between 1530 and 1543, which united England and Wales marked the culmination of a process that had begun during the Norman conquest in the late thirteenth century and culminated in the early sixteenth century with the introduction of Welshmen into full citizenship of the realm on the same terms as the English. The Welsh retained their own system of courts, the Great Sessions, until 1830, and this special legal system was combined with representation in the English parliament.[3] The identification of Wales with England was not complete: the Welsh language remained as the most obvious distinction between the two nations, but the ready acceptance in Wales of the Reformation, the aspiration of Wales in the civil war and the constitutional struggles of the seventeenth century to 'keep out of trouble',[4] and above all the industrialization of south Wales in the late eighteenth and nineteenth centuries, locked Wales firmly into the modern British state. This had cultural as well as social and economic implications, for it resulted in the influx of English people into the industrial areas, increasing the use of the English language and lessening the essential need for the Welsh language. But the debates over Irish home rule in the late nineteenth and early twentieth centuries had repercussions in Wales, especially when the idea of 'home rule all round' was canvassed as a means of resolving the Irish deadlock. Vyrnwy Morgan, in his survey of Wales and Ireland, was hostile to

Welsh home rule, which he dismissed as 'not general ... not imperative ... not even very articulate'; he believed that the best way forward was a more efficient administration of the various acts of parliament in Wales which could be best obtained through the creation of a Welsh Office of State with a minister responsible for Welsh affairs.[5]

Morgan was not an original or very deep thinker; but he identified the essentials of the modern debate about the place of Wales in the British state. He argued that what distinguished the Welsh experience in state building was the fact that there

> is hardly any trace of the dull leaden weight of an alien authority seeking to crush out of existence, or to suppress, the national aspirations of the people ... While preserving the outer form of subjugation, the Welsh have been allowed to indulge in the privilege of independence.[6]

Not everyone would agree with either the tone or the conclusion of this statement; but it conforms broadly with the agenda of Welsh politics in the nineteenth century, with its aim of seeking, not separation from, but equality with, England.[7] The question since 1914 has been whether this demand for equal treatment has been realized; whether it could be better sought through some form of Welsh home rule; or whether the administrative institutions of Wales, created by the British government, allow room enough for the Welsh, not only to pursue their political aspirations, but to express their sense of nationality.

After the Great War it seemed that this question was to have political and constitutional answers. A Speaker's Conference on Devolution appointed in October 1919, in the first flush of enthusiasm for change that swept the country in the last two years of the conflict, reported in April 1920 and called for parliaments to be established in Wales and Scotland, but was uncertain about how to deal with England: should it too be treated as one unit, or subdivided? The conference drew up a list of powers to be devolved under several headings (Regulation of Internal Commercial Undertakings; Order and Good Government; Agriculture and land, and the like).[8] The local legislatures should be given control of certain fiscal resources, such as traders' licences. The Welsh judicial system should remain the same, unless the Welsh legislature asked for changes to be made.[9] But the conference could not agree on the composition and character of the legislatures. Lowther himself favoured the lesser form of legislature, called 'Grand Councils', consisting of the members of the House of Commons returned to sit for the constituencies in the regions, and a council of peers consisting of a proportion of the members of the Lords chosen by themselves. He confessed later:

> The more I considered the proposal of one supreme and four independent legislatures, the less I liked it. The confusions which might arise, the multiplicity of elections, the novelty of five (possibly even more) Prime Ministers and Cabinets of probably divergent political views, the enormous expense of building four new sets of Parliament buildings and Government offices and providing all the paraphernalia of administration, frightened my economical soul ...[10]

In its legal system, Wales was not to be treated in quite the same way as Scotland; indeed   J. A. Murray Macdonald, one of the members of the conference, and a leading advocate of home rule all round, suggested that it was an 'open question' whether any good purpose would be served by giving separate institutions to Wales.[11] In the event the conference came to nothing. David Lloyd George, Prime Minister of the coalition government of Conservatives and Liberals that sponsored the initiative, rejected the whole concept of home rule, basing his case mainly on the injustice of the project to England.[12]

This might be dismissed as typical faint-heartedness on the part of the British political elite when it came to radical constitutional reform; and there is much truth in the accusation. But there was a problem for Welsh nationalist aspirations in particular. This was that Wales, unlike, it seemed, Ireland, could find space within the Victorian British state system. It was always tempting to choose a role on the larger stage of British politics. Tom Ellis, whose connections with, and sympathy for, Irish nationalism in the 1880s were well known, caused some disquiet in Welsh political circles when he abandoned the prospect of assuming the mantle of the 'Parnell of Wales' in favour of taking a government post. In 1892 he accepted the post of junior whip in the Liberal Government, a decision which he admitted would be a sore puzzle to the Welsh people, but one in which 'much salutary influence could be quietly and unostentationarily [*sic*] wielded in the service of Wales'.[13] This might appear to be a self-serving rationalization; but it was nothing of the sort. It raised the deeper problems and contradictions that underlay the strategy and aims of Welsh nationally minded politicians in the late nineteenth century. The issue was not really one of choice – whether to become a Parnell of Wales, or a member of the British political elite – but of a lack of choice. For, at bottom, there was an almost inexorable drive towards regarding the exploitation of the British state, and its growing powers, in the interests of Wales as the only (or at any rate the best) possible option. Welsh nationalist feeling was closely associated with Nonconformity; and Nonconformity wanted the British state to deliver certain reforms, especially educational policies which did not discriminate against Nonconformists in the interests of Anglicans, and the disestablishment of the Church of Wales. And what better choice to use the levers of the state than the British Liberal Party, itself deeply committed to the Nonconformist cause in England and Wales alike?[14]

This is not to say that the Welsh section of the British Liberal Party was always content with the kind of muscle it possessed in that party. In 1886 Tom Ellis suggested the use of Parnellite tactics of obstructing parliamentary business to draw attention to grievances.[15] But Ellis rose to prominence on a movement that developed, not from some claim that Wales must have political independence, but from the many and varied demands which the coming of democratic politics encouraged after 1867. Ellis was sensitive to the problems that England posed for Wales: referring to the need for an Irish settlement in 1886, he complained about the 'utter want of grace and sympathy, the two great qualities requisite for dealing satisfactorily with Celtic peoples'.[16] But what was the nature of Welsh nationality? And should it be translated into political form? In February 1890 David Lloyd George attended a meeting of the South Wales Liberal Federation where a resolution was moved by David Randell MP that:

> this Federation declares that the people of Wales should be entrusted with the management of the purely domestic affairs of the Principality, and recognizes in the movement to secure self-government for Wales, which received Mr. Gladstone's support at Manchester, the solution of the grave difficulties under which the Principality suffers, by reason of neglect of

succeeding Governments to meet the legislative requirements of its people.

Lloyd George rose to the occasion:

> When we consider what time is consumed enlightening the political intelligence of the average Englishman, and the slow rate of Parliamentary progress ... we cannot avoid the conclusion that one, if not two, generations would have passed away before the Imperial Government could have redressed the Welsh national grievance of today. Welsh Home Rule alone can bring within the reach of this generation the fruits of its political labours.

Lloyd George set out the other grounds for Welsh home rule. Wales was a nation as much as was Ireland; more so, since Ireland had lost 'one of the title deeds of her nationality – its ancient language. But Wales has preserved her charter of its integrity'. Wales had 'no Ulster' to disrupt her national claim. Wales could not be accused of desiring separation. Wales had no record of crime in its pursuit of nationality. This was an age when the people of Europe were infused with the Christian spirit, seeking an end to man's inhumanity to man; would Wales be content to be simply the standard bearer for another nation, or would the red dragon lead forth a nation 'to do battle for the right, as of old?'.[17] In a later speech, in Aberystwyth, he extolled the virtues of the Welsh nation. Wales was a separate nationality which 'ought to be the starting-point in the study of every Welsh question'. It had survived for 2,000 years 'in spite of every human effort to crush its vitality'.[18] Wales had literature, music; English culture, by contrast, consisted of football and horse-racing. The University of Wales was a model for others to emulate, and one over which the heir to the throne need not be ashamed to preside.[19]

But there was an ambiguity here. In a footnote to his biography of Lloyd George, du Parcq noted that Lloyd George was here referring to the recent installation of the Prince of Wales as Chancellor of the University of Wales.[20] Welsh nationalism and membership of the British state, then, despite Lloyd George's jibes at the philistine English, were not incompatible. Lloyd George pressed in parliament for home rule all round. And even while Lloyd George was making his claim for Welsh home rule, developments were taking place which would have a greater significance for Wales in the British state than the ephemeral call for home rule.

This was the gradual, at times hardly planned, devolution of administrative powers to Wales, and the recognition of Wales as a special area for certain administrative purposes. This was demanded as early as 1890 by Alfred Thomas, Liberal MP for Glamorgan East, who proposed the creation of a separate Department of State for the conduct of distinctly Welsh affairs, presided over by a minister acquainted with the national characteristics of Wales. He proposed his 'National Institutions (Wales)' bills in 1891 and 1892, involving a Secretary of State for Wales, a National Council for Wales and a Welsh Standing Committee, but these bills were not even discussed in the House.[21] In 1893 Asquith, as Home Secretary, rearranged the inspectoral divisions of Wales under the Workshop and Factories Act to meet the call (made by Tom Ellis in particular) for the government to acknowledge the 'administrative unity of Wales'.[22] Asquith treated Wales as a unit for the purpose of the Mines Regulation Act. In 1907 the Liberal government created a Welsh Department of Education;[23] in 1911 the National Insurance Act was passed providing the next opportunity for the delegation of legislative functions, but it was a sign of Lloyd George's flagging interest in specifically Welsh affairs that he confessed that he did so 'with regret and no real enthusiasm', but admitted that it was 'one of those questions in which you have got to defer to sentiment'.[24] These were piecemeal adaptations, with no concerted purpose beyond that of administrative convenience and the vague desire of requiting 'sentiment'. But they established, if not a pattern, then a trend that continued after the Great War. Thomas Griffiths, Labour MP for Pontypridd, claimed that Wales fought in the war for the rights of small nations, adding (not without a touch of banality) that it therefore deserved its own Health Minister. Christopher Addison, for his part, accepted the case for a separate Welsh Board of Health. In 1919 a Welsh Council of Agriculture was established, giving statutory recognition to an advisory body that had existed since 1912.[25] But few real powers were devolved to Wales, for the government simply did not recognize its claim for special treatment as being on the same footing as those of Scotland and, in its day, Ireland. And Whitehall civil servants were temperamentally averse to territorial administrative devolution, preferring to use the functional model. No party would countenance the idea of a Secretary of State for Wales.

Yet there was an important development implicit in these arrangements, however piecemeal and *ad hoc* they might be; and that was that Wales was being redefined with regard to her place in the British state in a way that was grappling her close to the state, while seeming to recognize her separate nationality. Not the least effective way of doing so was the use of patronage; Tom Ellis was consulted about the appointment of Nonconformists to positions of influence.[26] To grant administrative devolution, on however small a scale, was a beginning from which came the Welsh Secretary of State and the Welsh Office in 1964. But this, it could be argued, was a means of binding Wales more closely to the state administrative machine, while apparently doing the opposite. This was creating a Welsh dimension to the British state; it was not recognizing Welsh nationality in any political or cultural sense, though it did appease national sentiment by allowing some local initiative, while all the time keeping a watchful eye on the behaviour of the local administrative machine. Was it for this that the Welsh cultural and political revival of the late nineteenth century spread its wings?

Cymru Fydd, founded in 1894, embraced Welshmen who wanted to give new voice to Welsh cultural identity, to foster 'self respect and self reliance'. Yet it too regarded the union with England as 'inevitable'; it was one that provided the best opportunity that Wales could have 'to deliver her mission ... to the world ... it is by influencing England that Wales can influence the world'. 'The voices of England and of Wales should be joined, not in unison, but in harmony.' Wales would be the new Greece of the United Kingdom: 'captive Greece', said the Roman poet, 'took her savage conqueror prisoner'.[27]

In 1925 a new party, Plaid Cymru, the Welsh Nationalist Party, was founded to pursue the goal of the creation of a Welsh state, and to do so in order also to promote the Welsh language, culture and way of life: 'religious, cooperative, highly individualistic, and opposed to the consequences of urbanization and industrialization'. A Welsh nation state, the playwright and Welsh-language enthusiast Saunders Lewis declared in 1939, needed 'economic and political recognition', in order for it to remain a living and valuable aspect of Welsh life, otherwise it might simply remain a 'functionless survival'.[28] Saunders Lewis, together with Lewis Valentine and J. D. Williams, all party leaders of Plaid Cymru, struck what they saw as a necessary blow against the state when in 1936 they set fire to a government school at Penyberth in Caernarvonshire. But this kind of direct action was frowned upon by the party in its later existence,[29] even though the perpetrators, once sentenced to jail, gathered widespread support in Wales and even from David Lloyd George.[30] The arrival of Plaid Cymru on the political scene was not the new dawn for which its supporters had hoped.[31] The Labour Party was making its inroads into the Liberal areas of Wales, and was establishing itself as the party of Wales – or at least of the most heavily populated area of Wales, the industrial south-east. Constitutional reform seemed irrelevant when set beside the industrial depression that enveloped South Wales in the inter-war years; and even the intermittent, but significant, process of administrative reform faltered. In 1938 Neville Chamberlain turned down a proposal for a Secretary of State for Wales, and the Labour Party was hardly likely to dissent from Aneurin Bevan's claim that the Welsh problem was the same as the British problem, in that it was one of unemployment and regional decay. But the Second World War stimulated a new, if hardly fervent, interest in the possibility of regional decentralization of government. Departments were given regional organization, and by 1946 there were thirteen regional offices in Wales, excluding the Welsh Departments of Education, Health and Agriculture.[32]

But despite this concession to the special position of a Celtic nation of the United Kingdom, Wales soon felt the impact of the growing power of the state machine, as the state expanded its activities, assumed a greater role in public affairs, and began to run down the regional organization of government departments. In any case, Whitehall, and especially the Treasury, disliked regional organizations; ministers, for their part, claimed the right to control policy and expenditure 'for which they are answerable to parliament'. Uniformity was the key.[33]

Nevertheless, the recognition of Wales as not just another region of the United Kingdom was, however weakly and unwillingly, conceded. In 1949 a nominated Council for Wales and Monmouthshire was established, composed of representatives from local authorities, industry and other interests. The office of Minister for Welsh Affairs was created in 1951, by the Conservative government, as an appendage of the Home Office. In 1957 a Minister of State was appointed to work in association with the Minister for Housing and Local Government:[34] a concession which the Cardiff *Western Mail* described as the mountain labouring and bringing forth a molehill.[35] Wales entered the second half of the twentieth century with a kind of haphazard, partly negotiated, partly imposed, set of acknowledgements that Wales was not merely an appendage of the British state, but had certain recognition of national identity, including (in 1942) a Welsh Courts Act which removed some of the penal clauses against the Welsh language dating from the Acts of Union.[36] But common to this rather incoherent set of changes was the fact that they were conceded only if they were considered as of no threat to the fundamental unity of the state. This is only to make the point that all states are in some degree negotiated, in some degree imposed; but what changed, or seemed to change in the case of Wales and the state, was the appearance in the 1950s and early 1960s of pressure which – in the context of the debate over Britain that was emerging at the same time – resulted in the most important acknowledgement by the state that Wales was indeed a distinct region with its own special character and problems.

This issue was raised in parliament on 4 March 1955 by the Labour member for Merthyr Tydfil, S. O. Davies, in introducing the second reading of his bill for Welsh devolution. Davies acknowledged that Wales was 'frequently regarded as being just a region, just an area somewhere within the United Kingdom', but he recommended Members to accept his bill, declaring that it had support outside the rural areas of Wales, including Monmouthshire and Cardiff (at which point the Member for Cardiff West, George Thomas, interrupted with the remark: 'the Honourable Member will not get much support there').[37] Cledwyn Hughes, seconding the bill, spoke of 'grave dissatisfaction' in Wales because she had not got firmer control of her own affairs; devolution gave 'some measure of the status which befits a nation and which statehood alone can give'.[38] This widened the debate. For the government Major Gwilym Lloyd George (Secretary of State for the Home Office and Minister for Welsh Affairs), remarked:

> I cannot help feeling that the issue which confronts us today can be very simply stated in two words, 'nation' and 'State'.... The vitality of the Welsh nation can be better preserved if the Welsh people remain within the framework of Great Britain.

Lloyd George agreed that all members were keen for the welfare of their native land; but this was best served by the government, which was seeking to meet the needs of Wales: his own position as Minister for Welsh Affairs was proof of this. The Government of

Ireland Act of 1920, which Davies took as his model for Wales, was specific to the needs and circumstances of Northern Ireland; and he pointed out that Wales would be less well served under such a system, since her representation at Westminster must be reduced.[39] James Callaghan intervened to point out that 'in fact, in Northern Ireland, because of their poverty and unemployment, it has worsened the standards of the unemployed'.[40] The second reading of the bill resulted in a defeat by 48 votes to 14.

The point made (somewhat unconvincingly) by Gwilym Lloyd George – that a Minister for Welsh Affairs was a recognition in some degree of Welsh nationality – could, nonetheless, be taken further. In 1957 the Council for Wales and Monmouthshire put forward the case for collecting the various government offices in Wales into a new Welsh Office. This was ignored by the Conservative government, but complaints from Sir William Jones, a member of the Council, and its chairman Dr Huw T. Edwards provoked the official – if the rather diluted – response that pointed to the recent transfer of responsibilities for Welsh affairs from the Home Office to the Ministry of Housing and Local Government (which would mean that greater attention would be paid to Welsh needs).[41] In January 1959 the Council declared that Wales was 'a separate nation and not just a region, province or appendage of England'.[42] This must have surprised the former inhabitants of the Welsh village of Capel Celyn, which stood in the middle of a site marked by the Corporation of Liverpool for the construction of a new reservoir, a decision which aroused the opposition of even Welsh Labour MPs in parliament.[43]

The Labour Party, perhaps more in opposition to Conservative dislike of special Welsh institutional recognition than in any great spirit of radical reform, committed itself in 1959 to creating a Secretary of State for Wales with a seat in the cabinet, specific departmental duties and overall supervision of government departments in Wales.[44] Sooner than anyone could have expected, the question of regionalism and devolution of powers became the focus of a quite extensive political debate, as the 1960s witnessed a revived interest in regional problems and the appropriate response to them.[45] In 1963 the Labour Party, now at the end of its long march back to office, renewed its commitment to the Secretaryship of State, and when it came to power in 1964 it appointed James Griffiths to the post – a move which Richard Crossman, the new Minister for Local Government, dismissed as 'another equally idiotic creation... a completely artificial new office for Jim Griffiths and his two Parliamentary secretaries, all the result of a silly election pledge'.[46] Some Labour MPs opposed the transfer of administrative functions to the new Secretary of State, urging that his duties should be confined to oversight only. But Griffiths was able to wrest control of some functions: the Welsh Office was formed out of the regional branch of the Ministry of Housing in Wales, together with the Welsh division of the Ministry of Transport. But, even though Wales possessed a Department of Education (since 1907) and a Board of Health (since 1919), it took five years for these (obviously appropriate) functions to be transferred to the Welsh Office. By the mid-1970s the Welsh Office had won control of primary and secondary education, local government, economic planning and trade and industry.[47]

The Labour MP, T. W. Jones, declared that the establishment of the Welsh Office made Harold Wilson 'the first Prime Minister to have recognized in a practical way the nationhood of the Welsh people'.[48] But it could be argued that this marked a recognition not so much of the distinctiveness of Wales as of its firm institutional place within the British state. Admittedly, the creation of the Welsh Office and its entry into economic policy-making meant that Wales would be treated as a single economic unit. This in turn brought forth the creation of a Welsh Trades Union Congress. But these developments all took place within the traditional political system of the United Kingdom. There would be no democratic representative body that might breathe new political life into the emerging administrative and (therefore) policy-making activities of the Welsh Office. The Welsh TUC would negotiate with the Welsh Office; other pressure groups similarly orientated themselves to the new rising sun in the East. The people of Wales would, in this way, be left out of the equation. The 'outer form of subjugation' would be restructured; the institutions of union renegotiated. This is not to say that there was no such thing as Welsh politics. It existed on two levels: an intensely local, spoils-sharing, politics; and a distinctive choice that the Welsh people were presented with in United Kingdom elections – whether to return more Labour MPs to Westminster than those of any other party and thus sustain Labour's claim to be the party of Wales. And there was the ever-present Welsh Nationalist Party, Plaid Cymru, anxious to challenge Labour in its south-Walian stronghold, and even to win what were regarded as safe Labour seats. The fall of Carmarthen to Plaid

Cymru's Gwynfor Evans, in a by-election in July 1966 in which Evans doubled the share of the poll by getting 16,000 votes, placed Wales' first ever Nationalist MP in the House of Commons. There were many reasons for this. In March 1966 Labour won a General Election with a large majority, and it was safe for voters in Carmarthen to switch their allegiance. Local issues and personalities emerged. But it was a sign that Labour was regarded, in some places at least, as not working in Wales. By 1968 pit closures, economic insecurity and unemployment all put Labour under increased pressure.[49]

The concern about the consequences of the 'outer form of subjugation' was paralleled by an equally, if not more, intense debate about the inner form of freedom, as its supporters would have regarded the future of the Welsh language. In 1962 Saunders Lewis emerged from retirement to warn that the language must be saved: 'a revolution' must be launched to restore the language, which was a task 'more important than self-government'.[50] In 1962 the Welsh Language Society was founded, with some of its members prepared to take direct action to draw attention to the plight of the language.[51] Political nationalism also assumed a higher profile (though not one related to any further dramatic increase in its electoral representation).[52] Despite Plaid Cymru's unqualified commitment to constitutional methods, there were elements within Welsh nationalism that were prepared to take violent action. In 1969 two members of the Free Wales Army were killed planting a bomb during the Investiture of the Prince of Wales.[53] But the most important influence on the new perspective that developed in the politics of the United Kingdom was the challenge to Labour's hegemony mounted by the Scottish National Party, and in Wales by Plaid Cymru in the field of social and economic issues, which, though it could not seriously trouble Labour's hold on its industrial areas, nonetheless disturbed the complacency of Labour and encouraged the setting up in 1969 of a Royal Commission on the Constitution.

This Commission might have provided the platform for a radical reform, rather than a re-negotiation, of the place of Wales in the British state. The Commission was broadly sympathetic to the claims made by many of those who offered evidence, that Wales felt that it was the 'backyard of the United Kingdom', and it spoke in terms of winning back power from London.[54] The Commission's report, published in 1973, coincided with the Arab–Israeli war and the subsequent oil crisis which diverted attention away from its findings, which were, in any case, regarded as *jejeune* by the House of Commons.[55] The Labour government that came to power in February 1974 was hardly more enthusiastic about devolution than the Conservatives had been, but its minority position, and its fear of losing further ground to the Scottish National Party, pushed the government forward. In 1975 its proposals took shape with the publication of a White Paper *Our Changing Democracy: Devolution in Scotland and Wales*.[56] This proposed an Assembly for Wales but one without legislative powers. There would be 'a system devolving wide executive powers but within a constitutional framework much more akin to a major regional authority'; but this was qualified by the statement that Wales would have a 'novel' arrangement in that it would possess

> an administration analogous to that of local authority in that the assembly would itself be the Executive and would work via Committees; but the scale and scope of powers, including subordinate legislation, would go far beyond the local authority pattern.[57]

This compromise arose from divisions in the Labour Party on the question of whether or not the Assembly should have law-making powers. The assembly would be able to amend only Westminster legislation and would have no control over economic policy. Furthermore, it was decided that the Secretary of State for Wales, if he were to lose some of his functions, such as health and housing, to the Assembly, must be compensated by the acquisition of more economic powers, and in July 1975 he took over much of the responsibility for the Department of Trade and Industry in Wales, with powers of selective regional assistance.[58]

The government suffered the indignity of having its devolution legislation defeated in February 1977, but the centre of British politics had still to try to appease the periphery, especially after the Callaghan government's pact with the Liberals in March 1977, which operated formally until June 1978. The proposal to combine Scotland and Wales in one bill was replaced by a proposal of two bills, one for each country, and the Wales Act received the Royal Assent on 31 July 1978. It was to be tested in a referendum, which the hostility of some Labour MPs to devolution made conditional on the bill winning the support of at least 40 per cent of the Welsh (and of the Scottish) electorate.[59] Once again the 'outer form of subjugation' – the long experience of Wales as an integral part of the union – influenced the way in which the parties conducted the devolution campaign, as well as its eventual outcome. The pro-Assembly coalition – an all-parties group led by Labour and supported, with some reservations, by Plaid Cymru – placed the main emphasis of its recommendation on the belief that the Assembly would advance the claims of democracy in Wales, rather than on its role in the recognition of Welsh nationhood. But the Labour Party was divided on devolution; it all seemed unfamiliar to Labour Party members, who found it hard to see Welsh politics in terms solely of politics within Wales. Moreover, the nationalist aspect of the whole campaign, though played down by most devolution supporters, was enough to worry those who, again, saw the future of Wales as firmly in the direction of British politics, and of Wales' unequivocal integration with the British state.[60] In particular, interest groups in Wales which were part of wider United Kingdom organizations feared that the new administrative arrangements proposed for Wales would disrupt their long-standing and familiar relationship with central government.[61]

The devolution proposals of 1978 were resoundingly rejected by the Welsh electorate in the Referendum held on 1 March, St David's Day, 1979, by a majority of four to one. This did not damage the Labour Party in Wales, which in 1983 won 37.5 per cent of the vote, and then in 1987 45.1 per cent. Nationalism remained confined to its traditional areas in north-west Wales, while Conservatives – the forgotten party of Welsh history – polled 32.3 per cent of the vote in 1983, 29.5 in 1987 and 28.6 in 1992,[62] a creditable performance in the light of the increasing belief that the Celtic fringe nations were most markedly damaged by the decade of Thatcherism. But the Thatcher government appeared willing to make some gesture towards a recognition of Wales as having a special dimension in British politics: but only in the strictest form of governmental control. A Committee on Welsh Affairs was to be created, the new government announced, to 'provide opportunity for closer examination of departmental policy', and to make for greater openness in government.[63] The Conservatives had just sufficient MPs from Wales to give it its rightful built-in majority on the Committee (six out of eleven), and its Labour members included three strong anti-devolutionists.[64] The Committee would be seen as a means of demonstrating that Wales could be given her due in the normal machinery of the British parliament, rather than require her own devolved Assembly.[65]

One expectation was that the new Committee would offer some form of accountability for the operations of the Welsh Office, and especially for the large number of quangos in Wales. The growing power of the Welsh Office and of the Secretary of State for Wales raised questions about the place of Wales in the state. By the 1990s the Welsh Office had under its control some 2,300 civil servants,[66] and the direction of key functions in Wales, including roads (1964–5), health (1969), primary and secondary education (1970), higher and further education (1978) and agriculture and manpower policy (1978). This growth was partly to ensure a substantial role for the Welsh Secretary in the event of devolution; and partly to respond to that elusive but ever-present entity, 'Welsh sentiment'.[67] This process of acquiring new functions continued in the 1980s and 1990s, and it can truly be claimed that, in institutional terms, Wales acquired more recognition as a special nation in the United Kingdom than at any time in her previous history.

This could be taken as signalling that the 'outer form of subjugation' – that of the institutional development of the British state – had now been inverted; that the act of extending the institutions of the British state had, in effect, given Wales an inner form of freedom. This was argued by the Secretary of State for Wales, Peter Walker (whose banishment from the inner councils of the Thatcher cabinet might imply that Wales was still the backyard of the United Kingdom), on the grounds that he had used the Welsh Office as a kind of barrier, or at least a filter, to save Wales from the worst excesses of the Thatcher decade.[68] But a recent authority has argued that 'many of the policies carried out by the Welsh Office have been similar in intent and implementation to policies carried out elsewhere in the United Kingdom', and that 'the Welsh Office has negligible powers at best to vary the level of government spending, let alone the level of aggregate expenditure in the Welsh economy'.[69]

But by the 1990s the debate on Wales was moving away from a defence of the Welsh Office as the best expression of the exceptionalism of Wales in the United Kingdom, and towards a criticism of its power of patronage, of the 'democratic' deficit in Wales, of the vast budget – £2.4 billion, some 34 per cent of Welsh Office expenditure – which was spent by quangos in Wales. The Committee on Welsh Affairs had tried to assert some control over administration in Wales, but was met with 'a classic piece of administrative stonewalling';[70] when it came to examining the activities of quangos, the historians of the Committee conclude that 'members, or at least those who bothered to attend, were, by and large, content to employ the occasions as little more than reconnaissance exercises'.[71] The opinion of the Committee's second chairman, that it 'provided a democratic forum for the Welsh people',[72] was not shared by all, and the growth of quangos was alleged to have taken place at the expense of local government in Wales. One critic claimed that 'the steam-rollering of the Local Government (Wales) Act through the Westminster Parliament during 1993–4 is only the latest of a series of instances in which the wishes of a substantial majority of Welsh MPs have been overridden by their English counterparts'.[73] One contributor to a volume advocating the importance of a parliament in Wales described Wales as a 'stateless nation'.[74]

This raised all sorts of questions about what it meant for a nation to be without a state (or, for that matter, with one) in the contemporary United Kingdom, and what it meant to be a nation. Surveys revealed that most people living in Wales invariably thought of themselves as Welsh: 69 per cent in 1968, 57 per cent in 1979 and 69 per cent in 1981. In the same years the percentages describing themselves also as British were 15, 34 and 20. These figures suggest that the number of people describing themselves as Welsh and British rose in the year of most concern and excitement over the question of Welsh home rule, showing, perhaps, that both identities in Wales, British and Welsh, developed in a kind of oppositional symbiosis. The Welsh language was still the most obvious form of Welsh distinctiveness. Here again the Welsh Language Society, and Plaid Cymru, successfully negotiated with the British state.

By 1979 all the major political parties in the United Kingdom were committed to the implementation of a Welsh television channel, but in September 1979 the Thatcher government declared that, while Welsh language broadcasting would be enhanced, there would be no separate channel. In the spring of 1980 the Plaid Cymru president, Gwynfor Evans, announced that he would go on hunger strike unless the government honoured its pledge to Wales. For the first time in its modern history Wales was shaken by the kind of civil disobedience, albeit on a less dangerous scale, that had troubled Northern Ireland in the late 1960s, and in September the government reversed its decision, admitting that it had failed to persuade moderate, middle-ground, opinion 'that our judgement was right'.[75] This success was part of a general advance on the cultural front which raised the profile of the language in Wales, including the right to have Welsh used in the courts of law, thus reversing the Acts of Union of the sixteenth century which compelled the various courts of justice to conduct their business in English, and forbade persons to hold office unless they used the English language.[76]

But this could be interpreted (despite the excitement that it generated) as another example of the mechanism whereby the British state secured the compliance of its Welsh subjects – through a timely cultural and political concession. And it remained to be seen whether or not the doubts about the tendency to regard cultural linguistic nationalism as the true definition of Welshness would raise the alarm over any new proposals of devolution in the latter half of the 1990s, as they did in the second half of the 1970s. If this fear was, as one authority has described it, 'an act of political revenge of the overwhelming anglophone majority in Wales', then its motive force may not yet be expended.[77]

And it was possible that the anglophone majority would, yet again, have to make up its mind about this, and other issues, in the last years of the present century. The Labour Party promised to introduce devolution in Wales, again of a lesser kind than in Scotland. This it appears to be doing in a less than wholly enthusiastic spirit. But advocates of Welsh devolution now gave greater urgency to the democratic deficit,[78] to the need to make the Welsh Office and its many quangos accountable to some representative and responsible institution. Moreover, there seems to be a softening of what might be called unionist Wales to the use by the media of 'nationalistic' language – for example, to the News of Wales on BBC Wales describing itself as the 'National News of Wales', thus distinguishing itself from regional news programmes, which could not thus define themselves. Then there are the possibilities raised by an increased role for Wales in the European Union, with the concept of a 'Europe of the Regions', subsidiarity, and the need to take full advantage of the EU.[79] Wales, it was admitted, like Scotland had a better profile in Europe than did the English regions, thanks to the Welsh Secretary of State; but 'that advantage can only be consolidated when Wales acquires a directly elected Parliament'.[80]

It remained to be seen whether these were signs and portents of a real shift of opinion in Wales over the issue of its 'statelessness', or another example of the revolt of the intellectuals, and other elites, with little or no foundation in the general public. But, whatever the future of devolution in Wales, it is clear that Wales has experienced a very complex and significant shift in her relationship with the British state. When J. Vyrnwy Morgan spoke of the 'outer form of subjugation', at the beginning of one of the most turbulent periods in modern British history, he used the phrase in what might be broadly called a unionist sense – the sense that loss of native institutions were more than compensated for by the firm and good government from the centre. The development of administrative devolution in Wales has reversed this centralization in one sense, yet, arguably, has in another sense facilitated it. The Welsh Office is a buckle that helps bind Wales to England. Yet it also provides a focus for competing pressure groups, though not for the supervisory role of a Welsh Assembly. Some have argued that the outer form of subjugation is also a real form of subjugation, though not so much of Wales by England as of the Welsh people by non-accountable, non-representative, administrative bodies.[81] The stage is set for a battle, not between nationalism and unionism in Wales, not for some last great struggle – or even little struggle – between Wales and England, but between those who see devolution as one way of strengthening the institutions of the British state, and those who see it as a way of weakening the state, which can best be preserved by injecting new life into existing institutions of the union. But this debate is focused on Wales, and speaks in terms of territorial politics, though, arguably, it is at bottom concerned with functional government. The nations of the United Kingdom retain their identities; we are reminded that, if the Welsh can be called a stateless nation, then the United Kingdom can still be seen as a multi-national regime. There may be some doubts about what Wales was, or is; but there can be no doubt that, whatever it was, or is, or will be, it has at least played some role in mediating between state and society in one part of the United Kingdom.

Notes

1 J. Vyrnwy Morgan, *The War and Wales* (London: Chapman & Hall, 1916), pp. 50–1.
2 J. Vyrnwy Morgan, *A Study in Nationality* (London: Chapman & Hall, 1912), p. 415.

 3 G. E. Jones, *Modern Wales: a Concise History, 1485–1979* (Cambridge: Cambridge University Press, 1984), pp. 64–8.
 4 J. Davies, *A History of Wales* (London 1994), pp. 222–80, 284.
 5 Morgan, *A Study in Nationality*, pp. 431, 436–7.
 6 Morgan, *The War and Wales*, pp. 50–1.
 7 C. A. Davies, *Welsh Nationalism in the Twentieth Century: the Ethnic Option and the Modern State* (New York: Praeger, 1989), pp. 10–12.
 8 *Speaker's Conference on Devolution: Letter from Mr Speaker to the Prime Minister*, Cmnd 692 of 1920, pp. 4–5.
 9 Ibid., pp. 22–4.
10 J. Lowther, Lord Ullswater, *A Speaker's Commentaries*, 2 vols (London: Edward Arnold, 1925), vol. 2, p. 269.
11 *Speaker's Conference on Devolution*, p. 38.
12 D. G. Boyce and J. O. Stubbs, 'F. S. Oliver, Lord Selborne and Federalism', *Journal of Imperial and Commonwealth History*, 5, 1 (October 1976), pp. 53–81, at pp. 72–3.
13 N. Masterman, *The Forerunner: the Dilemmas of Tom Ellis, 1859–1899* (Llandybie: Christopher Davies, 1972), pp. 92–6, 181–2. See also R. Coupland, *Welsh and Scottish Nationalism* (London: Collins, 1954), pp. 227–32.
14 As Sir A. H. Williams put it in his *The Background to Welsh History* (Cardiff: Hughes a'i fab, 1950): 'an essentially English radical programme became a peculiarly Welsh national programme' (p. 96).
15 Masterman, *The Forerunner*, p. 185.
16 Ibid., p. 75.
17 H. du Parcq, *The Life of David Lloyd George*, 4 vols (London: Caxton Press, 1912–13), vol. 1, pp. 86–9.
18 Ibid., pp. 145–6. See also Coupland, *Welsh and Scottish Nationalism*, pp. 233–9.
19 Du Parcq, *Lloyd George*, pp. 147–8.
20 Ibid., p. 148. See also C. Wrigley, *Lloyd George* (Oxford: Blackwell, 1992), p. 58.
21 P. J. Randell, 'The Development of Administrative Decentralization in Wales from the Establishment of the Welsh Board of Education in 1907 to the Creation of the post of Secretary of State for Wales in October 1964', PhD thesis (University of Wales, Cardiff, 1967), pp. 2–8.
22 Masterman, *Tom Ellis*, pp. 193–4.
23 Randell, 'Development of Administrative Devolution', pp. 68, 70.
24 Ibid., pp. 76–8.
25 Ibid., pp. 90–108.
26 Masterman, *Tom Ellis*, p. 194.
27 W. Llewllyn Williams, *Cymru Fydd: the Young Wales Movement* (Cardiff, 1894).
28 A. B. Phillip, *The Welsh Question: Nationalism in Welsh Politics, 1945–1970* (Cardiff: Cardiff University Press, 1975), pp. 15–17; Coupland, *Welsh and Scottish Nationalism*, pp. 374–6.
29 P. Morgan, 'Welsh National Consciousness: the Historical Dimension', in W. J. Morgan (ed.) *The Welsh Dilemma: Some Essays on Nationalism*

in Wales (Llandybie: Christopher Davies, 1973), pp. 14–34, at p. 29; Coupland, *Welsh and Scottish Nationalism*, pp. 377–8.

30 G. A. Williams, *When Was Wales?* (London: Penguin, 1985), pp. 283–4.

31 But John Davies argued that 'merely by existing, the party was a declaration of the distinctiveness of Wales' (*A History of Wales*, p. 548).

32 Randell, 'Development of Administrative Devolution', pp. 152–3.

33 Ibid., pp. 153–4.

34 J. Osmond, *Creative Conflict: the Politics of Welsh Devolution* (Llandysul: Gomer Press, 1977), pp. 100–1.

35 Randell, op. cit., p. 243.

36 Morgan, 'Welsh National Consciousness', p. 29.

37 *Hansard, House of Commons Debates*, 5th series, vol. 537, cols 2439–41.

38 Ibid., col. 2450.

39 Ibid., cols 2469–73.

40 Ibid., cols 2525–6.

41 Osmond, *Creative Conflict*, pp. 101–2.

42 Randell, 'Development of Administrative Devolution', p. 246.

43 J. Morris, *The Matter of Wales: Epic View of a Small Country* (London: Penguin, 1984), pp. 376–7; Williams, *When Was Wales?*, p. 291.

44 Randell, op. cit., p. 248.

45 Ibid., p. 249.

46 R. Crossman, *The Diaries of a Cabinet Minister*, vol. 1, *Minister of Housing 1964–66* (London: Hamish Hamilton, 1975), p. 117. P. Madgwick, 'Territorial Ministries: the Scottish and Welsh Offices', in P. Madgwick and R. Rose (eds) *The Territorial Dimension in United Kingdom Politics* (London: Macmillan, 1982), Ch. 1. For Harold Wilson's account of the powers of the Secretary of State, see *Hansard, House of Commons Debates*, 5th series, vol. 702, cols. 623–32.

47 Osmond, *Creative Conflict*, pp. 103–4.

48 *Hansard, House of Commons Debates*, 5th series, vol. 702, col. 630.

49 Plaid Cymru's share of the vote in the next General Election, in 1970, rose to 11.5 per cent but then fell over the decade to 8.1 per cent in 1979, and then rose to 11.5 per cent by 1987. See Davies, *History of Wales*, p. 113; K. O. Morgan, *Rebirth of a Nation: Wales, 1880–1980* (Oxford: Oxford University Press, 1982), p. 393.

50 For a survey of the language question, see N. Thomas, 'The Language and Nationalism', in W. J. Morgan, *The Welsh Dilemma*, pp. 63–72.

51 Davies, *Welsh Nationalism*, pp. 45–6.

52 The General Elections of 1966, 1970 and 1974 (February) and 1974 (October) gave Labour a share of the vote of, respectively, 60.6 per cent, 51.6 per cent, 46.8 per cent and 49.5 per cent. The Conservatives' shares were 27.9, 27.7, 25.9 and 23.9, while Plaid Cymru's were 4.3, 11.5, 10.7 and 10.8. See D. Balsom, 'Public Opinion and Welsh Devolution', in D. Foulkes, J. Barry Jones and R. A. Wilford (eds) *The Welsh Veto: the Wales Act, 1978, and the Referendum* (Cardiff: University of Wales Press, 1983), Ch. 10, at p. 198.

53 Davies, *Welsh Nationalism*, p. 48.
54 *Royal Commission on the Constitution, 1969–1973*, vol. 1, *Report*, Cmnd 5460, (October 1973), pp. 3–7. See also generally Parts I and II, and Part III, Ch. 10. *A Memorandum of Dissent* was also published (vol. 2, Cmnd 5460–1, 1973).
55 J. Bulpitt, *Territory and Power in the United Kingdom: an Interpretation*, (Manchester: Manchester University Press, 1983), p. 184.
56 Cmnd 6348 of 1975.
57 Osmond, *Creative Conflict*, p. 141.
58 Ibid., pp. 247, 157. Morgan *Rebirth of a Nation*, describes the proposed devolution as possessing a 'fair range of powers' (pp. 388–9).
59 Bulpitt, *Territory and Power*, pp. 186–8.
60 D. Balsom, 'Public Opinion and Welsh Devolution', in Foulkes *et. al.*, *The Welsh Veto*, pp. 203–14. R. A. Wilford 'The Character of the Lobbies: Some Theoretical Considerations', ibid., pp. 109–17. J. Barry Jones and R. A. Wilford, 'The Referendum Campaign', ibid., pp. 118–51. H. Pritchard Jones, 'The Referendum and the Welsh Language Press', ibid., pp. 169–83.
61 J. Barry Jones and R. A. Wilford, 'Implications: Two Salient Issues', in Foulkes *et. al.*, *The Welsh Veto*, pp. 216–35, at p. 219.
62 D. Griffiths, *Thatcherism and Territorial Politics* (Aldershot: Avebury, 1996), pp. 38–9.
63 J. Barry Jones and R. A. Wilford, *Parliament and Territoriality: the Committee on Welsh Affairs, 1979–1993* (Cardiff: University of Wales Press, 1986), p. 11.
64 Ibid., pp. 12–13.
65 Ibid., p. 15.
66 From 225 in 1964 (Griffiths, *Thatcherism and Territorial Politics*, p. 52).
67 Ibid., pp. 50–1.
68 P. Walker, *Staying Power: an Autobiography* (London: Bloomsbury, 1991), pp. 202–4, 208, 210–11.
69 Griffiths, *Thatcherism and Territorial Politics*, pp. 114–15. For a discussion of the government's dismissal of criticisms made of its policy in Wales and the alleged danger of social unrest by the Welsh Committee of the House, see Jones and Wilford, *Parliament and Territoriality*, pp. 38–40.
70 Jones and Wilford, ibid., p. 63.
71 Ibid., p. 74.
72 Ibid., p. 83.
73 J. Osmond, 'Remaking Wales', in J. Osmond (ed.) *A Parliament for Wales* (Llandysul: Gomer Press, 1994), pp. 5–33, esp. pp. 9–14.
74 Ibid., p. 48.
75 Davies, *Welsh Nationalism*, pp. 49–50. For a survey of Welsh attitudes to direct action in this period, see W. L. Miller *et. al.*, *Democratic or Violent Protest? Attitudes to Direct Action in Scotland and Wales*, Strathclyde Papers in Public Policy, no. 107 (Strathclyde: Strathclyde University Press, 1982), pp. 10, 13, 42–51.

76 J. Davies, *History of Wales*, p. 66. For examples of cultural concessions in the Welsh Language Act of 1993, see Griffiths, *Thatcherism and Territorial Politics*, pp. 25–6.

77 D. Jones, ' "I Failed Utterly" : Saunders Lewis and the Cultural Politics of Welsh Modernism', *Irish Review*, vol. 19 (Spring/Summer 1996), pp. 22–43.

78 Osmond, in Osmond (ed.), *A Parliament for Wales*, p. 11.

79 Davies, *Welsh Nationalism*, pp. 97–8.

80 I. Bowen Rees, 'Political Identity in a Stateless Nation: the Relationship between Levels of Government in Wales', in Osmond (ed.), *A Parliament for Wales*, pp. 56–8.

81 For a defence of the quango system, see C. Betts (Welsh affairs' correspondent of the *Western Mail*), *Changing Wales: the Political Conundrum. Wales and its Politics in the Century's Last Decade* (Llandysul: Gomer Press, 1993), p. 57.

Chapter 3

The state in independent Ireland

Mary E. Daly

I

Many forces have shaped the independent Irish state. Among the most important are its revolutionary origins and the administrative system and political traditions that it inherited from the long years of British rule. To these we may add the impact of the country's socio-economic structure and the ideological influences of Irish nationalism and Catholic social teaching. The evolution of the state since independence has also been influenced by developments in other Western democracies, such as the emergence of the welfare state in Britain and in Northern Ireland after 1945, and by the changes that have taken place within Irish society, notably the transition to a more urban economy and the declining influence of the Catholic church. Since 1973 the European Community has provided funding for many government programmes and pressed for equal treatment in terms of pay and welfare entitlements. The history of the Irish state provides much evidence of contradiction and tension: between the impulse for change and the strength of continuity; between the liberal traditions of a weak state inherited from Britain and the more prescriptive approach derived from Roman Catholicism; between the theoretical claims for a 32-county Ireland and the reality of a 26-county state, and between the naive faith that the state could determine a country's economic destiny and the practical constraints applying to a small country on the periphery of Europe.

The Irish Free State marked a compromise between two conflicting alternatives: the thirty-two county Irish Republic which had been declared during the course of the abortive 1916 Rebellion and reaffirmed by Dáil Éireann in 1919, and the partitioned subordinate statelet provided in the 1920 Government of Ireland Act. In

December 1921, however, the Anglo-Irish Treaty conceded
Dominion status – a substantially greater measure of autonomy
than was envisaged in the 1920 Act, though something less than the
status of a republic. When the state was established in December
1922, the six counties that constituted Northern Ireland exercised
their right, under the Anglo-Irish Treaty, to opt out. As a result the
state's boundaries were reviewed. In 1925, however, the Irish and
British governments agreed to suppress the findings of the
Boundary Commission, and the minor changes that it recommended, were never implemented. The 1922 constitution established
a system of parliamentary democracy, with the executive drawn
from the majority party in the legislature or Dáil, an arrangement
that followed closely on the practice at Westminster.[1] The electorate
consisted of men and women aged over 21 years. Candidates were
elected by a system of proportional representation, a provision that
had been included in the 1920 Government of Ireland Act in order
to ensure adequate representation for minority interests. In contrast
to Britain, the new state had a written constitution. It also inherited
an administrative system that reflected that which had been recently
overhauled by Whitehall.[2]

Although Britain and Ireland formed a United Kingdom
between 1801 and 1922, the Irish state during these years displayed
marked differences from the state in Britain. As Alan Ward noted,
the union 'was approached in a strange way that did little to
eradicate the sense that Ireland was a separate political community'.[3] It had a separate administration, consisting of a Viceroy and
a Chief Secretary; the latter post generally carrying Cabinet rank.
The Under-Secretary, the most senior civil servant, oversaw all Irish
services; this was an extremely powerful position, particularly as the
Chief Secretary spent long periods in London. The Irish administration was more intrusive, more centralized and bureaucratic, than
its counterpart in England and Wales. Ireland had a state-funded
system of primary education many years before England and Wales
did, and the Irish Poor Law provided medical care through a system
of dispensaries for approximately one-third of the population.
Oliver MacDonagh has argued that Britain used Ireland as an
administrative laboratory.[4] Both the police and the educational
system were regulated from Dublin, whereas in England and Wales
they were overseen by local committees that included elected
representatives. The ratio of constabulary to population was more
than double the ratio in Britain and the proportion of soldiers was

higher. The soldiers and constabulary were concentrated in areas with above-average civil and agrarian unrest.[5] The number of inspectors employed by the Irish Local Government Board to oversee local authorities was also proportionately higher than in England and Wales.[6]

These practices reflected Ireland's quasi-colonial status. Faced with the dilemma of placing education and the police under control of the local Anglo-Irish elite or under the nationalist majority, who were often regarded as incapable of honest and efficient administration, Dublin Castle favoured a centralized bureaucracy as the lesser evil.[7]

By the second decade of the twentieth century a plethora of commissions and boards oversaw services such as primary and secondary education, economic development along the western seaboard, and land purchase and expenditure on public works.[8] Since appointments to these boards generally went to government supporters, their membership reflected British, but not Irish, political opinion. Indeed the so-called 'Castle Boards' offered a covert mechanism for preserving the authority of the Anglo-Irish ascendancy after it had lost electoral influence.[9]

The attitudes of Irish nationalists towards the state were coloured both by past experiences and by perceptions of British rule. Powerful grass-roots movements such as the Catholic Association and the Irish Party ensured that Irish nationalism received a precocious lesson in the effectiveness of mass organization, and in how to play and indeed bend the rules of parliamentary politics. Whether such familiarity with the mother of parliaments led to a certain contempt for the parliamentary system is a moot point. Many Irish people, both unionist and nationalist, had a rather equivocal attitude towards the state, and at various times, such as during the years of the land war, the plan of campaign and the Ulster crisis, a substantial number openly defied the authorities. Yet such actions were not necessarily regarded as incompatible with asking the government for money. During the Anglo-Irish war of 1919–21 local authorities who had sworn allegiance to Dáil Éireann often attempted to obtain loans or grants from the Local Government Board.[10]

Most nationalists believed that British rule in Ireland had inflicted considerable damage on Irish society during the course of the nineteenth century. The crimes for which it was held responsible included the decline of the Irish language, the Great Famine and the collapse of Irish industry: the latter were seen as the consequences of *laissez-faire* economics. Many nationalists believed that a more active state that took account of Irish needs would end emigration, reverse the decline of the rural population, and revive Irish industries and the Irish language.[11] Such expectations were fuelled by the belief that the interventionist policies favoured by the Irish parliament of the late eighteenth century (commonly known as 'Grattan's parliament') had resulted in economic prosperity.

Despite such inexorable pressures for an interventionist state, there were countervailing forces. In 1922 the Irish Free State was overwhelmingly Catholic and rural. Employees accounted for 44.5 per cent of the labour force, but they were outnumbered by the sum of employers (6.1 per cent), assisting relatives (20.7 per cent) and the self-employed (22.7 per cent). The rights of private property were regarded as sacrosanct; most farmers had become property owners only within the previous generation. (Such attitudes did not extend to the landlord class, who were regarded as having obtained their property by confiscation.) Although old-age pensions were universally welcome when introduced in 1908, the Irish Party believed that such a generous level of payments could not be maintained after Home Rule. It also regarded the Liberal Government's provisions for health and unemployment insurance as too expensive, and anyway unnecessary in a predominantly rural country. As to the needs of the urban working class, the section relating to Ireland in the *Royal Commission on the Poor Laws* argued that these needs could best be met by the rural resettlement of those affected.[12]

Such attitudes reflected the prevailing belief that Ireland's destiny was other than to become an urban and industrial society. They also mirrored the view of the Catholic Church, that responsibility for providing for sickness and poverty should rest in the first instance with the family and with private charities, the state helping out only where these agencies had failed. Such views reflected the Church's fear of socialism. The attitude of the Irish Catholic Church was also coloured by the fact that, during the nineteenth century, there were numerous disputes between Church and state over their respective roles in education and in providing for orphans and the sick. By the end of the nineteenth century, however, the state had gone to considerable lengths to accommodate the wishes of the Catholic Church and the religious sensibilities of the population. A non-denominational national school system was now denominational in practice if not in theory, the majority of schools being under clerical management; the state provided subsidies to private secondary schools that were segregated on the basis of religion and gender but did not interfere in their administration, and the Irish university system (again non-denominational in theory) tacitly recognized the sectarian divisions on the island. Catholic sisters were employed as nurses in many of the country's workhouses; Catholic priests served in workhouses as chaplains, while religious orders managed reformatories and industrial schools that were funded by the state.[13]

II

The Catholic and rural ethos of the Irish Free State was significantly enhanced as a consequence of the 1920 Government of Ireland Act which established the separate state of Northern Ireland. Territorial definition was only one of the problems facing the Irish Free State in 1922. Its survival was threatened by civil war, as was its future as a democracy. The extent of British authority over the new state was unclear, because dominion status was evolving.[14] Dáil Éireann approved the Anglo-Irish Treaty by 64 votes to 57. In the General Election of June 1922, 36 anti-Treaty candidates were returned; the remaining 128 seats went to pro-Treaty candidates. Yet opponents of the Treaty argued that neither the legislature nor the electorate could reverse the earlier declaration of a republic. As Éamon de Valera stated, 'The majority have no right to do wrong.'[15] Other republicans argued that the Irish Republican Army derived its mandate from the 1916 rebellion rather than from an elected assembly. When republican forces resorted to civil war in June 1922, they threatened not only the constitutional basis of the state as enshrined in the Anglo-Irish Treaty but the very survival of democracy.

Although the civil war ended in 1923 with a victory for government forces, incidents such as an attempted army mutiny in 1924 and the assassination of Home Affairs Minister Kevin O'Higgins in 1927 suggested that a stable electoral democracy was not yet assured. In 1923 the anti-Treaty deputies absented themselves from Dáil Éireann arguing that the assembly was illegal. (They also refused to take an oath of allegiance to the crown.) In 1927, however, after the assassination of Kevin O'Higgins, the government succeeded in persuading the abstentionist deputies to take their seats, by threatening to require all candidates for election to give a commitment to do so. In 1932 the Fianna Fáil party, which represented the defeated side in the civil war, took power peacefully, having emerged victorious in the General Election. During the 1920s the government curtailed the power of the army by a sustained programme of demobilization, and by ensuring that authority rested firmly in the hands of the cabinet. It also established the state's legitimacy in the eyes of the civilian population, introducing an unarmed police force that achieved widespread respect, and a court system that marked a compromise between the British system and the less orthodox courts organized by the first Dáil.[16] Compliance with rate collection, which was the most extensive form of direct taxation, slowly increased. In County Leitrim, the worst offender, only 23 per cent of rates were collected in 1927–28; two years later the figure reached 99 per cent.[17] The incidence of robberies on banks and post offices, the majority of them perpetrated by paramilitary forces, fell sharply.

Between 1922 and 1938 the remaining constraints on Irish sovereignty disappeared. Initially this was achieved in concert with other dominions, which also were concerned to enhance their autonomy *vis-à-vis* Westminster. Yet after 1931, when the Statute of Westminster confirmed that no law enacted by the United Kingdom parliament should extend to a dominion unless the dominion consented, the Irish Free State was on its own.[18] In 1933 the government removed the oath of allegiance to the crown taken by all deputies and senators, and abolished legal appeals to the privy council. The 1936 External Relations Act removed the King from the constitution. In 1938 Britain agreed to evacuate its three remaining naval bases, paving the way for Ireland to declare its neutrality when war broke out in 1939.[19]

At Britain's insistence the 1922 constitution reflected the terms of the Anglo-Irish Treaty. Nevertheless, as Leo Kohn noted, it retained a ,strong republican flavour, particularly in its acknowledgement 'that lawful authority comes from God to the people'.[20] The 1937 constitution ended such ambiguity by removing all references to royal prerogatives and providing for a directly elected President as Head of State. Yet this did not entirely clarify the position. Despite drafting an overtly republican constitution, de Valera did not declare a republic. He argued that it was important to retain a vestigial link with the crown (under the 1936 External Relations Act the crown accredited Irish diplomats and consular agents) in order to provide a bridge towards a united Ireland, and that the term 'republic' should apply only to a 32-county state. Opposition deputies showed little sympathy with such nuances. In 1949 the Inter-Party Government (representing all parties except Fianna Fáil) repealed the 1936 Act. Ireland became a republic and left the Commonwealth. It had not been active in Commonwealth affairs since 1932.[21]

Defining the boundaries of the state was more problematical. Irish nationalism has displayed a consistently wide gulf between the rhetoric of a 32-county Ireland and practical measures that might make this a reality. In 1922 when some teachers in northern Catholic schools preferred to remain under the Dublin educational system, the Irish Free State proved reluctant to pay their salaries; it also rejected approaches from nationalist local authorities in County Down that wished to come under its jurisdiction. During the 1930s the Fianna Fáil Government rejected suggestions from northern nationalists that deputies representing Northern Ireland constituencies be permitted to take their seats in Dáil Éireann.[22] It was alleged, with some justification, that the systematic removal of all constitutional ties to Britain and the Commonwealth 'might have been designed to consolidate Partition'.[23] Yet the aspiration towards a united Ireland, however vague, remained powerful. Articles 2 and 3 of the 1937 constitution should be seen both as a reflection of this contradictory stance and as an attempt to assuage the nationalist conscience; the clauses were probably the minimum that would have been acceptable to the majority of the electorate at the time. Article 2 states that '[t]he national territory consists of the whole island of Ireland, its islands and the territorial seas', while article 3 acknowledges that 'pending the re-integration of the national territory' the constitution would apply only to the Irish Free State. While Ulster unionists, not surprisingly, regard these clauses as evidence of the Irish state's irredentist tendencies, hard-line republicans from the southern state are more likely to justify their involvement in Northern Ireland affairs with a reference to the declaration of a 32-county republic in 1916.[24] In 1990, however, the Irish Supreme Court stated that article 2 of the constitution 'consists of a declaration of the extent of the national territory as a claim of legal right. The restriction imposed by article 3 prohibiting the enactment of laws applicable to the counties of Northern Ireland, pending re-integration of the national territory, in no way derogates from this claim.'[25]

III

The birth of the Irish Free State at a time of civil war meant that civil liberties were curtailed as government resorted to internment, established military courts and imposed mandatory sentences of capital punishment for a wide range of offences. In addition, the political climate of the early 1920s, when opposition politicians questioned the legitimacy of the state and abstained from the Dáil, meant that the government showed little sympathy with dissenting views. Such attitudes owed something to the legacy of constitutional nationalism. Between 1895 and 1910 less than 40 per cent of Irish parliamentary seats were contested.[26] In the 1918 General Election 25 of the 73 successful Sinn Féin candidates were returned unopposed; in 1920 all the seats for the parliament of Southern Ireland were filled without an election. Irish politicians do not appear to have fully appreciated the merits of an active opposition. According to Tom Garvin, 'most Irish people, whether Protestant or Catholic, were majoritarian rather than pluralist democrats'.[27] In that respect the split of Sinn Féin into two rival parties may have been fortuitous. Nevertheless during the 1930s much of the opposition to the government from both right and left was expressed in extra-parliamentary fashion by organizations such as the quasi-fascist 'blueshirts' and the IRA, a tradition that reflects the legacy of earlier movements such as the Land League. Both the Cumann na nGaedheal and Fianna Fáil Governments resorted to authoritarian measures to deal with dissent. In October 1931 the Cumann na nGaedheal Government established a military tribunal to meet the threat posed by left-wing republican organizations and used some of these powers to sue the *Irish Press*, the organ of the Fianna Fáil Party, for seditious libel. After 1932 Fianna Fáil employed similar powers under the Offences Against the State Act against the blueshirts and the IRA. During the Second World War over 500 republicans were interned without trial, because the government feared that the IRA's bombing campaign in England and its contacts with Germany jeopardized national security. Six men were executed; three died on hunger strike.[28] Internment was reintroduced during the IRA's 'Operation Harvest', between 1956 and 1961. In 1972 the Offences Against the State Act was strengthened to deal with the renewed threat posed by the Provisional IRA, though internment was not used.

During the 1920s the government abandoned several experimental features of the 1922 constitution because it believed that a strong executive was essential to democracy. These features included the appointment of extern ministers who would not necessarily be members of the Oireachtas (the two Houses of Parliament) and would not share in collective responsibility, and the provision that 50,000 voters might petition the Oireachtas to enact a specific measure; if it refused, the matter would be put to the people in a Referendum. Cumann na nGaedheal also ended direct elections to the Upper House or Seanad, and limited its powers. The Fianna Fáil Government continued this trend, abolishing the Seanad in 1936 and replacing it with a weaker body that could delay non-money bills for 90 days only, against the 20 months laid down in the 1922 constitution. Although the new Seanad was to be elected from five panels representing vocational interests, as the electorate (with the exception of the university seats) consisted of members of the Oireachtas and local councillors, it came to be dominated by party politics.[29]

No efforts were made to compensate for a weak upper house by increasing the powers of the Dáil, or Lower House. In April 1933 de Valera informed TDs that the Cabinet needed more time away from its parliamentary duties in order to tackle national problems; he suggested that the Dáil should be given 'say six months holidays to get that work done'. During the 1930s the government tried to avoid having to submit details of its industrial policy to scrutiny by the Dáil.[30] In September 1939, following the outbreak of the Second World War, the government introduced the Emergency Power Bill, which gave it powers 'for securing the public safety and preservation of the State in times of war'. This meant that many measures that would otherwise require specific legislation, and consequent detailed scrutiny by the legislature, could be implemented by decree. These powers were used extensively to strengthen state censorship – even to the extent of censoring Dáil debates – to freeze wages and to restrict personal freedom and economic activity. Although there was an obvious need for emergency powers, they would appear to have been used more extensively than circumstances dictated, and many of them were retained after the wartime emergency ended.[31]

The powers of the executive were not limited to any significant extent by the Head of State. The 1922 constitution provided for a Governor-General as the King's representative in Ireland, though unlike other dominions the Governor-General was an Irishman, whose name was proposed by the government. Despite this concession, the office undoubtedly rankled, and even the Cumann na nGaedheal Government favoured a low profile. There was no Irish state-opening of parliament (nor is there to this day), and the practice of the Governor-General addressing both Houses of the Oireachtas was quietly dropped in 1923.[32] Although the 1937 constitution provided for an elected President, he/she was not described as Head of State. The constitution merely stated that the President 'shall take precedence over all other persons in the State', and the office continued to be viewed with many of the reservations associated with the office of Governor-General. The President possesses only two powers that can be exercised with absolute discretion: the power to appoint some of the members of the Council of State (the remainder are ex-officio) and the power to grant or refuse a dissolution of the Dáil. The President may refer a bill to the Supreme Court in order to test its constitutionality if advised to do so by the Council of State; in other respects the President can act only on the approval or advice of the government.[33] Until the election of Mary Robinson in 1990 the office was seriously underfunded.

To a strong executive, a weak legislature and a weak Head of State, we may add a weak system of local government. During the nineteenth century the Irish state displayed strong centralist tendencies. Before 1922 Irish nationalists seem to have regarded local democracy as a stepping stone towards a national parliament. The leadership of Dáil Éireann regarded many local authorities as inefficient and corrupt, and it criticized their unwillingness to place the national interest ahead of local concerns. In 1924 rural district councils, the lowest tier of local authorities, were abolished. In 1933, Seán T. O'Kelly, Minister for Local Government and Public Health, informed the Cabinet that as county councils had become 'an expensive anachronism' they should be abolished, though the cabinet disagreed. Local authorities appear to have been subjected to more stringent controls after 1922 than under the local government board. Between 1923 and 1931 a total of 36 local authorities were dissolved, including four county councils and Dublin and Cork Corporations; a further six county councils were suspended between 1932 and 1942. During the first 20 years of independence local elections, which were scheduled to take place at three-year intervals, were postponed on four occasions. In 1942 responsibility for major executive decisions, including the allocation of local authority housing and most junior appointments, was transferred from elected councillors to the new office of County Manager. Senior posts had been filled by the local appointments commission since 1926. Although these reforms resulted in a more efficient and a more honest system of local government, councillors and back-bench TDs complained bitterly at the growth of bureaucracy and the increase in central control. The irritation often expressed by local authorities at the directives emanating from the Department of Local Government and Public Health, echoed the resentment felt by nineteenth-century Irish boards of guardians towards the local government board. Old attitudes die hard and tensions between central and local interests appear to have transcended a common commitment towards Irish independence.[34]

As Joseph Lee noted, the emasculation of local democracy was inextricably linked with the impotence of Dáil Éireann.[35] Because TDs had limited power to scrutinize and modify legislation or the estimates of government departments – which are generally debated at a relatively late stage in the financial year, i.e. when most money has already been earmarked and often spent – deputies tended to spend their time responding to local needs: querying a constituent's entitlement to a pension, lobbying for the completion of a local housing scheme or attempting to secure industrial investment. This again reflects continuity with the past: as Theo Hoppen has shown, the parish pump was a potent factor in Irish political life during the nineteenth century.[36] The Irish electoral system, with its multi-seat constituencies, where members of the same political party are often in competition for votes, has been an additional factor in perpetuating such practices.[37]

IV

The administration of the Irish state has frequently been described as powerful, secretive and having many similarities with that of the British civil service. The 1924 Ministers and Secretaries Act replaced 47 departments, boards and commissions with 11 departments, though a further array of boards and state corporations soon appeared. The 1924 Act followed British practice by affirming that responsibility rested with the Minister, and by giving the Department of Finance control over expenditure and personnel. All proposals that necessitated expenditure had first to be considered by Finance before being submitted to the Cabinet. Despite considerable pressure on politicians to use public employment as a reward for loyalty, neither the establishment of the Irish Free State, nor Fianna Fáil's taking office in 1932 were marked by a purge of civil servants. Indeed 21,000 of the civil servants initially employed by the new state had previously served under the British administration, against a mere 131 who had worked with Dáil Éireann. After 1924 recruitment for all positions was handled by the Civil Service Commission. The continuity between the Irish civil service under the union and the administration of the Irish Free State – and the considerable (even excessive) powers exercised by officials in the Department of Finance – have come to be accepted almost as truisms in the history of twentieth-century Ireland. Indeed the baleful hand of the Department of Finance and the long-distance influence of the Treasury (for many years an open telephone line linked the Department of Finance offices in Merrion Street to the Treasury in Whitehall) have come to be seen as key reasons for the economic failings of the independent Irish state.[38] Both arguments should be qualified. Although the overwhelming majority of Irish civil servants were trained within the British administrative system, most senior officials retired during the early 1920s. Their successors tended to be Irish-born and Catholic; the majority had not attended university. Before 1922 these men had deeply resented the cultural and social superiority of the elite who monopolized the senior positions, particularly as few of these posts were held by Irishmen. Although the Irish civil service began to recruit its own first-division in 1924 – administrative officers who were university graduates – most senior positions were filled by promotion from lower ranks. Only one-quarter of secretaries of government departments between 1923 and 1968 were university graduates.[39] Consequently the new Irish administration never developed the cosy links with the universities that characterized the British civil service. The Garda Síochána, or Irish police force, also abolished the distinction that had existed in the RIC between cadets (who tended to be drawn from Anglo-Irish families) and rank-and-file policemen in favour of promotion from the ranks.[40]

The extent to which the Department of Finance controlled public expenditure must be examined within the context of the state's involvement in the economy. Irish nationalism had a strongly mercantile flavour, which was enhanced by the belief that the *laissez-faire* policies favoured by successive British governments had damaged the economy. There was a determination to reverse many of the changes of the post-famine era such as the falling population, emigration, the switch from tillage to pasture and the decline of traditional manufacturing industries. Between 1922 and 1932, however, the government chose to consolidate its economic ties to Britain and to keep taxes and expenditure under tight control in order to maintain the competitiveness of agricultural exports. This programme disappointed many interest groups and it proved increasingly unpopular after 1929, when international recession halted emigration. The Fianna Fáil Government that took office in 1932 favoured a combination of economic and political nationalism at a time when many other countries were pursuing self-sufficiency programmes as a means of combating recession. By reducing economic dependence on Britain, it promised to create jobs both in agriculture and in industry. The new protected industries would be scattered throughout small towns, under native ownership and control, and they would employ men rather than women. This agenda reflected a naive confidence in the state's ability to override market forces and to defy the laws of economics. It also reflected the not-uncommon desire on the part of a new state to control its economic destiny, and the belief that the ideal Ireland consisted of small farms and small towns – the antithesis of urban and industrial Britain.

Imports were restricted by tariffs, quotas and licences. Farmers were offered guaranteed prices for favoured products such as sugar beet. Flour millers, tobacco manufacturers and producers of animal feeds were required to use a designated quota of Irish raw materials. A state-owned company was established to exploit turf as a source of fuel in place of English and Welsh coal. Other state companies processed sugar beet, manufactured steel and produced industrial alcohol from potatoes – the latter at enormous cost. Foreign-owned firms were prevented from manufacturing in Ireland except under licence. The government introduced legislation enabling it to regulate working hours and conditions, to gender quota and even to ban women from working in a specific industry, though these latter powers were never exercised. The objectives often proved to be mutually inconsistent. In order to attain self-sufficiency in tyres it was necessary to permit a foreign-owned company (Dunlop) to establish a plant; a state investment bank helped foreign companies to bypass the legal restrictions on operating in Ireland. The desire to create the maximum number of jobs meant that the government could not reject firms with a majority of female workers, or those that insisted on locating in Dublin.[41]

The economic programme of the 1930s cast a long shadow. Although it soon became apparent that many objectives were unattainable, successive governments found it difficult to abandon the aspirations. From 1938 until the late 1950s economic policy was caught between the contradictory goals of maintaining close trading links with Britain and extending self-sufficiency. In a vain effort to reverse rural depopulation, farmers were offered guaranteed prices for labour-intensive produce such as eggs and butter, which were exported at a loss. After 1949, when the state-controlled Industrial Development Authority began to seek overseas investors, foreign companies were still required to obtain a licence and to locate in the west of Ireland. Firms employing a predominantly female workforce were not welcome until the late 1970s.

Trends in public expenditure mirrored the wider economic policy. Expenditure remained low until 1932. Since the 1930s all political parties (with the possible exception of the Progressive Democrats) have favoured an interventionist economic policy. This reflects the fact that Irish political parties have tended to be catch-all parties, not clearly polarized between left and right. As a consequence of this consensus the government's share of GNP increased from approximately 19 per cent of the national product in 1926 to 67 per cent by 1985. Between 1931 and 1933 it rose by three or four percentage points, with farm subsidies (to compensate for depressed prices consequent on a trade war with Britain) and more generous support for housing and the unemployed accounting for the increase. Public expenditure fell in real terms during the 1939–45 emergency because of a shortage of materials, in marked contrast to the sharp rise that occurred in countries that were at war. As shortages eased and as Marshall Aid funds became available, public expenditure rose from 33.5 per cent of GNP in 1949–50 to 41.3 per cent in 1951–2; the additional spending went on social investment such as housing and hospitals. After 1952 public spending was curtailed because of successive balance of payments' crises and the difficulty in financing national loans.[42]

None of the policies pursued after 1932, other than the return to close trading links with Britain, met with the approval of the Department of Finance. However, Finance's views did not really prevail until the late 1950s when a succession of fiscal crises, coupled with a record level of emigration, prompted a reconsideration of the prevailing policies. As Garret FitzGerald has noted, *Economic Development*, the report written by T. K. Whitaker, secretary of the Department of Finance, marked a return to the policies of the 1920s (or rather an attempt to do so).[43] It recommended abandoning protection, an end to subsidies for unprofitable farm produce, a shift of public investment towards productive purposes and away from hospitals and houses, and the abandoning of social objectives, such as decentralization, in favour of achieving a higher rate of economic growth.

Between 1959 and 1964 the Irish economy achieved an annual growth rate of over 3 per cent. Manufacturing industry employment and industrial exports rose sharply as foreign-owned firms took advantage of the booming world economy. Although *Economic Development* had emphasized that the government had only limited power to transform the economy, the high growth-rate of the early 1960s encouraged a new wave of interventionist measures. The Second Programme for Economic Expansion (1964–70, but abandoned in 1968), laid down detailed and often unrealizable projections for individual industries. The gap between the state's faith in its ability to achieve an economic miracle and the reality itself was probably reached in 1978 with the publication of the Green Paper 'Development for Full Employment' and the ambitious programme of expenditure and tax cuts introduced by the Fianna Fáil Government in 1977.[44]

The share of national income taken by the public sector began to rise from 1963, and it accelerated after 1973. The Common Agricultural Policy and the regional and social funds provided new sources of income. Irish voters were aware that social security payments were less generous than the Community norm, and clamoured for adjustments. Ireland, like most other European countries, tried to reverse the economic recession that was triggered by the 1973 oil crisis by running a deficit on public expenditure. By 1975 the public sector's share of GDP was above the Community average; statistics suggest that by the early 1980s Ireland had the second largest public sector share in the EEC. The national debt soared from little more than half of GNP in 1973 to one-and-a-half times GNP by the mid-1980s, though it has fallen significantly since that time.[45]

Recent decades have seen the decline of economic nationalism in favour of a more open economy. This process began in 1957 with the removal of restrictions on foreign investment. Other landmarks were the 1965 Anglo-Irish Free Trade Agreement, which re-established free-trade between Britain and Ireland, membership of the EEC in 1973, and the decision to join the European monetary system in 1979. In 1988 the value of exports and imports amounted to 140 per cent of GDP in comparison with 60 per cent in 1960;[46] foreign-owned manufacturing and service industries account for a substantial share of employment and exports. This growing internationalism has been seen as an opportunity to assert Irish independence from Britain, which now accounts for a much smaller share of Irish trade. When sterling was devalued in 1931, 1949 and 1967, the Irish pound automatically followed suit. Ireland was given no advance warning of this decision in 1931 or in 1949. In 1980, because Britain had opted not to join the European monetary system, parity between the British and Irish currencies, which had lasted for over 150 years, was broken. The political dimensions of this decision are best captured by the remark of a senior official in the Department of Finance that '[en]try into the EMS was a sign that the Irish economy had come of age'.[47]

Did the government's intervention assist or damage the economy? In 1913 GNP per capita in Ireland was close to the European average, at approximately 60 per cent of the UK's level. By 1985 Ireland ranked below all countries in Western Europe except Portugal and Greece.[48] Some economists believe that there is a tendency for economies to converge, i.e. that less prosperous countries catch up on the leaders. Ireland seems to be an exception. Over the years 1950–1988, although Ireland achieved a higher rate of economic growth than did Britain, it failed to catch up with the more prosperous European economies, as also had other poor countries such as Spain and Portugal.[49] One possible explanation lies in Ireland's close economic links with Britain, another poor performer. State policies may also have been important. The uncompetitive mentality fostered in the 1930s, and the practice of subordinating economic development to cultural, political and social objectives, resulted in a less than efficient use of capital and a low growth rate. For decades successive governments insisted that trans-Atlantic air services land at Shannon airport on the west coast, even though this meant losing American carriers which would have brought additional tourists. Expenditure on roads and sanitary services was often used to create short-term jobs in backward regions rather than to relieve traffic congestion and water shortages in expanding areas. The Land Commission continued to create small-holdings despite the evidence that people were emigrating from similar farms because they could not earn an adequate livelihood.

During the 1930s the government was widely criticized for failing to consult industrialists and trade unionists about its economic programme. In time, however, these interests were accommodated by the state. The 1946 Industrial Relations Act established a Labour Court, consisting of employer and worker representatives with a neutral chairman appointed by the government, to adjudicate on wage demands and provide conciliation services. This provided a mechanism for employer and labour interests to negotiate national norms for increases in wages and salaries. In 1970 this process was replaced by a more formal Employer–Labour Conference. During the 1960s the government established consultative committees for individual industries to enable them to adapt to free trade. Since the 1970s the government has become more involved in the process of wage bargaining, offering tax concessions and commitments of public expenditure in return for moderate increases in pay.[50] This would appear to grant employers, trades union and farming interests a greater influence over economic policy than that of rank-and-file TDs.

The improved performance of the Irish economy in the 1990s has sometimes been attributed to this co-operation between the state and corporate interests. In 1985 Katzenstein suggested that the success of several small European economies (not including Ireland) could be attributed to strong corporate institutions and high levels of government assistance, though he believed that it was also essential that the economies were exposed to international competition.[51] Mancur Olson, however, has argued that vested interests have often resulted in a less efficient economy, though this thesis has been hotly contested.[52] The protectionist economic climate of the 1930s created a host of vested interests that resisted change in later years. From 1938 Irish industrialists successfully resisted efforts to reduce protection, and when Ireland began to welcome foreign investment in the late 1950s overseas companies were discouraged and even prohibited from competing in the domestic market in order to protect existing industrial interests.[53] However it would be unfair to adopt a wholly negative attitude towards the state's involvement in the economy. Ireland's success in attracting overseas investment is due to a successful government industrial promotion agency and to the tax and other financial incentives provided, together with the measures taken to adapt the educational system to meet market needs. While it is easy to criticize past efforts to create employment and to sustain small farms, they may have contributed towards the overall stability of the state. This is certainly true of the measures introduced during the 1930s when emigration was not an option.

V

Since 1922 the state has become much more involved in providing medical, educational and welfare services. In the 1920s state services were often limited to the poor, whereas child benefit, hospital care and fees-paid third-level education are now universally available. By the 1980s 40 per cent of the population received some form of social welfare benefit.[54] Although the expansion of state welfare services is a feature common to most Western democracies in this century, the process was somewhat delayed in Ireland. The 1930s saw the establishment of vocational schools and the introduction of means-tested unemployment assistance and means-tested pensions for widows and orphans. During the 1940s considerable attention was given to planning the future structure of health and welfare services. This was prompted both by the British blueprints for a post-war welfare state, which would apply in Northern Ireland, and by the evidence that was emerging of the extent of urban poverty, the high level of infant mortality in working-class families, and the apparent failure to tackle tuberculosis. The establishment of separate Departments for Health and for Social Welfare in 1947 provides the most concrete evidence of the government's intent.[55] Yet the actual changes were limited: more hospitals were built, and the 1952 Social Welfare Act increased the numbers covered by social insurance; in 1953 the state provided free medical care for babies for the first six weeks and free maternity care for the majority of women. Health and social welfare services were further extended during the 1970s. The Irish education system underwent no significant changes, however, between 1930 and the late 1960s.

The failure in the late 1940s to introduce an Irish variant of the welfare state was due to two factors: cost, and ideological objections. In 1943 it was calculated that replicating the planned British social security system would cost 28.9 per cent of Irish national income, against an estimated 15.2 per cent of Britain's.[56] By the 1970s a more prosperous economy was in a better position to finance such services; moreover, attitudes had changed. During the nineteenth century Church and state had come into conflict over their respective roles in education and healthcare. Any alteration to the status quo threatened to destroy the delicate equilibrium that had evolved. During the years 1900–20 the Catholic Church had opposed plans to raise additional revenue for the national schools through local taxation, because this would entail ceding control to local education committees. The fact that the membership of local authorities was overwhelmingly nationalist and Catholic does not appear to have blunted the Church's suspicion. When the Dáil Éireann Department of Local Government closed workhouses and replaced them with county hospitals and county homes in 1921 and 1922, the clergy demanded that the new institutions be controlled by religious rather than lay matrons.[57] When the 1930 Vocational Education Act was introduced, the reservations expressed by the Catholic Church at the establishment of non-denominational schools under lay control were allayed by appointing clergymen (often as chairmen) to vocational education committees and by restricting the curriculum to ensure that the schools would not compete with private secondary schools.[58]

Although none of the measures introduced by the government between 1932 and 1939 directly affected Church interests, the growing state involvement in economic matters prompted sections of the Catholic Church to launch an attack on bureaucracy and the power of the state. Catholic social teaching, expressed in the 1931 papal encyclical *Quadragesimo Anno*, suggested that responsibility for social and economic programmes should be entrusted to vocational interests, as opposed to being managed by the state. A government-appointed commission that sat during 1939–43 examined the possibility of developing vocational structures in Ireland.[59] Although its recommendations were ignored, the commission's comments concerning the excessive power of the state left their mark. Several contributors to a 1949 symposium which considered the White Paper on social insurance criticized the 'tendency to enhance the work of the State and to weaken the sense of personal responsibility', the 'persistence of British administrative techniques' more than twenty-five years after Ireland's independence, and suggested that the proposals were inappropriate for a peasant economy.[60] In what would appear to have been a pre-emptive strike against a comprehensive welfare state, Dr John Dignan, Catholic bishop of Clonfert, who was Chairman of the

National Health Insurance Society, in 1944 published a plan to reorganize social services on vocational lines.[61]

This ideological debate came to a head with the 1951 Mother and Child Scheme, one of the most prominent landmarks in the history of independent Ireland. As a first step towards providing a comprehensive state medical service, the government proposed to provide free ante- and post-natal care for women, and free care for children up to the age of 16. The plan aroused the wrath of the medical profession and the Catholic Church, who objected to the provision of a free service to all, irrespective of need, and to the fact that it would be provided by doctors who were salaried public servants. Other issues, such as the possibility of women being given advice on contraception, that might be contrary to Catholic teaching also featured in the dispute. The scheme collapsed because of the opposition of these interest groups, and a lack of support from the Inter-Party Government; many of its members had been among the most vociferous critics while in opposition. The expansion of a state medical service gave rise to similar conflicts in France, Switzerland and Sweden around this time.[62] The readiness of the Irish state to capitulate on this matter is an indication of the influence of the Catholic Church and the medical profession, and also of the fact that it was not countered by sustained popular support for an expanded health service: the proposal to introduce the Mother and Child Scheme originated within the civil service.

Following his resignation from office, the former Minister for Health, Noel Browne, published the correspondence that had taken place between himself, the Catholic hierarchy and the Taoiseach, John A. Costello, concerning the Mother and Child Scheme.[63] This revealed for the first time the extent to which government ministers, including Browne, consulted and even deferred to the Catholic hierarchy. When the Catholic Church raised objections to the much more modest health scheme proposed by Fianna Fáil in 1952–3, the matter was resolved in private talks held at the presidential residence, Áras an Uachtaráin. In 1923 when the first application for divorce came before the government of the Irish Free State, the President of the Executive Council, W. T. Cosgrave, sought the views of the Catholic Archbishop of Dublin.[64]

Éamon de Valera is known to have consulted members of the Society of Jesus and other Catholic clergy when the 1937 constitution was being drafted, though their influence over the final document was limited; he resisted demands that he 'make a definite break with the Liberal and non-Christian type of state'. Although in article 44 the state recognized the 'special position' of the Roman Catholic Church 'as the guardian of the Faith professed by the great majority of the citizens', and also recognized the major Protestant Churches, the Jewish Congregation 'and the other religious denominations existing in Ireland at the date of the coming into operation of this constitution', the practical import of this clause (which was repealed in 1972) is unclear. Article 44 also guaranteed freedom of conscience and the free practice of religion, and provided a guarantee that the state would not discriminate between schools that were managed by different religious denominations.[65]

The role of the Catholic Church within the Irish state is a complex subject. The overwhelming majority of the population attended church regularly; many leading politicians were dedicated, even devout Catholics, yet subservience to the Church's wishes was never total. Conformity with Church teaching was invariably greater in moral matters than in foreign policy, or in the overall political system, where the influence of a liberal parliamentary democracy prevailed. In 1922 Irish republicans defied a strongly-worded pastoral letter from the Catholic hierarchy which urged them to accept the Treaty. Yet, surprisingly, no anti-clerical party emerged; rather the dissenting republicans sought to make amends by their religious fervour. Legislation introduced during the 1920s prohibiting divorce and contraception, and providing for the censorship of films and publications, was not inflicted on an unwilling public by the Catholic Church. Most support for these measures came from the laity, and until the 1950s the government was more likely to receive requests for more stringent censorship than for its relaxation. While it has been suggested that the prohibitions on divorce and contraception were major sources of grievance within the Protestant community, this interpretation gives undue weight to the senate speeches of W. B. Yeats, who was by no means a representative figure.[66]

The pages of the *Church of Ireland Gazette* suggest that the topic of greatest concern within the Protestant community during the 1920s and 1930s was the introduction of compulsory Gaelic in national schools and as a requirement for employment in the public service. Some families responded by educating their children outside the state. During the 1940s Thomas Deirg, Minister for Education, actually attempted to prevent them from doing so.[67] The desire to restore the Irish language reflected the continuing influence of nineteenth-century romantic nationalism, which saw language as an essential characteristic of nationhood. Such views were regularly rehearsed by the founding fathers of Irish nationalism, such as Thomas Davis and Patrick Pearse, whose writings featured prominently in the new school textbooks. D. P. Moran, a journalist who favoured a rather exclusive form of Catholic nationalism, wished to see an Irish-speaking nation because he believed that the language would act as a barrier 'against the latest novelties from London and Paris'.[68] Although the Gaelic League aroused considerable popular interest in the language, by 1914 it was apparent that voluntary efforts would not secure its revival. The League successfully lobbied to have Irish made a required subject for matriculation in the National University of Ireland from 1911. The introduction of compulsory Irish in the national schools after 1922 was a logical extension of this approach.

Making the schools responsible for reviving the language was yet another instance where Irish nationalism showed excessive confidence in the power of the state. It was widely believed that the national schools had been responsible for the collapse of the Irish language during the previous century; consequently they were now saddled with its restoration. During the 1920s and 1930s the curriculum was gradually curtailed and standards reduced in order to provide greater opportunities for teaching Irish. Indeed the Department of Education's activity on this front masked the absence of a wider educational policy. The curriculum was also used to foster a sense of nationalism, with reading texts and history books presenting an image of Ireland's centuries' long campaign for independence. Representatives of the Protestant Churches protested that many of the textbooks reflected Roman Catholic doctrine and expressed unacceptable sentiments; in response the Department of Education commissioned more suitable books, including a history of Ireland for use in Protestant schools. The practice of using the state schools to promote national identity was by no means unique to Ireland: throughout the nineteenth century the public schools in France successfully inculcated a secular republicanism, as did the American public schools. It would have been remarkable had the Irish Free State not followed suit, given the almost clinical exclusion from national school textbooks during the nineteenth century of material relating to Ireland's history.

Censorship of films and publications was another mechanism that was used to define the image of the new nation. According to

Kevin Rockett American films that depicted 'alien images and ideas such as triangular relationships leading to the destruction of the nuclear family, the temptations of jazz dancing and the like', were either banned or cut, as were British films with a strong nationalist theme. In 1933, when protective tariffs were imposed on English periodicals and newspapers, the circulation of English dailies had reached 180,000–200,000. Irish writers, such as Frank O'Connor or Brinsley McNamara, who challenged the image of a wholesome Catholic and patriotic nation, appear to have been particularly targeted by the censorship board, as were works that promoted modernism, secular values and contraception. Such censorship was not unique to Ireland. It was widely believed that traditional standards of morality and social behaviour had collapsed during the First World War and its immediate aftermath; censorship was seen as a mechanism for restoring traditional values. In Ireland this mood was enhanced by the moral and intellectual insecurity that followed the Anglo-Irish war and the civil war. Morover, cultural politics served as a unifying force between the pro- and anti-Treaty factions; both agreed on the need to protect the new state from alien cultural influences.[69]

VI

It is not surprising that the Irish state was nationalist, introspective and Catholic during its early years. Indeed, given its revolutionary origins, the impact of cultural nationalism and the socio-economic composition of the population, a more confessional and less democratic state might have been predicted. Many of the key characteristics of the 1930s persisted until the 1960s and beyond. Such stability indicates that they met the wishes of the majority of the electorate, or at least of those who did not emigrate; it was a reflection also of the country's isolation and economic stagnation. A more open and more dynamic society would have resulted in pressures for change. By the late 1950s, however, 'the all-too-prevalent mood of despondency about the country's future'[70] prompted moves towards a more open economy. During the 1960s Ireland responded positively to the more liberal international climate and to the novelty of a prosperous economy. Censorship was relaxed; the ban on contraception was partly undermined with the availability of the contraceptive pill; a state television service exposed the population to new ideas. Membership of the United

Nations was marked by efforts to define Ireland's role as an unaligned country. In 1967 a committee on the constitution recommended the removal of the clauses referring to the special position of the Catholic Church, an end to the absolute ban on divorce, and the replacement of articles 2 and 3 with the declaration of a 'firm will that its territory be reunited in harmony and brotherly affection between all Irishman'.[71] The committee's recommendations were ignored. The outbreak of violence in Northern Ireland reawakened the ghosts of the Anglo-Irish war in the form of the 1970 arms crisis and the emergence of the Provisional IRA. However, it also prompted a reconsideration of the nature of the Irish state, specifically its attitude towards Northern Ireland and the unionist tradition. The 1985 Anglo-Irish Agreement affirmed the Irish government's role in Northern Ireland affairs while simultaneously acknowledging the need for the consent of the Northern Ireland population to a united Ireland.

The initial response to the prosperity of the 1960s was a higher marriage rate, a baby-boom and a decline in the number of women in paid employment. Growing urbanization did not immediately lead to a decline in religious practice; indeed the 1960s was a strong decade for Irish Catholicism. When the government announced plans for a network of state-funded co-educational and non-denominational comprehensive schools, designed to improve access to secondary education and to meet the needs of a growing economy, the Catholic hierarchy unleashed a storm of criticism. Ultimately most additional places were provided in existing private-sector denominational secondary schools. Government expenditure on education rose considerably without any corresponding increase in control; indeed the Church has succeeded in retaining a strong role in education despite a significant reduction in the number of religious personnel. In recent decades, however, the Irish state, in common with other Western nations, has faced demands from its citizens for greater personal freedom and equal treatment: the right to non-denominational schooling, access to divorce, contraception, equal treatment for women and recognition of gay rights. Change has been effected most readily through litigation in the Supreme Court and the European Court and through the directives of the European Commission. Indeed the Supreme Court's decisions in the McGee case, which challenged the constitutionality of the law prohibiting the importation of contraceptives, revealed the potential of the 1937 constitution as a liberating force.[72] By comparison, politicians and the electorate rejected referendums and bills that would have liberalized the position regarding divorce and contraception, and in 1983 a 'pro-life' referendum was carried by a large majority. Given that the European Community embodies a strong tradition of Christian Democracy and consequently of Catholic social teaching, and in the light of recent evidence that nationalism is by no means a spent force, it would be foolhardy to predict that the Irish state will automatically evolve into a liberal secular state. It is equally probable that the state will continue to play an active role in economic and social affairs.

Notes

1 B. Farrell, *The Founding of Dáil Éireann* (Dublin: Gill & Macmillan, 1971), p. 68.
2 On the years 1916–22 in general, see J. M. Curran, *The Birth of the Irish Free State, 1921–23* (Birmingham, AL: University of Alabama Press, 1980); on administrative continuity see R. Fanning, *The Irish Department of Finance* (Dublin: Institute of Public Administration, 1978), pp. 12–13; E. O'Halpin, *The Decline of the Union: British Government in Ireland, 1892–1920* (Dublin: Gill & Macmillan, 1987).
3 A. Ward, *The Irish Constitutional Tradition. Responsible Government and Modern Ireland, 1782–1992* (Dublin: Irish Academic Press, 1994), p. 30.
4 O. MacDonagh, *Ireland: the Union and its Aftermath* (London: Allen & Unwin, 1977), pp. 33–52.
5 K. T. Hoppen, *Elections, Politics and Society in Ireland, 1832–1885* (Oxford: Clarendon Press, 1984), pp. 371–3 and 414. In 1835 the ratio of police to people was 1 to 3,203 in Britain and 1 to 942 in Ireland; for soldiers the figures were 1 to 647 in Britain and 1 to 418 in Ireland. In 1881 the figures were, for police, 1 to 833 in Britain and 1 to 374 in Ireland; for soldiers, 1 to 455 in Britain and 1 to 194 in Ireland.
6 M. E. Daly, *The Buffer State: the Historical Roots of the Department of the Environment* (Dublin: Institute of Public Administration, 1997), p. 33.
7 V. Crossman, *Local Government in Nineteenth-Century Ireland* (Belfast: Institute of Irish Studies, 1994), pp. 2–7.
8 R. B. McDowell, *The Irish Administration, 1801–1914* (London: Routledge & Kegan Paul, 1964).
9 L. W. McBride, *The Greening of Dublin Castle: the Transformation of Bureaucratic and Judicial Personnel in Ireland, 1892–1922* (Washington: Catholic University of America Press, 1991), pp. 26–7.
10 Daly, *The Buffer State*, Chapter 2.
11 M. E. Daly, 'The Economic Ideals of Irish Nationalism: Frugal Comfort or Lavish Austerity?', *Éire-Ireland* (Winter 1994), pp. 77–100.

12 Daly, *The Buffer State*, p. 41; R. Barrington, *Health, Medicine and Politics in Ireland, 1900–1970* (Dublin: Institute of Public Administration, 1987), pp. 24–66.

13 D. H. Akenson, *The Irish Education Experiment: the National System of Education in the Nineteenth Century* (London, 1970); N. Atkinson, *Irish Education: a History of Educational Institutions* (Dublin: Allen Figgis, 1969).

14 T. Garvin, *1922: the Birth of Irish Democracy* (Dublin: Gill & Macmillan, 1996); D. Harkness, *The Restless Dominion: the Irish Free State and the British Commonwealth of Nations, 1921–1931* (London: Macmillan, 1969).

15 D. O'Sullivan, *The Irish Free State and its Senate* (London: Faber & Faber, 1940), p. 59.

16 P. Duggan, *A History of the Irish Army* (Dublin: Gill & Macmillan, 1991); M. G. Valiulis, *Almost a Rebellion: the Army Mutiny of 1924* (Cork: Tower Books, 1985); L. McNiffe, *A History of the Garda Síochánáa: a Social History of the Force* (Dublin: Wolfhound Press, 1997); M. Kotsonouris, *Retreat from Revolution: the Dáil Courts, 1920–24* (Dublin: Irish Academic Press, 1994).

17 Daly, *The Buffer State*, pp. 141–2.

18 Harkness, *Restless Dominion*.

19 P. Canning, *British Policy towards Ireland, 1921–1941* (Oxford: Clarendon Press, 1985); D. McMahon, *Republicans and Imperialists: Anglo-Irish Relations in the 1930s* (New Haven: Yale University Press, 1984).

20 L. Kohn, *The Constitution of the Irish Free State* (London, 1932), as cited by Garvin, *1922: The Birth of Irish Democracy*, p. 17. On British demands concerning the drafting of the 1922 constitution, see Curran, *Birth of Irish Democracy*, pp. 201–18.

21 J. Bowman, *De Valera and the Ulster Question, 1917–1973* (Oxford: Clarendon Press, 1982), pp. 147–60; I. McCabe, *A Diplomatic History of Ireland, 1948–49: the Republic, the Commonwealth and NATO* (Dublin: Irish Academic Press, 1991).

22 C. O'Halloran, *Partition and the Limits of Irish Nationalism: an Ideology under Stress* (Dublin: Gill & Macmillan, 1987), pp. 131–77; Daly, *The Buffer State*, p. 113; Bowman, *De Valera and the Ulster Question*, pp. 133–4.

23 A statement by Frank McDermott TD, founder of the National Centre Party, quoted in Bowman, *De Valera and the Ulster Question*, p. 128.

24 See e.g. Kevin Boland, *Up Dev!* (Rathcoole: published by the author, no date), p. 25.

25 Christopher Mc Gimpsey and Michael Mc Gimpsey *v.* Ireland and Others, *Irish Law Reports*, Supreme Court (1990), p. 442.

26 F. S. L. Lyons, *The Irish Parliamentary Party, 1890–1910* (London: Faber & Faber, 1957), pp. 132–4.

27 Garvin, *1922: The Birth of Irish Democracy*, p. 32.

28 D. Keogh, *Twentieth-Century Ireland: Nation and State* (Dublin: Gill & Macmillan, 1994), pp. 110–11.

29 Ward, *The Irish Constitutional Tradition*, pp. 206–24; 243–7.

30 M. E. Daly, *Industrial Development and Irish National Identity, 1922–39* (New York and Dublin: Syracuse University Press and Gill & Macmillan, 1992), pp. 103–4.

31 D. O Drisceoil, *Censorship in Ireland, 1939–1945: Neutrality, Politics and Society* (Cork: Cork University Press, 1996), p. 253; SV9 List of Orders and Statutory Instruments made under Emergency Powers Act and continued 1946; SV12 List of Orders and Statutory Instuments made under Emergency Powers Act and continued after 30 September 1949.

32 B. Sexton, *Ireland and the Crown, 1922–1936: the Governor-Generalship of the Irish Free State* (Dublin: Irish Academic Press, 1989), pp. 91–2.

33 Ward, *The Irish Constitutional Tradition*, pp. 286–95.

34 Daly, *The Buffer State*.

35 J. J. Lee, *Ireland 1912–1985: Politics and Society* (Cambridge: Cambridge University Press, 1989), p. 547.

36 Hoppen, *Elections, Politics and Society*, p. 436.

37 P. Sacks, *The Donegal Mafia: an Irish Political Machine* (New Haven: Yale University Press, 1976).

38 Fanning, *Finance*; Lee, *Ireland 1912–1985*, pp. 563–77.

39 M. E. Daly, 'The Formation of an Irish Nationalist Elite? Recruitment to the Irish Civil Service in the Decades Prior to Independence, 1870–1920', *Paedagogica Historica. International Journal of the History of Education*, 30, 1 (1994), pp. 381–401.

40 Mc Niffe, *A History of the Garda Síochaná*, pp 67–69. One set of cadets was recruited in 1923.

41 Daly, *Industrial Development and Irish National Identity*.

42 M. O'Donoghue and A. A. Tait, 'The Growth of Public Revenue and Expenditure in Ireland', in J. A. Bristow and A. A. Tait (eds) *Economic Policy in Ireland* (Dublin: Institute of Public Administration, 1968) p. 288; J. O'Hagan, 'An Analysis of the Relative Size of the Government Sector: Ireland 1926–52', *The Economic and Social Review*, 12, 1 (October 1980); N. F. R. Crafts, 'The Golden Age of Economic Growth in Western Europe, 1950–1973', *Economic History Review*, 48, 3 (August 1995), p. 440.

43 G. FitzGerald, 'Mr Whitaker and Industry', *Studies*, vol. 48 (1959), pp. 138–50.

44 *Development for Full Employment*, Prl 7193 (Dublin: Stationery Office, 1978).

45 J. O'Hagan, 'Government Intervention', in J. O'Hagan (ed.) *The Economy of Ireland* (Dublin, 1991), p. 82; K. A. Kennedy, T. Giblin and D. McHugh, *The Economic Development of Ireland in the Twentieth Century* (London: Routledge, 1988), pp. 87–91.

46 In the 1920s the figure was 80 per cent. (Kennedy *et al.*, *The Economic Development of Ireland*, p. 178).

47 Fanning, *Finance*, pp. 207–11, 442–56; 'Symposium on the European Monetary System', *Journal of the Statistical and Social Inquiry Society of Ireland*, 24, 3 (1980–1), p. 1.

48 Kennedy *et al.*, *The Economic Development of Ireland*, pp. 13–15.

49 N. Crafts and G. Toniolo, 'Postwar Growth: an Overview'; and C. Ó Gráda and K. O'Rourke, 'Irish Economic Growth, 1945–88', in Crafts and Toniolo (eds) *Economic Growth in Europe since 1945* (Cambridge: Cambridge University Press, 1996), pp. 1–37, 388–426.

50 E. O'Connor, *A Labour History of Ireland, 1824–1960* (Dublin: Gill & Macmillan, 1992), pp. 156–7; W. K. Roche, 'The Liberal Theory of Industrialism and the Development of Industrial Relations in Ireland'; and N. Hardiman, 'The State and Economic Interests: Ireland in Comparative Perspective', in J. H. Goldthorpe, and C. T. Whelan (eds) *The Development of Industrial Society in Ireland* (Oxford: Clarendon Press, 1992), pp. 291–359.

51 P. J. Katzenstein, *Small States in World Markets: Industrial Policy in Europe* (Ithaca: Cornell University Press, 1985).

52 M. Olson, 'The Varieties of Eurosclerosis: the Rise and Decline of Nations since 1982', in M. Olson, *The Rise and Decline of Nations* (New Haven: Yale University Press, 1982); Crafts and Toniolo, 'Postwar Growth: an Overview', in Crafts and Toniolo, op. cit., pp. 10–11, 73–94.

53 P. Bew and H. Patterson, *Seán Lemass and the Making of Modern Ireland* (Dublin: Gill & Macmillan, 1982).

54 F. Kennedy, 'Symposium on the Report of the Commission on Social Welfare', *Journal of the Statistical and Social Inquiry Society of Ireland*, 25, 4 (1986–7), p. 28.

55 Barrington, *Health, Medicine and Politics*, pp. 137–94.

56 B. F. Shields, 'Irish Social Services: a Symposium', *JSSISI*, vol. 17 (1942–3), p. 135.

57 D. Miller, *Church, State and Nation in Ireland, 1898–1921* (Dublin: Gill & Macmillan, 1973); Daly, *The Buffer State*, pp. 77–8.

58 S. Ó Buachalla, *Education Policy in Twentieth-Century Ireland* (Dublin: Wolfhound Press, 1988), p. 64; J. H. Whyte, *Church and State in Modern Ireland, 1923–1970* (Dublin: Gill & Macmillan, 1971), p. 38.

59 J. Lee, 'Aspects of Corporatist Thought in Ireland: the Commission on Vocational Organisation, 1939–43', in A. Cosgrove and D. McCartney (eds) *Studies in Irish History: Presented to R. Dudley Edwards* (Dublin: University College Dublin, 1979), pp. 324–46.

60 'Symposium on Social Security', *JSSISI*, 18, 3 (1949–50), pp. 249, 262, 264. The quotations are of statements by J. C. M. Eason, a business-man, and Joseph Johnston, economics professor at TCD. Neither man was a Catholic.

61 Rev. J. Dignan, *Social Security: Outlines of a Scheme of National Health Insurance* (Sligo: Champion Publications, 1945).

62 Barrington, *Health, Medicine and Politics*, pp. 195–221; Whyte, *Church and State in Modern Ireland*, pp. 120–272; J. Deeney, *To Cure and to Care* (Dublin: Glendale Press, 1989); N. Browne, *Against the Tide*, (Dublin: Gill & Macmillan, 1986); E. McKee, 'Church–State Relations and the Development of Irish Health Policy: the Mother-and-Child Scheme', *Irish Historical Studies*, 25, 98 (November 1986), pp. 159–94. E. Immergut, *Health Politics: Interests and Institutions in Western Europe* (Cambridge: Cambridge University Press, 1992).

63 Reproduced as Appendix B in Whyte, *Church and State in Modern Ireland*.
64 R. Fanning, 'Fianna Fáil and the Bishops', *Irish Times*, 13–14 February 1985; R. Fanning, *Independent Ireland* (Dublin, 1983), pp. 54–6.
65 Whyte, *Church and State in Modern Ireland*, pp. 52–6; D. Keogh, 'Church, State and Society', in B. Farrell (ed.) *De Valera's Constitution and Ours* (Dublin: Gill & Macmillan, 1988), pp. 103–19.
66 T. Brown, *Ireland: a Social and Cultural History, 1922–79* (London: Fontana, 1981), pp. 129–34.
67 Ó Buachalla, *Education Policy*, pp. 242–8.
68 J. Hutchinson, *The Dynamics of Cultural Nationalism: the Gaelic Revival and the Creation of the Irish Nation State* (London: Allen & Unwin, 1987); D. P. Moran, *The Philosophy of Irish Ireland* (Dublin: Gill & Son, 1905), pp. 15, 29, 111.
69 Ó Buachalla, *Education Policy*; K. Rockett, L. Gibbons and J. Hill, *Cinema and Ireland* (Syracuse: Syracuse University Press, 1988), p. 53; L. M. Cullen, *Eason and Son: a History* (Dublin: Eason, 1989), p. 347; M. O'Callaghan, 'Language, Nationality and Cultural Identity in the Irish Free State, 1922–7: the *Irish Statesman* and the *Catholic Bulletin* Reappraised', *Irish Historical Studies*, vol. 94 (1984).
70 T. K . Whitaker, *Economic Development* (Dublin, 1958), para. 12.
71 *Report of the Committee on the Constitution* (Dublin, 1967), Pr. 9817.
72 M. Robinson, 'Women and the New State', in M. Mc Curtain and D. Ó Corráin (eds) *Women in Irish Society: the Historical Dimension* (Dublin: Arlen House, 1978), pp. 66–9.

Chapter 4

The state and Northern Ireland

Richard English

I

The difficulties experienced by Marxist analysts of the state have been crisply reflected in debates concerning Northern Ireland. Conventional Marxists have persisted in arguments too reliant on simplistic readings of capitalism and of popular attitudes to carry much weight,[1] while even the more thoughtful exponents of the philosophy have considered it appropriate to modify their approach profoundly.[2] The idea that the state reflects (however autonomously) the interests of a dominant class has, to put it gently, been greatly complicated in Northern Ireland by the religious/ethnic division of society, and by the fact that since 1972 control of the state has not been in the hands of local political forces. Clearly, questions of social class have not been irrelevant to popular attitudes regarding the state; those at the sharpest edges of conflict concerning the state's very existence, for example, have been drawn substantially from the working class. Militant loyalism has been a largely self-sufficient working-class phenomenon; and (despite much discussion of the importance of middle-class Catholics) the most aggressive and sustained hostility from Catholics towards the Northern Irish state has been found among the working, and especially lower-working, class. But such considerations need not lead us into a Marxist framework. Some years ago Ralph Miliband's sophisticated attempt to build a general political sociology of advanced capitalist societies[3] challenged the pluralist-democratic view of the state, and did so with considerable intellectual power. But opponents of capitalism then and later have needed to do more than merely highlight its deficiencies. For challenges such as Miliband's to be effective, one would require the demonstration of a preferable alternative to the liberal-democratic capitalism which the pluralist-democratic view might be judged to defend. The existence of such an alternative on the left seems even less clear in the closing years of the twentieth century than it did thirty years earlier, when Miliband was writing his book. One does not have to endorse the full range of Francis Fukuyama's[4] views to accept the argument that liberal democracy has possessed many advantages over the large number of socialist experiments which have attempted to rival it, and the Northern Irish setting does not provide much reason to dissent from this view.

What the Northern Irish case study unquestionably does, however, is focus attention dramatically upon key issues relating to state definition. As ever with Northern Ireland, there is a problem of terminology. Was what existed during 1921–72 a state, a sub-state, a statelet? When considering London governments' dealings with Northern Ireland, are we more accurate in depicting them as UK governments, or as British governments trying to maintain as great a distance as possible from an expensive, puzzling and embarrassing place? Prior to 1969 Ulster was deliberately kept marginal from British central government. Indeed, for many years the British government's only discernible policy towards Northern Ireland was to minimize its involvement there. Following Northern Ireland's creation in the 1920s, sovereignty was still held by the UK; but Ulster was not discussed at Westminster. The post-1969 troubles have brought Northern Ireland back into closer attention, but there remains a strand of thinking within British government and state which aims to minimize London's involvement with Ulster and its problems.

To the dismay of unionists, then, it is perhaps the British state that we should be discussing. But how does that state act? Northern Irish experience demonstrates more persuasively than most the impropriety of considering the state to be a unitary actor. Army, police, judiciary and various sections of civil service and government have all contributed to state action in Northern Ireland, and often in contradictory ways. Before 1972 this was further complicated by the existence of two governments, those of Belfast and London. Consider, for example, the Northern Irish government's control over a quasi-military police force (the B Specials). London, the ultimate authority over Northern Ireland, had comparatively little control over this force, a fact which reflected the Unionist government's relative autonomy from London with regard to law and order. There are, therefore, in the case of Northern Ireland, problems over the defininion of what the state actually *is*, let alone what the interests of the British state might be in relation to the place. This automatically challenges much popular argument and assumption about the nature of the Northern Irish conflict, removing as it does the idea that the British state can be readily identified and its interests neatly pigeon-holed. The suggestion that the British state has a single, continuous, simple interest in Northern Ireland is mistaken. Indeed, it is the divergence of perspectives among British state actors which, on close inspection, becomes apparent. Divergence of perspective marked the negotiations leading up to the 1985 Ango-Irish Agreement,[5] and its extent comes into clearer focus as more evidence becomes available concerning key policies and initiatives. Historical and individual particularity are evident here, and they prompt us to be cautious regarding schematic readings of state action.

Another problem concerns questions of political violence and force, questions which are central to discussion of what the state actually is. Northern Ireland has represented a stark test of the Weberian state, the latter's claim to a monopoly of legitimate force having been seriously challenged by those of pro- as well as anti-state sympathies. And further problems have emerged. How should a liberal democracy act when facing determined political violence sustainedly directed against it by an illiberal minority? How can the state counter such violence while maintaining that distinction between legality and illegality which grounds the state's very self-definition? These questions have been ambiguously answered in Northern Ireland, the ambiguity heightened by a lack of agreement as to what precisely it is that the British have been facing in Northern Irish political violence.[6]

II

The maintenance of public order has been the state's most pressing objective in Northern Ireland for much of the post-1969 period, and it is one which has been fulfilled more successfully than might have been feared. Indeed, it might be rewarding to read the state and Northern Ireland in Hobbesian terms of facilitating self-preservation. For while Hobbes might be thought ultimately unpersuasive in accounting for why states emerge, his arguments do offer important insights regarding the advantages and achievements of actually functioning states, and as such are highly relevant to

Northern Ireland. A Hobbesian reading of Northern Ireland might, for example, concentrate on the popular reluctance to accept that what people (on various sides) claim as good or right is in fact merely what is or seems to be in their own particular interest. While people typically argue that an opinion (their own) deserves widespread acceptance within the community because it is right, Hobbesian scepticism would suggest that the persistence of differing opinions and of clashing interests is more plausible and appropriate. Moreover, according to this Hobbesian account, it might be suggested that acceptance of such a situation would allow for action by the state to prevent such clashing interests from leading to war. Whether such action would involve the pluralist reconciliation of conflicting interests attempted by London governments since the mid-1980s is debatable: as Hobbes's work powerfully argues, moral relativism need not lead to liberal pluralism. But the practical surrender by most of Northern Ireland's population to the authority of the state has allowed the latter's economic and military strength to preserve comparative peace in conditions otherwise likely to produce something far closer to civil war.

If one were to pursue this line of enquiry, with political philosophy guiding interpretation of the state, then it might also be recalled that Hobbes held that the state should ensure a level of welfare for all citizens, but that once this was attained policies should not be forced upon citizens. Again, he considered that extensive intervention in people's lives may be necessary in order to protect the survival of all. From another angle, nationalists in some areas of Northern Ireland in the late 1960s and early 1970s may have felt that, as the sovereign or her representatives were attacking them, they were justified in rebelling. Nationalists might also contend that, during the post-1969 years, their submission to the authority of the state has been more pragmatic than enthusiastic, and that the state's claim to legitimacy remains fundamentally flawed in many respects. The notions that the state should embody communally shared meaning, and that the law should be considered legitimate throughout the society, remain elusive in Northern Ireland. It is not that Irish partition inevitably produced either a regime destined to collapse or the starkness of division between Catholic and Protestant which did in fact develop after the 1920s. Catholic rejection of the state need not have been so sharp. 'If the Unionist Government had preserved PR, at least for parliamentary elections, and Stormont had developed as a forum for vigorous public debate, as seemed likely in 1926, the representatives of the Catholic minority might well have legitimized the institutions of the province by their support.'[7] Indeed, one authority has recently argued that even as late as 1968 it was possible that concessions could have produced a solution, thereby avoiding the troubles that ensued.[8]

Again, therefore, one is led to the conclusion that inevitabilism and schematic teleology have less place in analysis of the state than do contingency and the interaction of particular and uniquely combined developments. The collapse of Stormont was not inevitable, but was rather the outcome of developments within and between Catholic and Protestant politics in Northern Ireland, British politics, Republic of Ireland politics and international events further afield. Local initiatives and individual decisions helped create a crisis that was avoidable. The particular development of the collapse owed much to the demagoguery of figures such as Eamonn McCann and Ian Paisley – each of them persistently engaging, despite their unfortunate contributions to modern Ulster politics – and also to crucial fault-lines of conflict, such as policing. The latter arguably represents a particularly important register of the relations between the state and those governed under it; in Northern Ireland during the late 1960s and early 1970s it was frequently an index of hostility rather than harmony, with the state's coercive apparatus being famously contentious.

If the rights of those governed by the state are properly reflected in the obligations which bind the state's agents, then, as far as many Catholics are concerned, what happened in the last years of Stormont clearly involved a breakdown of the state's proper performance. These Catholics considered (and consider) there to have been (and to remain) considerable injustices in Northern Ireland. The pursuit of justice has impressive historical credentials among those studying politics. But even a character as far removed from Ulster's prejudices as Aristotle provides no escape from local partisanship on this question: justice may be the good in the political sphere, and may consist in that which promotes the common interest, but what *is* the common interest and (more importantly) who is to define it in so fiercely divided a polity?

This has been the essence of the Northern Irish conflict – the question of power – and it is one which focuses on possession of the state. Catholic hostility towards the state emerged in connection with civil rights' abuses, but clearly goes well beyond such abuse. By 1972 most civil rights' complaints had been dealt with in Northern

Ireland, and those yet unresolved (such as employment disadvantage) were probably beyond straightforward redress. Yet nationalist disaffection was not eroded as a consequence, and much nationalist argument has focused on the radical reordering, if not the destruction, of the Northern Irish state. The ambiguous stance of so many Northern Irish Catholics regarding the state – pragmatically asquiescent, but ultimately desirous of radical change – owes much to the historical experience (and even more to later interpretations) of 1921–72 statehood. Parliament is crucial to the British state, and the problems which developed in Northern Ireland owe much to the fact that the Westminster system proved ill-suited to a Belfast setting. The non-alternation of government ruined the parliamentary arrangement, with majoritarianism ensuring the marginalization of nationalists: the minority could not, foreseeably, become the majority. Yet for alternation one requires the absence of sizeable anti-system parties, and a degree of consensus on national values; and these conditions appeared not to exist in Northern Ireland.

Thus the idea that the state is legitimate because it represents the popular will has been difficult to sustain in the Ulster situation. Northern Ireland existed within a liberal democracy but was not typical of such a culture. Indeed, the majority-rule system facilitated much that was far from liberal, though sustained through democracy. But the question was about power: unionist retention of it against the challenges of the internally disloyal and the externally aggressive, and nationalist pursuit of it through radical political change. Power carries practical implications regarding the distribution of resources, and possesses accompanying implications regarding prestige. There repeatedly emerge in Northern Irish political debate demands that the state should (or, according to taste, should not) recognize, validate, support or embody particular communal meanings and their symbols.

Such meanings in Northern Ireland relate to familiar enough broad allegiances, with religion, nation and class each playing a part. Nationalism should not be seen as the preserve of one particular class, and attempts to present it as such in the Irish case have tended to be unsuccessful. But the attainment of economic benefits has in various ways proved decisive in stimulating and sustaining (and possibly in ending?) the violent post-1969 conflict. State dependence is likely to prove a more lasting phenomenon than anti-state violence in the region; and, significantly, while people have criticized or rejected the particular state in which they have found themselves in Northern Ireland there has been no rejection of the idea of the state as such. People want to influence the existing state or to replace it with another one, rather than to do away with the state form itself.

Thus while both the UK and the Republic of Ireland have failed, respectively, to convince Northern Irish nationalists and Ulster unionists to embrace them, there has been no challenge to the 'state' as a political concept. Ulster's republicans have been as conservative here as have her loyalists. But there has been a profound problem with legitimizing either potential state in the eyes of its opponents in Northern Ireland. The UK has been rather hesitant in exploring the implications of its own multi-national quality. That state and nation are not coextensive might helpfully have been reflected upon in terms of the interconnectedness of the problems facing numerous parts of the state. But there has been a strangely narrow Anglo-Irish quality to the debate on Northern Ireland: as Graham Walker, for example, has pointed out, Scotland has not tended to generate a distinctive contribution to arguments over Northern Ireland despite the obvious family resemblances between the two regions.[9]

The most famous national question in Northern Ireland relates to the problem of Northern Irish legitimacy, or illegitimacy, in the face of the argument of Irish nationalists that their national rights are denied within the UK. But Ulster unionists also present a national problem. Do they constitute a nation themselves, entitled therefore to the ambivalent benefits of self-determination and international respect repeatedly claimed by their Irish nationalist opponents? Self-determination itself is probably of little benefit in approaching the existence of the state in Northern Ireland, the identification of an agreed self which can do the determining being the essence of the very problem. But the relationship between unionists, whether or not they embody a nation, and the state in Northern Ireland unquestionably does deserve consideration. The year 1972 was a crucial one here, with the unionist state being effectively prorogued along with its parliament. Rarely can the blurred division between state and society have been better illustrated than in 1921–72 Northern Ireland: the difficulty of measuring the extent of state autonomy from society is made clear when one considers the relationship between, for example, the Orange Order and the various agents of the state such as the police force and the civil service. Churches might also provide a pertinent example; and the fact that a similarly blurred line could easily be seen during the same period in different organizations in Southern Ireland merely reinforces the point still further.

Unionists have often tended to be (unnecessarily?) highly anxious about both the British and Irish states. During the years since the ending of Stormont, the Ulster unionists' relationship with the London-based government and state has clearly been in many ways awkward. The idea that loyalists, for example, might be pro-state does not imply any neat overlap of views, or lack of tension, regarding the state in its governmental or security guises. And just as intra-unionist tensions helped to define the state under Stormont,[10] so also the post-1972 unionist political family has been divided into competing camps regarding policy, on broad as well as specific questions. This has been striking in the development of the 1990s Northern Irish peace process, with the emergence of a clear division within as well as between unionist political parties and organizations. The roots of this division go back to the adoption by the state, in the 1980s, of an approach embodied in the 1985 Anglo-Irish Agreement and subsequent initiatives, whereby the British state has attempted to establish a symmetrical arrangement of Northern Irish politics. London and Dublin have each been involved in this, with the two traditions, identities and communities in Northern Ireland being afforded equal respect. Unionists and nationalists are simultaneously reassured that their interests are to be guaranteed, that both can effectively win at the same time. Thus, for example, the 1985 Agreement affirmed 'that any change in the status of Northern Ireland would only come about with the consent of a majority of the people of Northern Ireland', and recognized 'that the present wish of a majority of the people of Northern Ireland is for no change in the status of Northern Ireland'. Unionists thus (hopefully) comforted, it aimed to appeal also to nationalists, on the grounds that 'if in the future a majority of the people of Northern Ireland clearly wish for and formally consent to the establishment of a united Ireland, [the UK and Republic of Ireland governments] will introduce and support in the respective parliaments legislation to give effect to that wish'.[11]

The two states – UK and Irish Republic – have for over a decade sought to create a symmetrical political balance in relation to Northern Ireland. The identities, aspirations and traditions of unionists and nationalists have repeatedly been flattered with respectful references and rhetorical guarantees of equal legitimacy, from the Anglo-Irish Agreement to the 1993 Downing Street Declaration, the 1995 Framework Documents and the 1998 Belfast Agreement. In the last of these texts, the notion of balance reached fulfilment in the idea of a power-sharing assembly in Northern Ireland, with cross-border institutional bait for nationalists and a guarantee to unionists that the latter need not be seen in trojan-horse terms. In broad outline, such a framework is not particularly new. The idea that a solution to Northern Ireland's political ills would involve power sharing and some form of Irish dimension, coupled with a rhetorical commitment that Northern Ireland should remain part of the UK as long as a majority of its inhabitants wanted it to do so, can be found in British government thinking from the early 1970s. But a combination of factors (not least among which was war-weariness in the context of a lengthy paramilitary stalemate) have in the 1990s led more political players than before to endorse the idea.

If states are, at root, concerned to maintain public order, then the 1990s ceasefires can be seen as indicating the rationale behind each state's policy here. It should also be noted that the post-1994 ceasefires have involved a diminution rather than a removal of political violence, that there is no certainty of their remaining permanently effective and that the dramatic rise in post-1985 loyalist violence can be substantially attributed to that governmental policy which underpinned the 1990s peace process. Yet the 1985 Anglo-Irish Agreement and its subsequent offspring have held diverse apparent benefits for Britain, for a number of different players: the marginalization of militant republicanism, the softening of international embarrassment and criticism over Ulster and the improvement of relations with Dublin governments which would increasingly share responsibility for the troublesome region north of the border.

This inter-state feature of recent politics in Northern Ireland is crucial. Precisely how symmetrical the two states themselves have been in relation to Northern Ireland is surely open to question. The north plays a more significant role in Irish nationalist ideology than it does in British thinking, for example, and one feature of the politics of the last decade has been the frequent unionist perception that 'their' state and government were perhaps less committed to fighting their corner than Irish nationalists' state and government were to fighting theirs. Moreover, the unequal size and power of the two states have implications for the kind of role – economic, military – which might be played in the foreseeable future. But extensive cooperation between London and Dublin, and the now irreversible involvement of the Republic in the politics of the north, mark major developments. There have been harmonizing attempts before, most notably in the 1960s, and these do not inspire optimism. The apparent improvement of north–south relations in that decade was interpreted differently in London and Dublin: the former did not see in better relations the implied weakening of the border perceived by the latter. Yet the context has now been greatly altered, the Republic's overriding desire to achieve a stable and peaceful resolution now demanding a shift in its largely rhetorical ambitions regarding the north. As the latter were only sustainable precisely because of the impossibility of attempts at their realization, this might be considered a limited change of position. But that would be to underestimate the ideological significance of all-Ireland ambition within Irish nationalist sentiment and ideology.

Britain, too, has no real desire for the uncompromised rule of Northern Ireland, so the Republic's involvement does not cut against the grain of dominant interests in London. Much attention has been focused on the statement in November 1990 by the then Secretary of State for Northern Ireland, Peter Brooke, that the British government had no selfish strategic or economic interest in Northern Ireland. But to argue that, for many years, it did have such an interest would be mistaken anyway. The British state has little to gain from an expensive and internationally embarrassing Northern Ireland, and much to gain from good relations with the Republic over the issue. Ultimate sovereignty has been qualified, in practical terms, by the Anglo-Irish Agreement. But sovereignty had been problematic in Northern Ireland even prior to 1985: the idea that sovereignty resides in the people of the relevant region had been an awkward one for the British state, since a large minority of the population did not consider the state legitimate, and because this was a view at least partly shared by many outside observers as well. If the idea of the nation state has been partially eroded, then it has been so eroded from a starting-point of questionable solidity.

III

Brendan O'Leary has recently argued that during the years of the Conservatives' tenure of government, between 1979 and 1997, there occurred a period of 'ethno-national policy learning', with various arms of the state (civil service, police, military, elected officers) growing in understanding of the true nature of the Northern Irish situation: 'Amongst British policy makers the definition and understanding of the conflict has been transformed in the last eighteen years. It has been recognized as ethno-national, and bi-governmental, as well as bi-national, in nature.'[12] If its nature is truly 'bi', then some institutionalized joint sovereignty between London and Dublin might be judged the most appropriate target at which to aim. Typically pluralist logic would suggest here that some form of joint or shared authority between the relevant states might be attempted, and there have been sophisticated justifications of such an approach within the literature in recent years (not least from O'Leary himself).[13]

The 1998 Belfast Agreement wisely fell well short of such an aim, although the declaration in the document that unionist and nationalist political aspirations are equally legitimate offers some philosophical foundation for development in that direction. How do reflections on the state affect our reading of such initiatives? One of the most striking recent contributions to the debate on Northern Ireland has come from the realm of normative political theory, and relates directly to the question of the state. Shane O'Neill's attempt to reconcile John Rawls's impartialism with Michael Walzer's contextualism by means of Jürgen Habermas's discourse ethics, includes a valuable section devoted to consideration of justice in the context of Northern Ireland. O'Neill points to one possible problem confronting a state trying to appear symmetrically fair towards competing forces within a divided society such as that of the north:

> a particular liberal democratic state is not neutral ... between, on the one hand, those patriotic citizens who count as a consti-tutive aspect of their own good the justness of that state's institutions, as they have been shaped historically in a distinc-tive cultural context, and, on the other hand, antipatriotic citizens who, for whatever reason, have come to despise those same institutions and who long for their destruction .... The state cannot but favour patriotic citizens over its antipatriots.[14]

So much for parity of esteem, unless one considers the state's parity policy as embodying an attempt to create a new kind of state. This would perhaps accord with O'Neill's preferred approach 'to create an inclusive political culture with which all citizens can identify'.

Clearly, neither the British nor the Irish state has been informed by the desire to create a theoretically rigorous contextual impartialism. But both states might be thought to have attempted critical and impartial reflection on questions of justice, without abstracting too much from the concrete needs of the specific population in Northern Ireland. To that extent, they would be in line with O'Neill's arresting thesis.

Yet part of the problem with discussion of Northern Irish politics is that even such illuminating arguments as O'Neill's appear capable of being recast in more familiar (unionist or nationalist) terms, and this plainly robs them of some of their initial appeal. Thus O'Neill's suggestion that unionist 'blindness to otherness' constitutes the main obstacle to progress in the north[15] might be read by some as straightforwardly partisan, and as a formula capable of being reversed with equal plausibility. More significantly, it might be suggested that the expectations of even such a contextualized impartialism as that favoured by O'Neill are a little high for practical political analysis. He stipulates, for example, that what one seeks in situations such as the Northern Irish one is agreement based on rational motivation, rather than on prudential grounds made pressing by power relations and unequal bargaining. But is *any* agreement (in Northern Ireland or elsewhere) likely to be reached on such terms? Let us consider the 1998 Agreement, and particularly its endorsement by the main unionist party, the Ulster Unionists. Unionism in the 1990s cannot offer, as arguably it could before 1972, a way for London to ignore Northern Ireland. Its protests have therefore been less persuasive and powerful, and its historical blemishes less easily overlooked. In such a position, with a London government as powerful as that of Tony Blair in 1998, could it really be said that prudential grounds, power relations and unequal bargaining have played no part in what appears as rationally considered an agreement as one is likely to achieve? Similar arguments might be offered in relation to other groups, most notably perhaps Sinn Fein. Prudential grounds, power relations and unequal bargaining are virtually constant in Northern Irish, as in much other, political debate.

Normative theorizing has much to offer in clarifying the nature and terms of debate regarding the state and Northern Ireland. That its demands are arguably too constricting in political practice should not blind us to its value. Previous schools of theoretical prescription have also, as suggested earlier, found the messiness of state and Ulster unyielding of their desired results. Indeed, our reading of 'the state' as a political concept can be illuminated by the Northern Irish case study from a number of such angles. Marxist and other schematic approaches tend to be less persuasive than those based more firmly on historical and individual particularity. Inevitabilism deserves less stress than do contingency and an appreciation of the uniqueness of combined historical developments at any given point. The state is not a unitary, but rather a multiple and often self-contradictory, actor. Religion, well into the last decade of the twentieth century, remains frequently vital to the state: vital to its definition and to its conceptual foundation, as well as crucial in moulding popular allegiances for or against it. Elsewhere in the UK (most obviously, perhaps, in Scotland) religious affiliation has helped mould attitudes towards the state; but the case is most clearly proven in Northern Ireland. Again, attacks on existing states, even where acute, need not imply an attack on 'the state' as an entity; indeed, they may sharpen people's conception of the need for (the right kind of) state formation. Yet the notion of a simple nation state, with uncomplicated sovereignty, is indeed under challenge: both because of political changes now occurring, and because of an ever-greater understanding of the complications and qualifications previously inherent within the state but not always recognized there. The 'state', so Northern Ireland tells us, may need refocusing and reorganizing in less discrete, and more layered, fashion. But it is likely to be no less powerful as a consequence.

Notes

1 For critical scrutiny of traditional Marxist thinking on Northern Ireland, see R. English, *Radicals and the Republic: Socialist Republicanism in the Irish Free State, 1925–1937* (Oxford: Oxford University Press, 1994), especially pp. 135–8, 199–202.

2 See, for example, the way in which one of the most intelligent Marxist treatments of Northern Ireland – that of Bew, Gibbon and Patterson – has been amended. The 1990s radical revision of their 1979 book has effectively removed much of the Marxism from the text: P. Bew, P. Gibbon and H. Patterson, *Northern Ireland, 1921–1994: Political Forces and Social Classes* (London: Serif, 1995) and *Northern Ireland, 1921–1996: Political Forces and Social Classes* (London: Serif, 1996); cf. P. Bew, P. Gibbon and H. Patterson, *The State in Northern Ireland, 1921–72: Political Forces and Social Classes* (Manchester: Manchester University Press, 1979).

3 R. Miliband, *The State in Capitalist Society: the Analysis of the Western System of Power* (London: Quartet, 1973; 1st edn 1969).

4 F. Fukuyama, *The End of History and the Last Man* (New York: Free Press, 1992).

5 P. Bew, H. Patterson and P. Teague, *Between War and Peace: the Political Future of Northern Ireland* (London: Lawrence & Wishart, 1997), Ch. 2.

6 C. Townshend, *Making the Peace: Public Order and Public Security in Modern Britain* (Oxford: Oxford University Press, 1993), pp. 174–85.

7 C. O'Leary, S. Elliott and R. A. Wilford, *The Northern Ireland Assembly, 1982–1986: a Constitutional Experiment* (London: Hurst & Co., 1988), p. 21.

8 N. Ó Dochartaigh, *From Civil Rights to Armalites: Derry and the Birth of the Irish Troubles* (Cork: Cork University Press, 1997), p. 26.

9 G. Walker, 'Scotland and Northern Ireland: Constitutional Questions, Connections and Possibilities', *Government and Opposition*, 33, 1 (Winter 1998).

10 On this, see the excellent discussion in Bew, Gibbon and Patterson, *Northern Ireland, 1921–1996*.

11 T. Hadden and K. Boyle (eds.) *The Anglo-Irish Agreement: Commentary, Text and Official Review* (London: Sweet & Maxwell, 1989), p. 18.

12 B. O'Leary, 'The Conservative Stewardship of Northern Ireland, 1979–97: Sound-bottomed Contradictions or Slow Learning?', *Political Studies*, 45, 4 (September 1997), p. 675.

13 B. O'Leary, T. Lyne, J. Marshall and B. Rowthorn, *Northern Ireland: Sharing Authority* (London: Institute for Public Policy Research, 1993).

14 S. O'Neill, *Impartiality in Context: Grounding Justice in a Pluralist World* (Albany: State University of New York Press, 1997), pp. 25–6.

15 Ibid., p. 189.

Chapter 5

Federal and confederal ideas in Scottish political culture

Christopher Harvie

I

Scottish nationalism, interpreted as devolution, was the only 'blue water' between the British parties in the 1997 election. Behind it was a discontent with British political practice which – exceptionally – nearly became theory. But did the theory of *Scottish* politics play any part? Pragmatism rules, even among nationalists: Alex Salmond's declaration, 'If independence doesn't improve the standard of living of the Scottish people, I wouldn't be advocating it', does not make him another Patrick Pearse.

Nationalist movements can go some distance before acquiring a theoretical political base.[1] The novelist and activist Darrell Figgis, in *The Irish Constitution Explained*, found little specifically Irish about the Free State Constitution of 1922. Sinn Fein under its founder Arthur Griffith was monarchistic rather than republican, its Anglo-Irish *Ausgleich* derived from Hungarian precedents.[2] Although the 1937 'republican' Constitution stressed both Catholicism and Irish indivisibility, even de Valera had to accept Ireland's subordination to the United Kingdom's economy and did not feel out of place in the Commonwealth of Smuts and Mackenzie King.[3]

In Britain A. V. Dicey's dogma stubbornly persists: parliamentary sovereignty underwritten by public opinion, whether enthusiastic or resigned to acceptance. But this can be unpredictable. Erskine Childers's *The Framework of Home Rule* (1910) argued for Irish dominion status. Its Diceyite rejection of federalism in favour of an amicable separation, governed by convention, fitted the imperialist patriot of *The Riddle of the Sands* (1903), though not the republican-unto-death of 1922. Childers and Pearse were the contemporaries of Shaw, Yeats, Joyce, Synge and O'Casey, who seemed, like Dicey's own generation, the young Oxbridge democrats of the 1860s, to hunger after Isaiah's 'something I must have which speaks to me and my age!' When sovereignty rests on public opinion, enthusiasm can disrupt hegemonic power which is intellectually torpid. Together with Commons manoeuvre and the Reform League, Bagehot's 'Palmerstonian Constitution' was remade by *Essays on Reform* and its Mazzinian nationalism, by Trollope's *Pallisers*, George Eliot's *Felix Holt* and Matthew Arnold's *Culture and Anarchy*: works which articulated constitutional change and embedded it in elite discourse.[4]

Constitutional canniness and cultural effervescence mark the current literature of Scottish home rule. Lindsay Paterson's *Autonomy of Modern Scotland* (1994) is a history of that country's semi-independence, and has little to say about theory. In Richard Finlay's *Independent and Free* (1994) and Andrew Marr's *The Battle for Scotland* (1992), the manoeuvres of groups and individuals give the home-rule cause a coalition-without-end quality.[5] The approaches of Michael Keating and Arthur Midwinter, James Kellas and James Mitchell have an empirical character, being suffused with the legalism of the Scottish bourgeoisie. This whole movement is pacifistic – and not just by nationalistic standards, but by those of political agitation, from the Anti-Corn Law League to the Gay Christians.[6]

But Paterson's intellectual milieu is as lively as Pearse's Ireland, and in this excitement the *leitmotif* is 'autonomy'. The novels of James Kelman and Alasdair Gray, the films of Bill Forsyth, the music of Runrig or James Macmillan, the art of Peter Howson or Ken Currie, and not least a mass of historical and political writing, have shadowed 'the condition of Scotland' question. Gray's borrowing from the Canadian poet Dennis Lee – 'work as if you were living in the early days of a better nation' – has helped an intelligentsia, traditionally produced in abundance by the educational system, discover a 'better nation', which is certainly not Britain.[7]

This goes beyond ideology, though myth *qua* organizing ideology is important, as Robert Anderson, analysing the politics of education of Victorian Scotland, has shown. What the *literati* of the eighteenth century would have called the 'notion' of the 'democratic intellect', for example, creates a system of values and priorities which allows specialisms to co-operate; and establishes the limits of 'sovereign' action – the contingent structures within which a national elite has to manoeuvre.[8]

In 1981 William Miller argued that the struggle over Scottish autonomy had so skewed traditional parliamentarianism that 'the end of British politics' had occurred; and what has replaced it is a less stable model of British plus Scottish politics.[9] He confined himself, however, to the distortions of the Westminster model. This essay will try to locate the Scottish dimension. It will concern itself, in section two, with the role of public opinion in British constitutionalism. Section three will examine the changes in 'British' public opinion, and section four deals with the trajectories of current 'British' and 'Scottish' politics. This will frame, in sections five to eight, a history of the theory of Scottish politics, emphasizing its distinctive components, their development and response to historical change.

II

> Yince on a time there was a king, wha sat
> scrievan this edict in his palace-haa
> til aa his fowk: 'Vassals, I tell ye flat
> that I am I, and you are bugger-aa.'[10]

Andrew Marr uses the Lallans' internationalist Robert Garioch to highlight the self-satisfaction of Westminster. But although Dicey's 'flexible constitution' was unwritten, parliamentary Acts still provided constitutions for subordinate legislatures in a highly decentralized polity. The colonies were the most obvious examples, but in Scotland the legislatures – 'estates' – of education, law, kirk and local government had political traditions of negotiating with parliament on a quasi-sovereign basis. The latter has lost the strength of convention as it has accrued formal power; the elite's manoeuvrability commended by Joseph Schumpeter has calcified into what James Mitchell regards as the fetish of parliamentary sovereignty:

> The question of sovereignty, unresolved at the time of the Union, lies at the heart of the debate on Scotland's position in the United Kingdom ... The central position of parliament has been of paramount importance in Unionist thinking.[11]

Public opinion is unstraightforward. William Miller has shown that English–Scottish divergences are at most around 10 percentage points, though neither differs greatly from those of other European countries. But he does not explore adherence to the myth of 'Britishness', and possible relationships between the weakening of parliamentary and monarchic esteem and insecurity about jobs, family and social prospects.[12] Here significant divergence seems possible. The impetus for this, however, may not be Scottish. New Labour eschewed constitutional ideas (fiercely present in the late 1980s) and positive programmes in favour of conventional but unprecedentedly well-organized harrying of government, while *The Red Paper on Scotland* (1975) reached the age of 21 in May 1996, an event uncommemorated by its editor Dr Gordon Brown. Tony Blair's reliance on Tory malfunctioning, however, recalls an ominous warning from his political guru John Macmurray:

> The British differentiation of the cultural from the political union had its main source in the historical accident by which a Scottish king inherited the English throne. It was confirmed by the failure of the English attempt – totalitarian in conception – to force episcopacy on Scotland. Scotland remained free in fellowship, with her own type of established religion and her own distinctive type of law.... An epidemic of militant nationalism would not consolidate, but disrupt the political unity of Great Britain.[13]

'Free in fellowship' could advertise Blairite devolution, but post-1979 'British' nationalism of the sort Macmurray feared has roused the *'Braveheart'* syndrome, sounding a harsher note of ethnic resentment, and not just on the football or the rugby field.[14] It supplements three other areas of conflict: the evolving European regionalism which requires institutions to deal with those environmental, educational and economic development problems at present handled by London and Brussels; the 'anti-*Braveheart*' (but still internal) business of recovering the civic from the ethnic; and, finally, the conflict of both with the attempt by New Labour to reinvent the 'British state', this time in a quasi-federal mode.[15]

III

The ideological convergence of the front benches hints at Hilaire Belloc on the 1906 General Election:

The accursed power which stands on Privilege
(And goes with Women, and Champagne and Bridge)
Broke – and Democracy resumed her reign:
(Which goes with Bridge, and Women and Champagne).[16]

But constitutional pressures became so intense that by 1912 the Tories were, in George Dangerfield's words, 'determined to smash the Liberal party into an irremediable mess of blood and brains', and so threatened civil war.[17] Constitutional fora – from the Frankfurt Parliament of 1848 to the Scottish Constitutional Convention of 1988 – can lose momentum, but the underlying causes are easily brought to the surface again.

The issue of 'national culture' is unobtrusive partly because the peripheral elites have side-stepped Westminster in order to court Europe, avoiding the London–Oxbridge elite.[18] This could lead to the complexities of the Anglo-Scottish relation being discounted. The Scots scarcely figured in the European Science Foundation's massive research project 'Governments and Non-Dominant Ethnic Groups, 1850–1940', although it was originated by an Oxbridge Scot: Hugh Seton-Watson.[19] So how relevant to the Scots is that inquiry's key paradigm: the typology of the Czech revisionist Marxist Miroslav Hroch? Having seen his first two stages of mobilization – the intellectual movement and the capture of institutions – does the '*Braveheart*' syndrome, along with the 1997 Election and Referendum, some opinion polls and SNP election successes, announce the third stage, the mass movement?[20]

The answer to this lies, at least in part, in applying Hroch's criteria to British centralism. The intellectual matrix was contributed by Bagehot and Dicey, theorists of the 'flexible constitution' from 1865 to 1885, political-science versions of the literary 'Britishness' which Robert Crawford has found among the Augustan Scots *literati*. Dicey was partly of Scottish descent; Bagehot the product of the 'Scottish' University of London. They surrounded a simple concept with a complex culture: Erskine May, buttressed by *The English Constitution* and *The Law of the Constitution*, ensuring that Westminster continued to recruit, through collegiate and legal politics, from achievers on the 'periphery' and later from the labour movement.[21]

In Ireland, 1867–1922, this incorporation failed – only just – but the Scots and the Welsh conformed.[22] With the fumbling of Irish Home Rule in the 1880s and in 1911–14, the opportunity for a 'balanced' and participative restructuring was lost. 'Britishness' then recomposed itself around a welfarist paradigm, from T. H. Green's 'Liberal Legislation and Freedom of Contract' in 1881, via Fabianism, to T. H. Marshall's 'social citizenship' of 1950, which reached its apogee as a civic culture in Anthony Crosland's *The Future of Socialism* (1956), reflecting a wartime solidarity and a co-ordinating of key industrial sectors which co-opted even Tories, from Churchill to Heath.[23]

Responses to a welfarism under threat in the late 1970s, such as the Bennite 'alternative economic strategy', were left-Diceyan: a 'Norwegian' form of protectionist social democracy.[24] This failed, not least because 25 per cent of British manufacturing investment, in oil, was already dominated by foreign concerns.[25] The European-ism of the Social Democrat–Liberal alliance fared no better, because of exclusion from power, yet Mrs Thatcher's 'free economy and strong state' were equally compromised by Europe and by globalization – ironically carried through the medium of the English language.[26] And the market did not stop at the destruction of 'social citizenship', but attacked the solidarity within capitalism represented by the Fordist firm.

The mechanics of the old order persisted in the ease whereby a party majority could sell off publicly owned industry and shrink the welfare state, while maintaining an *ad hoc* Bagehotian cabinet in its media and finance networks. But Diceyan equality at law was subverted by the use of multinational capital and government cash to sustain huge court cases, while the 'public opinion–parliament–law–convention–public opinion–parliament' circuit no longer linked centre to periphery.[27] This atomization paradoxically *stressed* the national. As voluntarist civil society – families, localities, churches, small-scale capitalism – was weakened, individuals turned to the nation for welfare and for reassurance, being encouraged to do so by opportunistic interventions articulated and even financed by conservative groups linked to the USA, the Middle East and the NICs, media and city tycoons. Sir James Goldsmith's Referendum Party, with votes in southern England up to ten times higher than in Scotland, was one instance, comparable perhaps with the position of Joe Chamberlain before 1906. But the former was submerged in the torrent of English popular sentiment which followed the death of 'England's Rose' on 31 August 1997, with no parallel in the other nations of the United Kingdom.[28]

Anglo-British nationalism, abandoning its traditional under-statement, has been subject to a defensive ethnocentric historicism, emanating largely from Oxbridge, through the influence of the Peterhouse school, with Maurice Cowling's *Religion and Public Doctrine* becoming the liturgy of the neophytes.[29] David Cannadine, with his wife Linda Colley representing moderate constitutional reconstruction, mourns British history in headlong retreat, at least from school and classroom.[30] 'Britishness' has now taken on a 'chiliasm of despair' more usually associated with the peripheral nationalists or the labour movement.[31] Anthropology is another area characterized by divergence. Despite his *The Subversive Family* (1982), the Conservative constitutionalist and former Thatcher adviser Ferdinand Mount seems oblivious to the Franco-Scottish Emanuel Todd (himself an adviser, briefly, to President Chirac, before reverting to his Communist loyalties) whose *The Conditions of Progress* (1988) differentiates Celts from Anglo-Saxons in terms of family type, making a near-ethnic case for nationalism. For Mount, the Scottish political tradition could be dismissed in a daft quotation of Lewis Spence, the first and least successful National Party candidate.[32]

On the moderate left, decentralization and, in particular, Scottish devolution have now registered. *Scotland's Claim of Right* of 1987, and its influence on Charter '88, was the first Scottish constitutional initiative to impinge on London's consciousness since the days of the *Edinburgh Review*.[33] Yet the metropolitan response has been far from convincing. Will Hutton's *The State We're In*, a 'constitutionalist' interpretation of Britain's economic decline after the Charter '88 pattern, was deeply imprecise about regional institutions.[34] Dissent from the Anglo-British constitutional myth was central to Marr's *Ruling Britannia*, but his merriment could not conceal doubts about the invalid's will to recover. Although Mount took the hatchet to Bagehot, Dicey and Ivor Jennings, and put forward a case for 'minimalist' devolution, he assumed a continuing nationalism which appears implausible when viewed close-up.

Two historical shifts lie behind this. First, Conservative assaults on the central civil service and on local autonomy increased the powers of the devolved administrations in Scotland and Wales and their quangoes. The central elite devolving autonomy, Jim Bulpitt-style, to its regional brethren gave way to a centrifugal bureaucracy.[35] Second, Ireland's use of its European Union membership effectively realized the modernizing programme of Irish nationalism, endorsing secularization, orientating the country away from Britain, and positing a different future for regions with which it has now drawn level (with output up from 56 per cent of UK GNP in 1976 to 87 per cent in 1995).[36] For the Scots, Ireland has become a country to emulate, and a potential weapon for the SNP in the Catholic Labour heartlands of the central belt. The lesson of *Braveheart* is that Michael D. Higgins, the Irish culture minister, won the Battle of Stirling Bridge.

The continuity between Major and Blair is not a reprise of 1950s Butskellism. Its conventions – cabinet government, the manipulation of party by elite, corporative decision-making, parliamentary sovereignty, the indivisibility of the common law – are all in disarray.[37] After the Tory debacle, an uncompromising English nationalism – sponsored by the right? or by New Labour? – could attempt to repeat the crisis of 1906–14.[38]

The SNP result in 1997 was modest, but Scottish Toryism managed to get the worst of all possible worlds: even allowing for the 'honeymoon period', the most recent poll shows the SNP at 30 per cent, Labour on 46 per cent, with the Tories far behind at 12 per cent, in a vote for a devolved parliament, and the political feelings of the people are diverging in ways unalluded to by Miller or Mount. In 1989, the British rallied round the Royal Family (37 per cent); the Scots, however, trusted the Royals (20 per cent) much less than they did the National Health Service.[39] As unreconstructed 'social citizens', the Scots maintained a central element of historic 'Britishness'; but this, along with openness to regionalism and to European federalism, was no longer current in the south.[40]

IV

In the industrial epoch nationalism was propelled by economic motives, institutions became recruiters of cadres, and history was endowed with evolutionary perspective. Linda Colley has, up to a point, demonstrated this in *Britons*, in which the economic success of divinely approved Protestantism is shown to have created a new 'British' state ideology, less unionist than it was imperial: there was no 'English Empire', though there was a 'little England'.[41] The Irish interpreted this negatively, as the record of their own country's exploitation.[42] This *might* have changed had Irish participation in 'Imperial Britain' developed, but war and revolution enforced a republican reconstruction of history which lasted until the 1960s. The development of a European state and a reactive English nationalism are now having the same effect on the Scots.

Assessing their implications involves looking forward as well as back, and setting an increasingly independent Scottish party politics in this trajectory. Michael Forsyth's bold attempt to emulate Gerald Balfour in 1890s Ireland, by annexing cultural nationalism while denying political devolution, was a disaster. In 1997 Tory support at 17 per cent did not yield a single seat. The constellation is now radically different from that obtaining in England, with the Referendum vote – of 74–26 per cent on 11 September (compared with 52–48 per cent – on 1 March 1979) – allowing the SNP to wait for devolution, for proportional representation, and for Blair to become unpopular. The first Scottish Parliamentary Election will leave Labour with the prospect of a minority government, or a coalition with the Lib-Dems. But the election might even produce an SNP-led coalition. Most Scots voters polled during the Referendum campaign thought a Yes vote would weaken the union (Labour claimed it would strengthen it). Given conflict over powers and finance, growing discontent as welfare is cut and job security diminishes, the slippery slope beckons, even before the next British General Election.[43] If in 2000 a Referendum on the Euro finds the Conservatives and Labour divided, a Scottish SNP-led Government, touting the Irish precedent and getting support from incoming firms which fear being excluded from Europe, will find itself already halfway down it.[44]

The irony of this *Schicksalkampf* is that Scottish constitutionalism will have a 'British' continuity: a context in which cultural nationalism, unanticipated in the 1970s, could be decisive. The SNP – Europe-friendly, quietly republican and on most issues to the left of Labour – reflects familiar Scottish attitudes, and 'Independence in Europe' attracts more support than the SNP itself.[45] Since 1980 Scottish culture has registered at more or less all levels, blurring the lines within the intelligentsia between separatists and home rulers, republicans and socialists. This is partly because a previously class-based society is evolving life-styles which relate to one another through national institutions: the embourgeoisment and secularization of Scotland's Catholics; an emulation of Ireland and other small

EU states; a leftish suspicion of New Labour on unemployment and nuclear weapons; a shift into single-issue and environmental groups.[46] Two incalculables are youth and gender. A *Trainspotting* generation has emerged, presently apolitical, deeply insecure, but concerned about the environment and employment. Scotswomen, traditionally neglected by politics, are being promised an improved status in the parliament and the SNP is – though more by accident than by design – the only party in which women comprise one-third of MPs and MEPs.[47]

This political discourse has a dual focus: on the one hand there is domestic policy, and on the other a European polity at the limit of amalgamation through bureaucratic action.[48] The Scots helpfully *lack* some of Hroch's requirements – not the least of which is 'possession' of an ethnic-national conviction. From the Declaration of Arbroath in 1320, via the reformers and covenanters and Fletcher of Saltoun, to James Bryce and Seton-Watson, *père et fils*, the Scots have both philosophized about and dissented from nationalism, their civic and Calvinist impulses moving between diverse identities.[49] In 1945 Hamilton Fyfe, editor of the *Daily Herald* and brother of the principal of Aberdeen University, wrote *The Illusion of National Character*, marking Fyfe as even less friendly to nationalism than Elie Kedourie or Carlton Hayes, but also as implicitly endorsing Hugh MacDiarmid's contention that to reject conventional nationality is to express the political identity of the Scots.[50] This 'civic republicanism' has been as historically important – and as mutable (think of Tom Nairn's 'The Three Dreams of Scottish Nationalism'[51] and what followed) – as the more explicit Scoto-Europeanism I am going to discuss. But with the end of 'welfare Britain', civic republicanism is back on stage, while Anglo-Britain regresses to an early stage of Hrochian evolution.

V

There is an ambivalence about the SNP's nationalism. An ethnic element exists, as intractable and embarrassing as is Irish nationalism; but a party warned off kilts by one of its founders, R. B. Cunninghame-Graham (*chutzpah*, this, coming from so flamboyant a romantic) can only greet Mel Gibson with qualified satisfaction. Historians of the 'ancient Scottish constitution' – D. H. MacNeill and Compton Mackenzie in the past, Murray Pittock today – would regard the Declaration of Arbroath in 1320 as fitting into the aristocratic nationalism of the French–Papal alliance. This old order rode out the Reformation, with the estates – law, kirk, burghs, universities – remaining subordinate to the nobility, whose rights were upheld by George Buchanan's gentrified republicanism and by Andrew Fletcher's federal scheme for British union: anti-metropolitan but also deeply inegalitarian. In the 1750s, after the last Jacobite rising, this petered out into antiquarianism.[52] A particularism of the sort that flared up into national rebirth in Poland, Hungary or Finland was done down, according to Colin Kidd, in *Subverting Scotland's Past* (1993), by Whig 'improvement', which also commodified the feelings it could not eradicate into the commercial 'culture' of Burns and Scott.[53]

This was not, however, the only stream of ideology. Its competitor in some ways exemplifies that British tendency to construe federalism as a centralizing rather than a pluralistic doctrine. 'Federal Calvinism' used the F-word in the sense of a covenant between God and man *and* between man and man: a type of transcendental constitutionalism. Politically it encompassed the 'Godly Commonwealth' of the Presbyterians, with authority devolved to the local oligarchies of kirk sessions and elders, the base of a pyramid of presbyteries and synods, culminating in the General Assembly of the Kirk. In the late seventeenth century this took stronger root on the other side of the Atlantic.[54]

Marx and Engels imagined Scottish nationalism as an ideological lean-to, reassembled from the detritus of pre-national cultures.[55] Pittock and Kidd reanimated ethnicity because of the destruction of Marxism in 1989–91, but ethnic nationalism's subsequent short life makes this less convincing. Scottish politics did not decline with ethno-historical politics. David Marquand has written of the dynamism of the market, the 'universal pander', and its dissolving effect on existing conventions. The post-union Scots adapted both the covenant and the 'estates' – the Faculty of Advocates, the Convention of Royal Burghs, the General Assembly and the universities – to contain the market and direct the social feelings which Adam Smith termed expressions of 'sympathy'. When Adam Ferguson talks of 'social bands' he is essentially using a secular version of the language of federal Calvinism.[56]

The union, in Diceyite terms of unrestricted sovereignty, involved the supererogation of a basic law – 'federal' in the covenanting sense – by parliamentary absolutism:

The legislators who passed these acts assuredly intended to give certain portions of them more than the ordinary effect of statutes. Yet the history of legislation in respect of these acts affords the strongest proof of the futility inherent in every attempt of one sovereign legislature to restrain the action of another equally sovereign body.[57]

The Scots were forced to acquiesce in several substantial breaches of the union's terms, but most of the obligations to respect Scottish institutions survived, and Anglo-Scottish politics created compensatory conventions in a state in which regulation was in any case minimal. These consisted of explicit alliances with authority, for which patronage and local autonomy were the *quid pro quo*. As the political community broadened, an innovative popular literature appeared which acted as its exegesis. With access to the administration and to markets, the threat of 'luxury and corruption' to the polis prompted a reorientation of politics in the direction of entrepreneurship and socialization.

To quote the verdict on the union of Bailie Nicoll Jarvie in Sir Walter Scott's *Rob Roy* (1818) – in Scotland, the most popular of all his works, on stage as well as in print – does not just show the 'universal pander' being coerced to 'improve', but highlights a continuing Scottish role for political fiction. The 'ballads of the nation' in the Middle Ages – Blind Hary's *Wallace* and Barbour's *Brus* – were replaced by the novel as a constitutional narrative convention, articulated by a new type of patriot:

> Let ilka ane roose the ford as they find it. I say, 'Let Glasgow flourish!' whilk is judiciously and elegantly putten round the town's arms by way of bye-word. Now, since St Mungo catched herrings in the Clyde, what was ever like to gar us flourish like the sugar and tobacco trade? Will ony body tell me that, and grumble at the treaty that opened us a road west-awa yonder?[58]

Scott's bourgeois hero is allowed to articulate a virtuoso medley of local tradition, heraldry and economics, and his apparent demolition of the old order represented by his cousin Rob Roy is even more subtle:

> But I maun hear naething about honour – we ken naething hear but aboot credit. Honour is a homicide and a bloodspiller, that

gangs about making frays in the street; But Credit is a decent honest man, that sits at hame and makes the pat play.[59]

Honour and credit can mean the same thing. In Scott's play on words lies a concern that economic success guaranteed the union, but might also lead to the 'corruption' feared by Smith and Ferguson. This specifically Glaswegian patriotism differs from the militancy of British nationalism postulated by Linda Colley and by Nicholas Phillipson's 'politics of noisy inaction':

> Mr Jarvie answered some objection which Owen made on the difficulty of sorting a cargo for America without buying from England with vehemence and volubility. 'Na, na sir, we stand on our ain bottom; we pickle in our ain pock-neuk … let every herring hing by its ain head, and every sheep by its ain shank and ye'll find, sir, us Glasgow folk no sae far ahint but what we may follow.'[60]

Hume and Smith, though regarding cultural nationality as destructive, thought the 'local or provincial state' best-suited to economic development, while the British state handled defence and economic policy. The outcome was a diffused sovereignty which traded parliamentary power for patronage and local autonomy: the dualism of Phillipson's 'semi-independence' which underwrote the remarkable changes of 1745–1843.[61]

This settlement conflated Gramsci's 'traditional' and 'organic' intellectuals. Economic development was driven by landowners and advocates, and by the towns, individually and corporately: building harbours and new villages, promoting industry and regulating labour. The Kirk was also involved in education, poor relief, assembling statistics and extending social control. Cumulatively, this transformed the Buchanan–Fletcher gentry ideal into civics, and transformed Edinburgh from a congested slum into a 'polite' capital for the 'estates', centralized and professionalized after the end of the heritable jurisdictions in 1747.[62]

'Civic humanism' was maintained by the agitation of the militia during the 1760s. This was premature, too soon after 1745, but it modified another 'national' element. Scotticisms were eradicated to enable Scots to colonize British public life, but cultural goods were 'symbolically appropriated', notably by 'Ossian' MacPherson, Burns and Scott, into British cultural stock.[63] Coinciding with 'print capitalism', this compound of efficiency and cultural nativism – what I have called 'red and black Scotland' – became during the long French War of 1793–1815 the Scottish element of what Linda Colley describes as the 'forging' of Britain.[64]

This devolution was not federal, as Scotland lacked a broadly competent parliament, but as the Scots did not share a uniform law with England, they stressed the peculiarity of their institutions, almost to the point, as Scott observed, of unquestioning reverence:

> Every youth of every temper and almost every description of character is sent either to study as a lawyer, or to a Writer's office as an apprentice. The Scottish seem to conceive Themis the most powerful of goddesses.[65]

'Management' was confederal: relying on a local elite governing through distinct instruments. As 'improvement' proceeded, the legal and aristocratic elements diminished, which enhanced the importance of the pillar most open to popular control: the Presbyterian Kirk.[66]

British nation or British state? Colley argues for the emotional assimilation of nationalism, but is vague about the institutions which affected people's daily existence. The Reform Act of 1832 replaced a deeply unrepresentative Scottish electorate, but integration into a multinational state was a more awkward transaction.[67] While Tom Nairn sees a Scottish proto-nationalism sliding effortlessly into aristo-bourgeois imperialism, George Davie's more combative interpretation is of the Scottish enlightenment flaring up for a last time in the 1830s, attempting to make 'the reform of the Union parliament the occasion for rescuing from corruption a two-kingdoms' constitution distinctive of the country, placing the spiritual order once again on a level with the temporal' and falling silent after the Disruption of 1843.[68] The Scots in fact extended 'civic humanism' into the bourgeois epoch, not just through the 'federal' contest for control over the Kirk, but through John Galt and Thomas Carlyle's critiques of parliament.

VI

If political fiction is seen as a type of constitutional convention, then Galt's novels are as pivotal for Scotland as the Trollope–Bagehot combination would later be for England: the paradigms of an enduringly popular political literature, ranging from Henry Cockburn's *Memorials of His Time* (1854) to William Alexander's *Johnie Gibb of Gushetneuk* (1871) and, at a lower level, in the didactic output of the *Kailyard*. The essential premise of Galt's 'rich diet of unspoken criticism' is the supremacy of law over power, and the equation of law with community, in a sense closer to that of von Savigny than to the Hobbesian–Austinian approach of the English tradition.[69] A student of the 'civic' Machiavelli, and directly influenced by Dugald Stewart and Adam Ferguson, Galt applied 'the general principles of the philosophy of history' to 'the West' – the region bounded by Glasgow, Greenock and Ayr, following it from rural tranquillity to industrial insecurity.[70] In *Annals of the Parish*, his study of a small Ayrshire village, contract takes over from status, broadly 'improving' the community, but in *The Provost* (1822) corruption rules. Its eponymous autobiographer

> got the cart up the brae, and the whole council reduced to the will and pleasure of his majesty, whose deputies and agents I have considered all inferior magistrates to be, administering and exercising, as they do, their power and authority in his royal name.[71]

For Galt Westminster is not a solution but a problem, tackled in the last of his 'theoretical histories'. *The Member* shows politics – decision-making and power-broking – uncoiling itself from the rational business of industrial and urban development. In this he echoed Scott's concern in the *Malagrowther Letters* (1826) about assaults on Scottish distinctiveness by both metropolitan parties. Scott *qua* national remembrancer and print capitalist, with imitators throughout Europe, was marginalized by his near-paranoid Toryism; Galt was far subtler.

The Member sums up the message of the earlier novels in attacking the Hobbesian arrogance of Westminster. It centres on a Scots nabob who buys himself an English borough to steer patronage in the direction of his gannet-like family.[72] Parliamentary and constituency conflicts enforce an education in the evils of the system. When Archibald Jobbry meets Mr Selby, a colonial proprietor ruined (like Galt) by government default, he realizes his complicity, while Selby's ideas of reform promise to destroy the very basis of parliamentary sovereignty:

Till Governments, and Houses of Commons, and those institutions which the sinful condition of man renders necessary, are made responsible to a tribunal of appeal, whose decisions shall control them, there can be no effectual reform. The first step is to take away all will of its own from Government – for statesmen are but mere men, rarely in talent above the average of their species, from what I have seen – and oblige it to consider itself no better than an individual, even with respect to its own individual subjects. Let the law in all aspects be paramount, and it will matter little whether the lords or the vagabonds send members to Parliament ...[73]

Officialism strikes at Jobbry himself when he is caught up in a farm labourers' riot, taken for Captain Swing himself, and dragged off to jail. The experience almost moralizes him but, no Reformer and certainly no exemplary mouthpiece, he ends unregenerate, retreating to his estate and dedicating his memoirs to the Tory whip:

I had indeed a sore heart when I saw the Whigs and Whiglings coming louping, like the puddocks of Egypt, over among the right hand benches of the House of Commons, greedy as corbies and chattering like pyets.[74]

Although *The Member* was overshadowed by the issue of church government in the 1830s, its combination of moralism and vernacular rhetoric was to last, and also to be developed (though not in a way entirely helpful to Scottish identity) by Thomas Carlyle.[75] A vast subject in himself, Carlyle shared Galt's sense that society existed independently of party-political action. He was the contemporary of Thomas Chalmers and the ecumenical Edward Irving, whose universalist Catholic Apostolic Church presaged several attempts to re-erect secular versions of the Two Kingdoms ideology. His 'message' contained both a secularized religious impulse, and precise authoritarian reforms which anticipated later 'civics'.[76] Ironically, the British elite's absorbent abilities made Carlyle the main inspirer of that didactic but persuasive tradition, the realist novel of public life, from Disraeli to Meredith.[77] This marked, in Schumpeter's sense, the success of English politics, in the critical decade of the 1840s, in recruiting from the elites of the other nations – turning 'uneven development' into a positive advantage.[78]

VII

Victorian Scotland, in contrast to the Continent, where nationalist activity climaxed in 1848, seemed resigned to British unity. The 1850s and 1860s were the age of 'north Britain'. An energetic attack on the Scots deductive philosophy was delivered by H. T. Buckle in his third volume of *The History of Civilization in England* (1861):

> The Scotch literature, notwithstanding its brilliancy, its power, and the splendid discoveries of which it was the vehicle, produced little or no effect on the nation at large .... Its method, both of investigation and of proof, was too refined to suit ordinary understandings. Therefore, upon ordinary understandings it was inoperative. In Scotland, as in ancient Greece, and in modern Germany, the intellectual classes, being essentially deductive, have been unable to influence the main body of the people. They have considered things at too great an altitude, and at too great a remove.[79]

Buckle damned Scottish metaphysics for arresting the country's development through adherence to a primitive and vindictive theology: 'In no civilized country is toleration so little understood ... in none is the spirit of bigotry and persecution so extensively diffused.'[80] He was followed by John Stuart Mill, whose *Examination of Sir William Hamilton's Philosophy* (1864) devastated common-sense philosophy just when the Westminster essence was being distilled by Erskine May and Bagehot, by the political novel, and by the reformers of Oxford and Cambridge.

The Disruption of 1843 had permitted this by destroying what was, in effect, a devolved assembly. The battle for the autonomy of the Kirk, and thus for control of Scottish educational and social policy, had been about 'non-intrusionists' interpreting the Act of Union as a basic law, federal just as much as Calvinism was federal, a line taken by J. F. Ferrier at the time, and by the young Harold Laski in his pluralist phase.[81] With the secession of the Free Kirk and the split of Calvinism into three competing groups, institutional autonomy in education and poor relief was lost, and class and sectarian loyalties were strengthened, just when the railway and telegraph were cementing ties to the south:

A great national institution, indeed the most essential of all, was broken up and a fundamental element of Scottish identity destroyed ... the minister, once an administrator, an arm of the state, a prop of the social order, was now just a pastor and preacher.[82]

This was the moment for Tom Nairn's tartan monster to take to the glens. A Tory nationalism, compounded of *Blackwoods* and Balmoral and radiating from every baronial mansion in the tones of Eton and Oxford, continued the 'commodification' of Scottish identity, aided by the Crimean War and the Indian Mutiny, the Highland sports, tourism and the aniline dyes which produced the shrieking colours of modern tartan. A brief right-wing nationalist phase in the 1850s, in which *Blackwoodsmen* like W. E. Aytoun denounced Liberalism as wholly denationalized, gave way in later decades to a mixture of deference and militant Protestantism which thrived on Liberal and Presbyterian division.

Yet, in Lindsay Paterson's terms, practical autonomy remained substantial. The vesting of poor relief in an effectively 'independent' board, selected to represent Scottish interests and with wide interpretive powers, had parallels in different municipal practices, involving remarkable degrees of freedom in civic initiatives.[83] The young Dicey admitted this 'confederal' quality when he wrote in 1867:

> Irish and Scotch Members are from the necessity of the case representatives of a class, and do therefore exert a force out of all proportion to their numbers. Few governments would dare to legislate for Scotland or Ireland in the face of the united opposition of the Scotch or Irish Members. Any one who is unwilling to see the working classes legislate for the majority of the nation, as the Scotch Members legislate for Scotland, will prefer the direct supremacy of numbers to the indirect supremacy of a tribunate.[84]

Even imperialism was interpreted with a sense of ideological separateness. The Imperial Federation League, formed in 1884, briefly moved Scots autonomy in a federal direction. Energized (temporarily) by the Irish Home Rule crisis, Lord Rosebery in 1885 saw the re-creation of the Secretary of State as but one step in a much more drastic constitutional reconstruction:

I cannot understand people preferring separation to Home Rule. I detest separation and feel that nothing could make me agree to it. Home Rule, however, is a necessity for both us and the Irish. They will have it within two years at the latest. Scotland will follow, then England. When that is accomplished, Imperial Federation will cease to be a dream.[85]

The Scots *were* ardent federalists – in Canada and Australia. At home, the shift was more confederal, to another autonomous institution that could be defended. The Christian social civics of Chalmers and Thomas Erskine of Linlathen, frustrated by the Disruption in 1843, became secularized and transferred to the universities. George Davie described this in 1961 in perhaps the leading text of post-war nationalism, *The Democratic Intellect*.[86] Robert Anderson has pointed out that Davie's assertion of a specifically Scottish educational 'party' shows enthusiasm outrunning evidence, but education, like social welfare, retained both a 'semi-independent' mode of governance and a distinctive national ethos.

It was sustained by a party Liberalism which held to the conventions that Dicey described, while representing an economy which, with its large-scale exporting industries and commercial agriculture, was unusually market-oriented and thus *ipso-facto* independent of London governance. A popular politics relatively free of 'influence' was able to indulge in the Liberal high-mindedness of Gladstone.[87] His sense of 'Christendom' (the 'international public right' diffused among the European nations) and of self-government (initially among religious groups; latterly among nations) accorded both with the traditions of divided sovereignty and of international law interpreted, by Professor James Lorimer and Professor James Bryce, as juridical federalism.[88]

Laissez-faire started to break down after 1873 as a result of the land crisis, shifting political action in two opposed directions. 'Welfarist' interventions in the market, such as the Highland Land Act of 1885, and in the Scottish Office in the same year, presaged similar measures in farming and housing.[89] Although *ad hoc* in its origins, the Scottish Office bore some similarity to what John Stuart Mill proposed in his *Principles of Parliamentary Reform* of 1859: a professional legislative board which would remove initiative from parliament. Unpopular among the English elite, Mill echoed some Scots preoccupations: the enfranchisement of women and multiple votes for the educated. The Scottish Office developed along Millite lines, supplementing the semi-independence of the estates, and retaining an orientation either to Europe or across the Atlantic. This sustained a professional administrative culture far different from that of the Oxbridge–Westminster elite because it was based more on theory than on ascriptive authority.[90]

Yet the expansion of state activity coincided with a philosophical shift. Utilitarianism, briefly dominant at the universities, was ousted by Hegelianism, with its automatic attractiveness to the 'state-in-being'. The symposium *Essays in Philosophical Criticism*, edited by Andrew Seth and R. B. Haldane, and published in memory of T. H. Green in 1883, favoured welfarism and 'international public right', but Hegelians left and right did not view Scotland through pluralist lenses.[91] Haldane, philosopher turned Liberal War Minister and later Labour Lord Chancellor, was a master of Fabian manoeuvre as an educational innovator. Scottish self-government interested him not at all.

Such people did not talk of an evolving Scottish state but of 'civics'. This 'notion' continued well into the twentieth century, and was conceptually akin to the German *Rechtstaat*; a state under law, not necessarily under democracy, which promoted and exported public service-based innovation, creating radically new institutions. Such exemplars as William Weir and the National Grid, John Grierson and documentary film, John Reith and the BBC, and Walter Elliot and agriculture, can be seen as having followed the spirit of Haldane's 1918 inquiry into the Machinery of Government. Although such reforms were of British institutions, the focus of loyalty was functional, never unconditional, and balanced, in David Marquand's terms, by a very loud Scottish 'voice'.

This ethos outcropped in the theory of James Lorimer, an almost archetypal Hrochian nationalist. As Erskine's friend, Lorimer defended the autonomy of the Scots universities, revived Scottish architecture, and argued in favour of female suffrage and proportional representation. The civic notion of 'good' rather than 'popular' government is deeply engrained in his thought, and informed his international outlook when in 1885 he put forward the first scheme for a federal Europe in his *Institutes of International Law*. The origins of such supra-national concepts of 'imperium' can be seen in James Bryce's *The Holy Roman Empire* (1864), the prelude to his enormously influential *American Commonwealth* (1889), which anticipated the role of convention within the

European Union.[92] Such formulations of federal ideas extended to Conservative thinkers, and derived inspiration from another Scottish source, Alexander Hamilton's *Federalist Papers* (1778). 'Home rule all round' was propounded in the 1900s by the imperialist F. S. Oliver, ideas echoed by his friend John Buchan in his study of *Montrose* (1926), and in his novel *Witch Wood* (1928) in which he has a fictional Montrose restate the federal Calvinist ideal:

> There is but one master in the land, and its name is law – which in itself is a creation of a free people under the inspiration of the Almighty. That law may be changed by the people's will, but till it be so changed it is to be revered and obeyed. It has ordained the King's prerogative, the rights of the subject, and the rights and duties of the Kirk. The state is like the body, whose health is only to be maintained by a just proportion among its members. If a man's belly be his god, his limbs will suffer; if he use only his legs, his arms will dwindle. If, therefore, the King should intrude upon the subject's rights, or the subject whittle at the King's prerogative, or the Kirk set herself above the Crown, there will be a sick state and an ailing people.[93]

VIII

A figure who embodied the ambiguity of this period was Sir Patrick Geddes (1854–1932), pioneering sociologist and regional planner, who combined *virtu* with Comteian positivism, the social criticism of Carlyle and Ruskin, and 'cosmopolitan' Celtic nationalism. Geddes' regional planning movement both exploited and criticized Empire – through his links with the proconsuls, the Lords Pentland and Aberdeen, and with Zionism, and Irish and Indian nationalism.[94] When Hugh MacDiarmid added the international influences of 'modernism' – Pound, Spengler, Shestov and Joyce – to the 'Scottish renaissance', he was rehabilitating Geddes in a post-imperial Scotland.[95]

Geddes' paradigm fused nationality and urbanization, drawing on evolutionary ideas and the contemporary problems of Scottish cities in which nearly half the population lived. Karl Miller has noted the attraction of 'Venetianism' for Henry Cockburn as well as for John Ruskin.[96] 'Civics' was well-adapted to something which resembled a west-coast floating republic stretching from Bristol to Glasgow, dependent on the capital goods industries and steam traction. A confederation of huge multi-cultural cities, regional mineral-fields, and worldwide commercial contacts, this area of western Britain was Scots-dominated, and by 1910 Geddes regarded it as standing on the edge of a 'geotechnic' civics which would balance cultural nationalism, cosmopolitanism and technology.[97]

'Civics' in both its Haldanite and Geddesian form anticipated Marshallian 'social citizenship' – a political society democratic in recruitment although elitist in function. Hence its success in urban politics and colonial territories where first-comers tended to rule over natives and late-comers. Derived psychologically from the Calvinist distinction between the 'adherent' and the 'elect' in the 'body of the Kirk', civics made the assumptions specifically denounced by Graham Wallas in his critique of James Bryce:

> Mr Bryce refers to 'the democratic ideal of the intelligent inde-
> pendence of the individual voter, an ideal far removed from the
> actualities of any State'. What does Mr Bryce mean by 'ideal
> democracy'? If it means anything, it means the best form of
> democracy which is consistent with the facts of human nature.
> But one feels ... that Mr Bryce means by these words the kind
> of democracy which might be possible if human nature were as
> he himself would like it to be, and as he was taught at Oxford to
> think that it was.[98]

Wallas has been called the father of British political behaviourism, but the high-mindedness he criticized was more Scots-derived than Oxonian. Bryce's ideas of the law go back via Chalmers and Galt to Roman and medieval precedents, but also draw on the amalgama-tion of sociology, religion and technology, to be encountered among the Scottish anthropologists – MacLennan, Robertson Smith and J. G. Frazer, as well as Geddes. This scientist element was strong in Walter Elliot's *Toryism and the Twentieth Century* (1927) in which the sciences, social and physical, are assumed as the basis of expert government – 'biology is the logos of Toryism' – while the market component was almost completely sidelined.[99] The empirical influence of the 'legislative ethos' of early European sociology has been noticed by Noel Annan in the case of Rudyard Kipling, though he neglects the Scots contribution to the 1880–1920 period. Then, as in the eighteenth century, the organic and traditional intelligentsia combined into a powerful hybrid of journalists, politicians and social engineers, whose Hebraic notion of 'The Law' was drawn from the 'shopfloor' of technology as well as from Biblical tradition.[100] Given such undoubted 'fire and strength', and an active home-rule movement, why did it come to a standstill?

IX

Any culture-derived ideology which is connected only indirectly to sovereign institutions, by opposing sympathy and emotion to an over-rigid mechanism, will tend to produce complete contradiction – something to which the Tory cultural nationalist and political unionist – Hogg, Stevenson, Buchan come to mind – is peculiarly prone.[101] Out of this quandary can come two things: an internal division amounting to *stasis* when a rational politics of community and family challenges individuality, or a buccaneering and un-crupulous opportunism assaulting an ascriptive and lazy establishment. This issues in an obsession with the collapse of rationalism: the *doppelganger* from Hogg through Stevenson to R. D. Laing. And Scots have been prolific with modern versions of Hogg's Gil-Martin: the likes of Lord Beaverbrook and Rupert Murdoch, born out of Scottish religious politics and taking enthusiastically to the solipsism of the 'Scotsman on the make'. In 1825 Sir Walter Scott wrote to J. W. Croker: 'If you unscotch us you will find us damned mischievous Englishmen.'[102] Political intemperance has shadowed even the most dedicated careerists within the union.[103]

In terms of external forces, a dramatic challenge to Scots autonomy and to 'civics' came with the centralization enforced by the First World War, and the zenith of Britain's imperial might, rapidly followed by two decades of unbroken economic recession. Autonomy lost out after 1920 to centralized collectivism, the replacement of the administrative boards by civil service departments and, after the removal of anti-Tory Ireland from an increasingly Conservative Westminster, the marginalization of constitutional issues. Economic collapse subverted 'civics', but so too did the ethnic nationalism of Versailles which produced the National Party of Scotland in 1928. The martyrs of Easter 1916 became icons of the *literati*: MacDiarmid and Edwin Muir, enthusiasts like Ruaridh Erskine of Mar, and the occasional leftist maverick like John MacLean. Liberators, in the form of the Scots literary renaissance, these writers obscured mass-unemployment, housing deterioration, sectarianism, poor health and neglected education. Here the attitudes of John Wheatley, the most innovatory of post-war politicians, were collectivist and civic-autonomous without being nationalist. His Marxism went hand-in-hand with a concept, derived probably from Geddes, of

> Glasgow's golden future as a landscaped, healthy, prosperous municipality with its own home and foreign trading departments, and ships with the city's arms trading from the Clyde with other Socialist cities round the world.[104]

Wheatley fared no better than had the home-rule bodies in the 1920s which moved from federalism, in the Labour MP George Buchanan's Bill of 1924, to confederalism in the Bill drafted by the Scottish Home Rule Convention in 1926, which became the policy of the new National Party of Scotland in 1928. The depression allied the ethnic nationalists with collectivism of a sort. Further agencies of the welfarist type were invoked, not least in the plethora of civic bodies, from the Scottish National Development Council to the Saltire Society, set up in the 1930s. *The New Unionism* (1936) of the economist J. R. R. Porteous preached a corporate Keynesianism, which led Elliot to appoint him to the new Scottish Economic Committee. He would later join MacCormick's Scottish Convention and the SNP.

Social Credit, the nostrum of a Scottish engineer, C. H. Douglas, was for a time as influential within the Labour Party as within the NPS – or as it was in Canada or New Zealand.[105] Anti-bank propaganda perhaps appealed in a country whose banks shifted investments south in response to the slump, reflecting an attitude quite different from the peasant-based ideology of Ireland or the language struggle in Wales.[106] But in the 1930s the shift was back towards the federal, with the largely ex-Liberal Scottish Party combining with the NPS on such terms to form the SNP under John MacCormick, 1934–42. This ethos persisted in MacCormick's Scottish Convention in the late 1940s.

The federal tradition was not just exported, but could be repatriated also. Carlyle, John Muir, Thomas Davidson and, later, Geddes had helped, via Whitman, William James and Lewis Mumford, to create the ideology of the American progressive movement which issued in the New Deal.[107] Its cultural elements – regional planning, people's history and political folksong – influenced post-1945

Scottish radicalism, via John Grierson, Alan Lomax and Hamish Henderson, *without* taking the usual route through London.[108] Yet this federalism had something of its Anglo-American meaning of centralization, depending either on the regional policy of Big Government or on promoting working-class self-government. This reinforced the welfare citizenship of the 1935 Unemployment Assistance Board or, in cultural terms, of Reith's BBC, and was accelerated by the southwards shift of the print media, although there were counter-currents, such as the notion of 'imperial federation' characteristic of the Beaverbrook papers.

Labour's rapid growth in the 1920s provoked a Unionist–Liberal *anschluss*, which made the 'estates' chary of taking the initiative, though the Scottish National Development Corporation and a succession of planning bodies owed much both to the Convention of Royal Burghs and the Scottish Office. This was followed, during the Second World War, by the success of Tom Johnston's decentralization, legislative as well as administrative, under the umbrella of his Scottish Council of State, which involved physical planning, energy, and the health service. The emergence of Liberal and independent-Conservative anti-centralist forces followed, with MacCormick's Scottish Covenant Movement arguably underlying the Liberal as well as the SNP revivals of the 1960s.[109] Lord Cooper's observation on the lack of a tradition of sovereignty in Scots constitutional law, in his judgment on MacCormick *v.* the Lord Advocate in 1953, arguably reflected not just traditional Scottish constitutional doctrine but the progress that had been made in stretching the legal permissiveness of welfarist Britain.[110]

X

The Scottish Covenant Movement was the last important instance of the imperial federation/Act of Union as basic law approach, although its ghostly presence continued in Edward Heath's attempt to annex devolution through Sir Alec Douglas-Home's Committee of 1968–70 and in Professors Alan Peacock and Norman Hunt's note of dissent to the Kilbrandon Report, proposing a form of devolution-all-round, including the English regions.

The post-MacCormick SNP, under Robert McIntyre and Arthur Donaldson, demanded dominion status. But this – Sinn Fein-like – position faded into the background from which it had evolved, namely 'small-town radical party activism', in this instance fighting it out with the Liberals. Its protest role drew activists from the old ILP and CND, and it shared some 'small-is-beautiful' ideas with Plaid Cymru.[111] In the 1970s dominion status gave way to proposals for an Association of British States, while reactions to the setback of 1979–83 took the SNP to the left of Labour on most issues. Its expansion was checked by Labour's conversion to devolution, and the party's role in opposition, but it maintained its vote, not least through its 'Scotland in Europe' policy, adopted in 1988. This squared federalism and confederalism within a European frame, removing the threat of separation while capitalizing on England's alienation from Brussels.

The formerly 'left unionist' parties have also shifted. The language of *Scotland's Claim of Right* (1987), embodied in the Scottish Constitutional Convention of March 1989, reinvoked the position of the Church of Scotland on the dual sovereignty issue in 1842. By demanding entrenched clauses guaranteeing Scottish autonomy, it reanimated the popular sovereignty doctrine.[112] The SNP spurned the Convention, when its requirement for there to be an independence option in any subsequent referendum was refused; yet this doctrine (and the dropping of 'strong' English regional assemblies by Labour) moved the Scottish consensus closer to the SNP's position.[113]

After the 1997 election, are we closer to Hroch's third stage – though less through a mass movement than a decline of British loyalties? SNP support remains primarily rural, though the gradient (from 56 per cent of the vote in Banff and Buchan in 1997 to 11 per cent in Roxburgh) is much flatter than is Plaid Cymru's in Wales (from 52 per cent in Caernarfon to 1 per cent in Monmouth). About 25 per cent of Labour voters think themselves likely to transfer to the SNP; and support for independence, less than 20 per cent in the mid-1970s, is now around 35 per cent.

The political feelings of the Scottish and the metropolitan elites have diverged, not just because of a competitive 'bourgeois regionalism' in the Scots cities, although dealing with Europeans as a Scot (or Welshman or Irishman) is convenient. The persistence of a welfare ethos and a sense of 'fairness' give far higher prestige to trades unions, with Campbell Christie carrying more weight than any Scottish MP: a 'social-marketist' tendency which reinforces the country's European orientation.[114]

In 1995 a non-nationalist authority, Professor Christopher Smout, Historiographer-Royal for Scotland, put the chances of confederalism above those of devolution:

> you probably are going to have a devolution situation, and that will be an unstable one. And that is likely to lead either to a Major situation, where Britishness wins, or to some form of independent situation, where Scottishness wins. But these two things will remain in the Scottish psyche. I think the divorce will be quite painful.[115]

The paradox is that while constitutional self-awareness has matured, the autonomy of the Scottish 'community' has been diminished, not just by the external control of capital. In certain aspects – diet, drugs, violence, prostitution – its distinctiveness is negative. But the degree to which new Scottish approaches to the totality of a society have married themselves to politics, as a means towards an ecological integration of technics and civics – a concept pioneered by Patrick Geddes – is distinctive. To recover the trajectories of Scottish discourse on politics, religion, philosophy and culture, while British conventions deteriorate, brings autonomy perceptibly closer.

To sum up: a distinctive Scottish politics resided in the authority devolved within the state to subsidiary bodies – the churches, the lawyers, education, local government – framed by a public doctrine which converted the laws which govern these bodies into positive conventions capable of invoking loyalty, rather than parliamentary privileges increasingly deemed intolerable. Traditionally, the divergence between Scottish and English discourses has been treated warily by the devolved administration, whose role took on quasi-confederal aspects, influencing the country's European orientation. Since 1979 this has become increasingly controversial, with the dissolution of the British state provoking a much more explicit nationalism on both sides of the border. This in turn has encouraged the historicizing of a specifically Scots politics.

Notes

1 See F. O'Toole, *The Observer*, 7 April 1996. This chapter had its origins in a paper delivered to the Political Studies Association in Glasgow, 10 April 1996.

2   A. Griffith, *The Resurrection of Hungary* (Dublin: United Irishman, 1904).

3   D. Figgis, *The Irish Constitution Explained* (Dublin: Mellifont Press, 1922), pp. 21, 55. In a conversation in 1976 with Dr Garret FitzGerald, the former Taoiseach described the old President's nostalgia for the 'White Commonwealth' of the 1930s.

4   See C. Harvie, *The Lights of Liberalism: University Liberals and the Challenge of Democracy 1860–1886* (London: Allen Lane, 1976).

5   L. Paterson, *The Autonomy of Modern Scotland* (Edinburgh: Edinburgh University Press, 1994); R. J. Finlay, *Scottish Politics and the Origins of the SNP, 1918–1945* (Edinburgh: John Donald, 1994); A. Marr, *The Battle for Scotland* (Harmondsworth: Penguin, 1994).

6   M. Keating and A. Midwinter, *The Government of Scotland* (Edinburgh: Mainstream, 1983); J. Kellas, *The Scottish Political System*, 3rd edn (Cambridge: Cambridge University Press, 1989); J. Mitchell, *Conservatives and the Union* (Edinburgh: Edinburgh University Press, 1990) and *Strategies for Self-Government: the Campaigns for a Scottish Parliament* (Edinburgh: Polygon, 1996).

7   A. Gray, *1982 Janine* (Edinburgh: Canongate, 1984), p. 185.

8   R. Anderson, *Education and Opportunity in Nineteenth-Century Scotland* (Oxford: Clarendon, 1983), pp. 1–2.

9   W. L. Miller, *The End of British Politics* (Oxford: Oxford University Press, 1981).

10   G. Belli (translation by R. Garioch), cited in A. Marr, *Ruling Britannia* (London: Michael Joseph, 1995), p. 230.

11   J. Schumpeter, *Capitalism, Socialism and Democracy* (London: Allen & Unwin, 1942); Mitchell, *Conservatives and the Union*, p. 13. The traditional 'functional-romantic' doctrine of British constitutionalism is to be found in P. Norton, *Does Parliament Matter?* (Hemel Hempstead: Wheatsheaf, 1993).

12   Cited in the 'Programme' for the Political Science Conference held at Glasgow University, 10–12 April 1996.

13   J. Macmurray, *Conditions of Freedom* (London: Faber, 1950), p. 66.

14   J. Lloyd in *Scotland on Sunday*, 5 May 1996; I. Lindsay, 'The Uses and Abuses of National Stereotypes', *Scottish Affairs*, vol. 20 (Summer 1997), pp. 133–48; *Deutschlandfunk* report, 12 January 1994; and see H. Drucker (ed.) *Mackintosh on Scotland* (Oxford: Blackwell, 1980). School polls in the 1997 campaign bore this out. The result at Royal High in Edinburgh, for example, put the SNP at 212, the Liberal Democrats at 117, Labour at 93 and the Conservatives at 38: see *The Times*, 24 April 1997.

15   Harvie, *Lights of Liberalism*; N. Annan, *Our Age* (London: HarperCollins, 1994 [1992]).

16   H. Belloc, 'On a General Election' in *Stories, Essays and Poems* (London: Dent, 1938), p. 414.

17   G. Dangerfield, *The Strange Death of Liberal England* (London: MacGibbon & Kee, 1966 [1935]), p. 76.

18   K. Stolz, 'Scotland in the European Union' (PhD dissertation, Universität Freiburg, 1996).

19 F. M. L. Thompson (general editor) *Comparative Studies on Government and Non-Dominant Groups in Europe, 1850–1940*, 8 volumes (New York and Aldershot: NYUP and Dartmouth, 1992–3): vol. 6, *The Formation of National Elites*, edited by A. Kappeler.

20 M. Hroch, 'Social and Territorial Characteristics in the Composition of the Leading Groups of National Movements', in Kappeler (ed.), *Formation*, pp. 257–76; M. Hroch, *Social Preconditions of National Revival in Europe* (Cambridge: Cambridge University Press, 1985 [1968]).

21 T. E. May, *Laws, Privileges, Proceedings and Usages of Parliament* (1844).

22 R. Crawford, *Devolving English Literature* (Oxford: Clarendon, 1993); T. Garvin, 'Great Hatred, Little Room: Social Background and Political Sentiment among Revolutionary Activists in Ireland 1890–1922', in D. G. Boyce (ed.) *The Revolution in Ireland, 1879–1923* (London: Macmillan, 1988), pp. 91–114.

23 G. Almond and S. Verba, *The Civic Culture: Political Attitudes and Democracy in Five Nations* (Princeton: Princeton University Press, 1963).

24 F. Cripps *et al.*, *Manifesto: a Radical Strategy for Britain's Future* (London: Pan Books, 1981).

25 C. Harvie, *Fool's Gold: The Story of North Sea Oil* (Harmondsworth: Penguin, 1995, revised edn).

26 See the editorial in the *Independent on Sunday*, 5 May 1996; C. Harvie, 'Thoughts on the Union between Law and Opinion, or Dicey's Last Stand', in D. Marquand and C. Crouch (eds) *The New Centralism* (Oxford: Blackwell, 1989); and A. Gamble, 'The Free Economy and the Strong State', in R. Miliband and J. Saville (eds) *The Socialist Register* (London: Merlin, 1979).

27 I take Dicey's view from R. A. Cosgrove, *The Rule of Law: Albert Venn Dicey, Victorian Jurist* (London: Macmillan, 1980), Chapters 4 and 5; and see D. Marquand, *The Unprincipled Society* (London: Cape, 1988), Chapter 7.

28 The Scottish vote for the Referendum Party averaged less than one-third of the English level; at most about 12,000 Scots turned out for services commemorating the Princess of Wales on Saturday 6 September, compared with estimates of 1–2 million at the funeral in London. Also see D. Cesarani, 'The Changing Character of Citizenship and Nationality in Britain', in D. Cesarani and M. Fulbrook (eds) *Citizenship, Nationality and Migration in Europe* (London: Routledge, 1996); and the 'New Times' edition of *Marxism Today*, October 1998.

29 See, for example, J. C. D. Clark, *The Language of Liberty, 1660–1832: Political Discourse and Social Dynamics in the Anglo-American World* (Cambridge: Cambridge University Press, 1994), a Cowling-inspired work whose concentration on English religious ideology practically displaces from consideration all other national traditions.

30 D. Cannadine, 'The Past in the Present', in L. M. Smith (ed.) *The Making of Britain: Echoes of Greatness* (London: Macmillan and Channel 4, 1988), p. 14.
31 P. Johnson, *Wake Up, England! A Latter-Day Pamphlet* (London: Weidenfeld & Nicolson, 1994); A. Roberts, *Eminent Churchillians* (London: Cassell, 1995); and see *The Times, Spectator* and *Daily Telegraph, passim.*
32 F. Mount, *The British Constitution Now* (London: Mandarin Books, 1993), p. 10; and see his pro-devolution article in the *Evening Standard*, 16 November 1996.
33 B. Crick (ed.) *National Identities: the Constitution of the United Kingdom* (Oxford: Blackwell, 1991).
34 W. Hutton, *The State We're In* (London: Cape, 1995).
35 J. Bulpitt, *Territory and Power in the United Kingdom* (Manchester: Manchester University Press, 1993); J. Osmond, *Welsh Europeans* (Bridgend: Seren, 1996).
36 Statistics from *Britannia World Data, The World in 1990*, etc. (London: Economist Publishing Co.).
37 *The Times*, 6 April 1996.
38 Marquand, *Unprincipled Society.*
39 *Scotsman*, 9 February 1998 and *Guardian*, 15 November 1989.
40 N. Ascherson, *Games with Shadows* (London: Verso, 1986); T. Nairn, *The Enchanted Glass: Britain and its Monarchy* (London: Verso, 1988); Marr, *Ruling Britannia.* Not to speak of two adoptive Scots: O. D. Edwards, who edited the book version of *A Claim of Right for Scotland* (Edinburgh: Polygon, 1992), and B. Crick, *Political Thoughts and Polemics* (Edinburgh: Edinburgh University Press, 1990).
41 L. Colley, *Britons: Forging the Nation, 1707–1837* (London: Yale University Press, 1992).
42 Garvin, 'Great Hatred', pp. 96–7, 101.
43 See C. H. Lee, *Scotland and the United Kingdom: the Economy and the Union in the Twentieth Century* (Manchester: Manchester University Press, 1995), and my review of the book in *The Scottish Historical Review*, 1997.
44 See 'Bagehot' (Peter Jones) in *Economist*, 12 April 1996.
45 *Scotsman*, March 1996.
46 The Referendum returns showed a particularly strong support (high turnout: high majority) for devolution in the New Scotland of the central belt outwith the cities: Fife 61:76, Central 65:76, Lothian 61:75.
47 *A Woman's Claim of Right for Scotland* (Edinburgh: Polygon, 1994); and see E. MacAskill in the *Guardian*, 30 November 1996.
48 A. Calder, 'By the Water of Leith I Sat Down and Wept: Reflections on Scottish Identity', in H. Ritchie (ed.) *New Scottish Writing* (London: Bloomsbury, 1996).
49 H. Seton-Watson, *Nationalism and Communism* (London: Methuen, 1964).
50 H. Fyfe, *The Illusion of National Character* (London: Watts, 1945); and see C. M. Grieve, *Albyn, or Scotland and the Future* (London: Kegan Paul, 1927), p. 46.

51 T. Nairn, 'The Three Dreams of Scottish Nationalism', in K. Miller (ed.) *Memoirs of a Modern Scotland* (London: Faber, 1969).
52 D. B. MacNeill, *The Scottish Realm* (Glasgow: Arthur Donaldson, 1957); C. Mackenzie outlines, at exhausting length, a neo-Jacobite national policy in *The North Wind of Love* (London: Chatto & Windus, 1962 [1945]), Chapter 1; M. Pittock, *The Invention of Scotland: the Stuart Myth and the Scottish Identity, 1638 to the Present* (London: Routledge, 1991), Chapter 5.
53 C. Kidd, *Subverting Scotland's Past* (Oxford: Clarendon, 1993).
54 A. Williamson, *Scottish National Consciousness in the Age of James VI* (Edinburgh: John Donald, 1979); see especially Chapter 3.
55 F. Engels, 'The Magyar Struggle', 13 January 1849, cited in C. Harvie, *Scotland and Nationalism* (London: Routledge, 1994), p. 26.
56 D. Marquand, 'How United Is the Modern United Kingdom?', in A. Grant and K. J. Stringer (eds) *Uniting the Kingdom? The Making of British History* (London: Routledge, 1995).
57 A. V. Dicey, *Law of the Constitution* (London: Macmillan, 1927 [1886]), p. 63.
58 W. Scott, *Rob Roy* (London: 1896 [1817]), pp. 254–5.
59 Ibid., p. 238.
60 Ibid., p. 327.
61 A. Smith, *The Wealth of Nations*, p. 318; N. Phillipson, 'Nationalism and Ideology', in J. N. Wolfe (ed.) *Government and Nationalism in Scotland* (Edinburgh: Edinburgh University Press, 1969), pp. 168–86.
62 W. H. Fraser, *Conflict and Class: Scottish Workers, 1700–1838* (Edinburgh: John Donald, 1988); M. Fry, 'The Disruption and the Union', in S. J. Brown and M. Fry (eds), *Scotland in the Age of the Disruption* (Edinburgh: Edinburgh University Press, 1993).
63 M. Chapman, *The Celts* (London: Macmillan, 1993).
64 Colley, *Britons*, pp. 117–31.
65 *The Journal of Sir Walter Scott* (Edinburgh: Oliver & Boyd, 1950), p. 31.
66 I. D. L. Clark, 'From Protest to Reaction: the Moderate Regime in the Church of Scotland, 1752–1805', in N. T. Phillipson and R. Mitchison (eds) *Scotland in the Age of Improvement* (Edinburgh, 1970), pp. 200–24.
67 Colley, *Britons*, pp. 341–74.
68 T. Nairn, *The Break-up of Britain* (London: Verso, 1977), pp. 118–20; G. E. Davie, *The Scottish Enlightenment* (Edinburgh: Polygon, 1990), p. 43.
69 I. Campbell, *Kailyard* (Edinburgh: Ramsey Head Press, 1981), pp. 48ff.
70 P. H. Scott, *John Galt* (Edinburgh: Scottish Academic Press, 1985), p. 76.
71 J. Galt, *The Provost* (Foulis,1913 [1822]), p. 23.
72 See Scott, *John Galt*; H. MacPherson, 'Carlyle', in *A Century of Political Development* (Edinburgh: Blackwood, 1908); S. J. Brown, *Thomas Chalmers and the Godly Commonwealth in Scotland* (Oxford: Oxford University Press, 1982).

73 J. Galt, *The Member* (Edinburgh: Scottish Academic Press, 1985 edn), p. 62.

74 Ibid., p. 119.

75 W. Donaldson, *Popular Literature in Victorian Scotland: Language, Fiction and the Press* (Aberdeen: Aberdeen University Press, 1986), p. 9.

76 C. Harvie, 'Carlyle the Radical', *Scotlands*, 3, 2 (1966).

77 C. Harvie, *The Centre of Things: Political Fiction in Britain from Disraeli to the Present* (London: Unwin Hyman, 1991), pp. 36ff.

78 Ibid., Chapter 3.

79 H. T. Buckle, *The History of Civilization in England* (London: Longmans, 1871 edn), pp. 465f.

80 Ibid., p. 140.

81 J. F. Ferrier, *Observations on Church and State* (Edinburgh: Blackwood, 1848); H. Laski, *Studies in the Problems of Sovereignty* (New Haven: Yale University Press, 1917), pp. 208ff.

82 M. Fry, *Patronage and Politics: a Political History of Modern Scotland* (Aberdeen: Aberdeen University Press, 1987), p. 52.

83 Anderson, *Education and Opportunity*, pp.358–61; I. Levitt, *Poverty and Welfare in Scotland, 1890–1948* (Edinburgh: Edinburgh University Press, 1988), Chapter 2; G. Best, 'Another Part of the Island', in H. J. Dyos and M. Wolff (eds) *The Victorian City: Images and Realities* (London: Routledge, 1973), vol. 1, pp. 389–412.

84 A. V. Dicey, 'The Balance of Classes', in A. O. Rutson (ed.) *Essays on Reform* (London: MacGibbon & Kee, 1967), p. 68.

85 Cited by G. Walker, *Intimate Strangers: Political and Cultural Interaction Between Scotland and Ulster in Modern Times* (Edinburgh: Edinburgh University Press, 1995), pp. 18–19.

86 G. E. Davie, *The Democratic Intellect: Scotland and her Universities in the Nineteenth Century* (Edinburgh: Edinburgh University Press, 1961).

87 Fry, *Patronage and Politics*, p. 93.

88 C. Harvie, 'Gladstonianism, the Provinces and Popular Political Culture', in R. Bellamy (ed.) *Victorian Liberalism* (London: Routledge, 1989), pp. 152–74.

89 H. J. Hanham, 'Mid-Victorian Scottish Nationalism: Romantic and Radical', in R. Robson (ed.) *Ideas and Institutions of Victorian Britain* (London: Bell, 1967), pp. 143–79; C. Harvie, 'Legalism, Myth and National Identity in Scotland in the Imperial Epoch', Paper given at a Symposium on Self-Determination and Self-Expression in Commonwealth Countries in July 1986 and published in *Cencrastus*, 26 (1987).

90 J. S. Mill, *Principles of Parliamentary Reform* (London: Longmans, 1859).

91 Where Goethe in the 1820s congratulated Carlyle on Scottish distinctiveness, G. Lúkacs wrote of Scott throughout *The Historical Novel* (London: Merlin, 1989 [1936]) as an English author. Goethe to Carlyle (1828), cited in J. A. Froude, *Thomas Carlyle: A History of the First Forty Years of his Life*, vol. 1 (London: Longman Green, 1885), pp. 414–20.

92 See Kleinknecht, *Imperiale und Internationale Ordnung: Eine Untersuchung zum Anglo-Amerikanischen Gelehrtenliberalismus am Beispiel von James Bryce (1838–1922)* (Göttingen: Vandenhoeck und Rupprecht, 1985), pp. 71–114.

93 J. Buchan, *Witch Wood* (Edinburgh: Nelson, 1928, reprinted 1950), p. 69.

94 H. Meller, *Patrick Geddes: Social Evolutionist and City Planner* (London: Routledge, 1990); D. Macmillan, *Art in Scotland* (Edinburgh: Mainstream, 1992); A. Gray, *Why Scots Should Rule Scotland* (Edinburgh: Canongate, 1992).

95 Harvie, *Scotland and Nationalism*, Chapter 3.

96 K. Miller, *Cockburn's Millennium* (London: Duckworth, 1966).

97 C. Harvie, 'Garron Top to Caergybi: Images of the Inland Sea', Address delivered to the Hewitt Summer School, July 1994, published in *Irish Studies*, 19 (1996).

98 G. Wallas, *Human Nature in Politics* (London: Constable, 1908), pp. 126–7.

99 W. Elliot, *Toryism and the Twentieth Century* (London: Philip Allen, 1927), p. 126.

100 N. Annan, 'Kipling's Place in the History of Ideas', *Victorian Studies*, 3 (1960).

101 C. Harvie, 'Second Thoughts of a Scotsman on the Make: Politics, Nationalism and Myth in John Buchan', *Scottish Historical Review* (1991).

102 Scott to Croker, 19 March 1825, in H. Grierson (ed.) *The Letters of Sir Walter Scott, 1825–1826* (London: Constable, 1935), p. 472.

103 *Scotsman*, 28 April 1996.

104 I. S. Wood, 'Scottish Labour in the 1920s', in I. Donnachie, C. Harvie and I. S. Wood (eds) *Forward: Scottish Labour Politics since 1888* (Edinburgh: Polygon, 1989), p. 34.

105 No research has been done on the Social Credit movement in Britain; but G. Walker shows how influential it was on Tom Johnston, in his *Thomas Johnston* (Manchester: Manchester University Press, 1988).

106 S. Hagemann, *Die Schottische Renaissance* (Frankfurt: Peter Lang, 1990); Harvie, *Scotland and Nationalism*, Chapter 3.

107 D. Anderson, *Lewis Mumford: an American Life* (New York: Macmillan, 1989).

108 H. Henderson, *Alias MacAlias* (Edinburgh: Polygon, 1993).

109 Walker, *Johnston*, Chapter 6.

110 Mitchell, *Strategies for Self-Government*, pp. 267–9.

111 Harvie, *Scotland and Nationalism*, pp. 173–8.

112 Mitchell, *Strategies for Self-Government*, pp. 127–33.

113 Campaign for a Scottish Assembly, *A Claim of Right for Scotland* (1988); and see J. Ross, 'A Fond Farewell to Devolution', *Radical Scotland* (December/January 1988–9); P. Lynch, 'The Scottish Constitutional Convention, 1992–95', *Scottish Affairs* (Spring 1996); G. Leicester, 'Fundamentals for a New Scotland Act: the Constitution Unit's Report on Scotland', *Scottish Affairs* (Summer 1996).

114 J. Kellas, *The Scottish Political System* (Cambridge: Cambridge University Press, 1990).

115 Interview of 28 June 1995, in M. Köthe, 'Schottland 1995: über den Umgang mit dem Thema der Nationalen Identität' (MA thesis, Universität Hannover, 1996), p. 223.

Chapter 6

Member states and the European Union[1]

Elizabeth Meehan

Pinning down the nature of the European Union (EU) and its constituent states is difficult because this relatively new compact does not fit readily into established schools of thought or concepts with which we are already familiar. It is hard, therefore, to find a language that conveys exactly what the analyst wants to say.[2] Studies of the EU are partial because of their dependence on what once may have been useful contrasts but are now 'false dichotomies' – 'primarily the debate between intergovernmentalism and supra-nationalism'.[3] Practising politicians may see the EU as the continuation of a 'process of mutually agreed [by states] gradual integration' or as the destroyer of 'the sovereign state'.[4] Yet, again, advocates of a new Europe may see the EU, not as too federal, but as not federal enough.

It is not argued here that the EU is a state-in-the-making (either federal or unified). Nor is it argued that macro-level changes and the growth of autonomous links between sub-state regions and the continental institutions combine to seriously undermine the status of states – at least for the foreseeable future. It is, however, argued that changes are taking place which alter conventional assumptions, have an impact on inter-state relations, and give greater international standing to sub-state regions than has been customary – all of which may have the dynamic potential to result in unforeseeable outcomes.

If people engaged in practical politics are concerned about the proper relationship that should obtain between the states that make up the EU, and between the central institutions and powers of the union, intellectual analysis focuses on what those relationships actually are and the directions they are likely to follow. Of particular note is the question of whether or not states are being undermined as the key shapers of the international system by global forces and Continental integration. There seems to be, however, an emerging consensus – incorporating elements even of the Realist school of international relations – that, irrespective of whether states 'have had their day' or 'are here to stay', their defining characteristics and core activities are changing. As indicated above, this chapter reflects that emerging consensus.

The chapter opens with a brief delineation of the contours of the political and intellectual debates about the future of states, particularly those that make up the EU. British political discourse about the relationship between member states and the EU often refers to the United States of America as constituting a model of what should be avoided or as indicative of what is threatening to the sovereign state in European integration. Hence, section two examines this comparison in a way that is argued to be more appropriate than what usually takes place. This section suggests that it is not self-evident that the experience of the USA demonstrates that the EU will displace the independence of its constituent states to the extent that 'Euro-sceptics' fear. The chapter then changes tack, using a different method to explore, in section three, the potential of the EU to become a 'super-state'; more accurately expressed, it considers the dynamics of central and state competences. Here the analysis takes as its starting point what are said to be the defining characteristics of states as they have developed since the Treaty of Westphalia to consider whether the central institutions of the EU are, indeed, acquiring such features at the expense of the member states. Both main parts of the chapter indicate a complex situation in which the continuation of state power and the development of some EU state-like powers coexist. The chapter concludes by suggesting that the difficulty encountered in explaining 'Europe' reflects changes, which are not exclusive to the EU, in the nature of states and the international order.

I

Political anxieties that the dynamics of European integration are fatally undermining practical independence and legal sovereignty are felt more acutely in the United Kingdom than among its partners. Though the French refer to 'l'Europe des patries', and the British to 'a Europe of the nation states', the two are not as close in outlook as the phrases might imply; think, for example, of the attitudes of political elites in the two countries towards economic and monetary union (EMU). Similarly, the opinion of the German Constitutional Court that the Maastricht Treaty established a 'federation of states' and 'not a state based upon the principle of one European nation'[5] does not mean that German political elites share the British conception of integration. The British resist moves towards 'ever closer union', even if only a quasi-federalist union, because of their tendency to equate federalism with centralization within a unitary state, often called 'super-state'. Hence Mrs Thatcher's 1985 statement that she 'would never commend to the House of Commons a federation which would be the equivalent to the United States of Europe'.[6]

The intellectual debate has been between the Realist school of international relations – for which states, by and large in traditional form, remain the key determinant of the shape of international society – and critics of that school. Critics approach the issue from what they see occurring both above and below the state in its current form. In identifying 'grand forces' which inhibit states' capacities to act independently, Gellner,[7] for example, argues that power comes no longer through territory but through industrial and economic growth. This source of power, uncoupled from territorial control, at once diminishes the need for clearly defined borders and impels supranational organization. Arrighi[8] is equally radical in his argument that the state system is being superseded by a system of free enterprise ('free, that is, from … vassalage to state power') and of 'suprastatal organizations'. Taking sovereignty in its legal sense, Rosas,[9] drawing on the view of Camilleris and Falk that 'the primacy of domestic law … is arguably one of the cardinal premises of state sovereignty', points out that the primacy of European law may 'cripple' the sovereignty of member states. In examining both international and European law, Rosas comes to the conclusion that 'the foundations of the traditional inter-state system are shaking'.[10]

A counter-argument comes in the form of the observation that states can hardly be thought of as insignificant when we see that the demand for independent statehood has not abated. On the other hand, there are those who believe that, despite exceptions, there is less concern than there used to be among governments in Western Europe – if not elsewhere – to achieve congruence between political and cultural borders and a greater willingness on the part of a single state to accept cultural diversity within its borders, and on the part of neighbouring states to live with the straddling of their borders by one nationality.[11] Nevertheless, this does not mean that the scope for action by states is uninhibited by sub-state cultural or national diversity. Allardt[12] suggests that governments need to allocate increasing amounts of their budgets to conflict management, since even limited upsets among small sub-state nationalities can reduce their capacities to be effective in the international sphere. Moreover, the existence of 'a supranational organization may strengthen the position of minor nationalities in a sovereign state which may be uni-lingual but in reality is multi-national'.[13] This is illustrated, from a more specifically legal point of view, by Kazancigil,[14] who points out that already, in the European Union, sub-national units have the status to conclude inter-regional agreements and establish direct links with central institutions.

The combined incursions from above and below into states' practical freedom of manoeuvre and monopoly of legal powers appear, indeed, to represent a pincer-like attack upon the very foundations of states in the conventional sense. These themes will be revisited; in the meantime, it is necessary to consider whether the advocates of 'a Europe of the nation states' have good grounds for their anxieties over the experience of the USA.

II

Most appeals to the USA's experience as constituting a lesson that integration is undesirable are anachronistic in the sense that they compare the EU and the USA as each is today. It is more appropriate to examine the two systems in comparable stages of development, even though these occurred in different periods. Thus, this section focuses on America in the eighteenth century, when the USA, too, was in an embryonic stage, and considers whether or not subsequent forces which encouraged centralization are reflected in the context of European integration. In such an approach, similarities certainly can be identified,[15] but there are also striking differences in the status of the respective constituent states and the impact of such differences on the forces of centralization.

Constituent states and institutions

In eighteenth-century America, debate about a constitution for the union, and its ratification, took place in a context in which states, though they enjoyed – and continue to enjoy – strong popular political allegiance,[16] had been independent for only a little over a decade; and, in that sense, their institutions were not so well established as are those of their modern European counterparts. These states were linked through the Articles of Confederation, ties which, as in the European Free Trade Association, were inter-governmental in character. Though the European Communities were born partly out of a realization of the weakness of European states and partly out of the belief that states could not regain their capacity to carry out their core functions except by 'pooling' some legal powers[17] in ties that were closer than inter-governmental links, the machinery of those states, and their authority in all its senses, were incomparably more entrenched than had been those of young ex-colonies.

This difference affected then, and affects now, the boundaries of discourse about the distribution of policy competences. The greater fluidity of American conditions both allowed and compelled advocates of union, notably the authors of *The Federalist Papers*,[18] to be particularly systematic in their arguments for the union as a new 'package'. In Europe, despite the initial analysis according to which post-war reconstruction entailed ceding sovereignty over some issues to common institutions, it is not possible for those who determine the course of integration to ignore the existing powerful state machineries and to start from scratch, as it were, in construct-ing a rational design for European union. Though federalists who support the idea of a full constitution for Europe, distributing powers and setting out citizens' rights, have occupied office in EU institutions,[19] it is hardly surprising that influential European outlooks have more in common with American anti-federalists who wished to reform, not revolutionize, the Articles of Confederation.

Thus, the apex of the 'government' of the EU and the govern-ments of the member states are not separated as they were by the Constitution of the USA: they are, as it were, the same – notwith-standing the relative independence of the European Commission, discussed later. The composition of the European Council (heads of member-state governments who consider strategy) and the Council of Ministers (ministers of member-state governments who make final decisions about common – like the American 'Union' – policies) means that, as the anti-federalists had hoped would be the case in America, the EU is regulated by the states that make it up. This 'confederal' characteristic of the EU is bolstered by its decision-making rules which allow member states to decide whether decisions should be taken unanimously, by qualified-majority voting or by a simple majority. It was the capacity of a single state effectively to veto progress by withholding consent – which is what happened, particularly during the time in which France was represented by General de Gaulle – that led to the introduction of forms of majority voting. Now, the Amsterdam Treaty, as a result of pressure from the British Prime Minister, undermines the qualified-majority principle by allowing a state to block its use where it believes that core interests are at stake – thus potentially reintroducing the problems of the late 1960s[20] or, from the intergovernmentalist point of view, restoring power to protect core national interests.

This structure of European government reflects a view about the promotion of popular and state interests similar to that of the anti-federalists in the USA. Proponents of 'a Europe of the nation states' believe that the interests of all people of democratic, legally sovereign territories can be distilled into the public interest as articulated by their governments and represented at EU level by domestically elected and accountable office-holders. This is similar to the US anti-federalists' claim that, in fact, they were the 'true federalists' because, if rights and powers were to link an entire people directly with the centre, by-passing states as the foci of allegiance and the channels of accountability, the new republic would not be a *federal* republic but a *consolidated* one.[21] Claude Cheysson took a similar view about Europe, believing that citizenship in the form of direct links between the peoples of Europe and the centre 'places us in the supranational, whereas European Union does not'.[22]

In emphasizing states as the key to America's being federal, not consolidated, the anti-federalists were arguing that theirs would be a system in which the 'representatives had the same feelings as the voters'.[23] Thus, a state's failure to comply with union policy might occasionally merit 'a light remedy' from elsewhere in the system. But it was more likely to warrant a thorough investigation of causes (the fault probably lying with the Union) than central coercion through, for example, the proposed authority of the Supreme Court to rule unchallengeably on 'all questions of law and equality'.[24]

While it is true that the European Court of Justice (ECJ) has comparable authority over those areas brought into its jurisdiction by the treaties, the US anti-federalists' preference for state action over union action is echoed in one of several understandings of the notion of subsidiarity in the Maastricht Treaty. This is the view, espoused by governments, that subsidiarity entrenches the sovereignty of member states[25] by obliging the Commission to demonstrate convincingly that proposed actions meet certain tests, showing that there is a common problem which, by its nature, cannot be solved except by common action. All other matters remain the responsibility of domestic governments, to be pursued according to national interests.

The contrast between European states governing the union themselves and the separation of union and state powers in America does make a difference to patterns of what the anti-federalists called *consolidation* and what 'Euro-sceptics' call *centralization*.

Forces of centralization

A number of material factors played a part in the nineteenth century in transforming the fear that centralization was antithetical to the liberty of individuals and states into a belief that union government was the principal effective guarantor of rights and collective well-being. Industrialization and urbanization brought problems that could not be handled by states alone. Most dramatically, there was the Civil War and subsequent reconstruction. The Fourteenth Amendment, on Equal Protection, enabled judicial review by the Supreme Court of states' rules about rights. In terms of general political discourse, the growth of the party system contributed to the 'nationalization'[26] of social and racial issues.[27]

Some underlying forces comparable to those which 'consolidated' or 'nationalized' policy questions in the USA are present in the EU, but with less evidence of similar political consequences. While the causes and effects of what might be labelled a 'Continental civil war', between 1939 and 1945, played an important part, as had the War of Independence, in the first stages of integration, it seems unlikely that there will be another 'civil war', reinforcing centralization, in the first quarter of the twenty-first century (i.e. comparable to the US Civil War nearly a century after the ratification of the Constitution). Such a European war would confound the many accounts of international relations which claim that modern interests and conditions almost eliminate the likelihood of liberal democracies entering into major armed conflict with one another.

It might be argued that American forces of industrialization and urbanization have a counterpart in the European beliefs that individual states cannot control the dislocations of the transition to the Single European Market, and cannot deal, alone, with such adverse human consequences of industrial restructuring in an integrated market as: the 'export' of unskilled manufacturing to poor and peripheral countries or regions; the confinement of skilled manufacturing to the heartlands; potentially excessive migration by poorly equipped people from the peripheries to the centre to seek better-paid employment; and, consequent to the inability of the skilled-labour market to accommodate them, mounting pressure on the social services of host countries. Concern about 'social dumping' partly explains interest in the idea of a so-called 'Social Charter'.

Proponents of the strongest form of Charter hoped for a directly applicable Bill of Rights for European workers and citizens. Their hopes were opposed by employers and several of the governments, being dashed most vociferously by the UK government. The first upshot was a 1989 Solemn Declaration on a Community Charter for Basic Social Rights for Workers and an accompanying Action Programme. This was not a programme to establish a direct link between the peoples of Europe and the centre, but a set of proposals requiring inter-governmental negotiation in the Council of Ministers – for Directives, and their further implementation in the states, and non-binding Recommendations. The next phase was the Maastricht Treaty and its controversial Social Agreement, again resisted by the British who negotiated an 'opt-out' protocol. Following the election in 1997 of a Labour Government, the UK 'opted-in' and the Social Agreement is now a main part of the 1997 Amsterdam Treaty. But, even so, many proposed actions arising from it will have to secure unanimous agreement, thereby maintaining the powers of member-state governments. The Amsterdam Treaty goes much further than its predecessors in setting out what citizens may expect in the way of fundamental principles of human rights and is innovative in methods of redress for citizens in cases of breach of rights by either states or common institutions. But it remains to be seen whether this treaty has the potential to strengthen the direct link between peoples and the centre at the expense of their indirect links through member-state-based nationality or lawful residence. Moreover, while the Amsterdam Treaty extends the definition of forms of discrimination, and hence widens the scope of persons with potential rights, decisions as to whether to put new regimes into practice remain in the hands of the

EU's legislature – that is, the member states in the Council of Ministers.

In addition to the possibility that material forces may encourage the centralization of powers and a more direct relationship between citizens and the new centre, there is the question of whether there is a centralizing dynamic in the logic of Community rules comparable with that of American federalism. This brings us back to the ubiquitous and chimerical concept of subsidiarity.

The Federalists saw the distribution of powers in the proposed US Constitution as a 'happy' combination in which aggregate interests were for the Union to deal with and particular interests fell to the states concerned.[28] Thus, as Parish points out,[29] 'Americans embraced subsidiarity almost two centuries before the word was invented' – and, it might be added, in a way similar to that in which modern regionalists understand the term, since people applied the same principle to civil associations and government at the district, local and state levels for most of the nineteenth century.

But the anti-federalists had anticipated a centralizing tendency in what we now call subsidiarity. It was 'true', conceded one of them,[30] 'that the powers of the union were limited to certain objects'; but these were 'the most important ones'. Moreover, the limitation was more apparent than real, since it would be for 'the union to decide' upon all the laws that were 'necessary and proper' to bring about those objects. This was soon put to the test in a controversy about whether the authority to create a national bank could be inferred from any specified federal powers to take 'necessary and proper' action, or whether creating a national bank was merely 'convenient'.[31] And, the more fully integrated the internal market became, the more correspondingly significant became the clause of the US Constitution which authorizes the centre to regulate international, or inter-state, commerce. The centralizing effects of its use have 'spilled-over' into many areas.

In the EU, Article 235 of the Treaty of Rome allows measures to be introduced which are not expressly authorized in the treaty, if complementary steps are necessary to the realization of goals that are specified. For example, Directives for equal pay for work of equal value, equal treatment in other conditions of employment, in state social security schemes and in occupational pension schemes, were able to be brought into force under Article 235 in order to bring about the intentions of Article 119 on equal pay. The existence of this provision cannot threaten the governments of

European states as much as would have been the case in America since, as noted earlier, the final decision-making body is composed of the states themselves.

Nevertheless, there is, according to Adonis,[32] still an expansionary logic, analogous to the US Commerce Clause, that may be beyond the control of member-state governments. In contrast to the different comforts of subsidiarity for governments, on the one hand, and for regionalists and 'social partners', on the other, Adonis argues that it is far from devolutionary and cannot be, as Jacques Delors described it, 'a constant counterweight to the natural tendency of the centre to accumulate power'. He points out that the measures accompanying the Social Charter, incorporate subsidiarity merely in how they are implemented, not in their substance. But it was to the principle and substance of some proposed rights that the UK government objected, whatever the level of implementation. Even the criterion that common action should depend on necessity – or, more loosely, on the greater effectiveness of co-operation than of independent action – makes sense, he argues, only in the context of an understanding that policy is made at the common level and administration is carried out in the states.

But, again, it is worth thinking of this argument in the light of the fact that final decisions at the common level are made by states themselves, albeit on the basis of proposals emanating from the Commission. Here, whether or not particular state interests have to be submerged depends upon whether the issue in question is one in respect of which states have agreed in advance that unanimity, qualified-majority or simple majority voting will apply. Though they agreed to qualified-majority voting to achieve a fully integrated market, social rights other than those on health and safety brought forward on the basis of the Social Charter required unanimous consent – as will the new ones.

That the British were allowed to 'opt-out' of the Social Agreement, numerous other protocols in the Maastricht Treaty, further special arrangements in the Amsterdam Treaty and some acceptance[33] of 'flexible integration', all seem to point to two things. One is the possibility that material forces have occasioned a degree of fragmentation instead of the universalization experienced in the USA. The other is that they reinforce an impression that implicit, undesired or unexpected centralizing tendencies of European integration can be moderated by the political process. On the other hand, things are not as they were. As Laffan[34] points out, the Union alters the exercise of national political authority in a web of collaboration and co-operation. This interaction between different sources of authority is also indicated in the second approach of this chapter to the topic, to which discussion now turns: consideration of theories of the state, and of the possibility that there might emerge a state called 'Europe'.

III

It is almost a truism to say that notions of the state are contested. Nevertheless, Pierson has succeeded in distilling from various approaches several defining characteristics which are used here to explore the extent to which the EU is state-like and whether this diminishes the status of its member states. In his view,[35] the most important features of state mechanisms are:

1   (monopoly) control of the means of violence;
2   territoriality;
3   sovereignty;
4   constitutionality;
5   impersonal power;
6   the public bureaucracy;
7   authority/legitimacy;
8   citizenship; and
9   taxation

These mechanisms overlap and it is not always possible to deal with them as discrete aspects of the relationship between member states and the EU. For example, foreign policy in the EU is linked with security policy, which could enable it to be discussed in connection with force as well as, in Pierson's account, with territoriality. Territoriality in the context of the EU could be construed as an aspect of citizenship as much as of international relations. Hence, the groupings which follow.

Control of the means of violence, aspects of territoriality, foreign policy

Control of the means of violence may refer to the maintenance of internal security or the use of force to guarantee or extend territorial boundaries;[36] that is, primarily the police, other aspects of the administration of justice and the armed services. Pierson notes that, though actual force may not be 'normal' or may be used by non-state actors, the 'right' to use force and the effectiveness of its monopolization by the state are important to theories of the state. Linked to the possibility of forceful protection of territory is the role of foreign policy – increasingly more important than military strategy, if it is indeed correct that war has a smaller place in the interests and values of modern liberal democracies. Foreign policy, 'by broad agreement', is a 'function of the nation-state', and is even 'synonymous' with it.[37] Over the last twenty years, policing, foreign policy and external security have found their places on the EU's agenda.

Recent agreements on such matters simultaneously increase the scope for common action and reaffirm something of the state monopoly. The inter-governmental Justice and Home Affairs Pillar (the 'Third Pillar') of the Maastricht Treaty has been divided, immigration, asylum and related aspects of policing (and of drug-trafficking) being transferred to the common arena of the 'First Pillar'. But individual states retain power in the sense that further policy developments will require unanimous decision making. Policing of criminal activities and co-operation between national police forces remain matters for inter-governmental negotiation and agreement to conventions under the 'Third Pillar'. What Duff[38] calls a 'coy Declaration' reminds us that 'states retain sovereignty in these matters'. Yet, conventions will be allowed to come into force more easily than before; limited judicial review of conventions has been introduced, and ties with the common 'Pillar' of Maastricht have been strengthened.[39]

New arrangements for foreign policy (at first, European Political Co-operation) and for security policy (the Common Foreign and Security Policy Pillar – Maastricht's 'Second Pillar') remain tentative and 'driven by domestic rather than international pressures'.[40] The Amsterdam Treaty asserts that there is a collective 'goal of safeguarding the territorial integrity of the Union'.[41] But it is not clear what follows from this.

A new role for the European Commission in brokering inter-state agreement on joint actions will be hampered by arrangements for flexibility (and, hence, increased 'constructive abstention') and by 'uncertain funding arrangements which will defy financial planning'.[42] Such an outcome illustrates the force of Whitman's remark[43] that the identification of foreign policy with states makes its development in the EU problematic.

On the other hand, the then European Community (EC) played 'an increasingly active role in the core of economic diplomacy'[44] (known not as foreign, but as 'external policy'). But, the monopoly of international strategic power remaining in the hands of the USA, in negotiation with the USSR, resulted in the EC being called a 'civilian power'.[45] For similar reasons, Hedley Bull said in 1982 that ' "Europe" [is] not an actor in international affairs' and would not be so even if it were to create a 'supranational' defence identity – defence implying weakness rather than strength.[46]

In 1998, the EU still lacks most of the means associated with monopoly of the right to use external force, though there has been a significant shift in the potential for its internal use – bearing in mind that some policing will be by inter-governmental agreement, albeit 'looser' than before, and even common policies will be common only because the member states themselves have agreed to this.

Sovereignty, constitutionality, impersonal power, the public bureaucracy, authority or legitimacy

As Pierson points out,[47] more than one sense of 'sovereignty' is associated with the idea of the state. One – popular sovereignty – is related to citizenship, discussed later. Another is the territorial dimension of sovereignty, the relevant internal and external implications of which are partly dealt with above and, in other ways, below. A third development in sovereignty is its apportionment to different institutions through the separation of powers, a theme that is relevant to all the items in the heading above.

As Pierson indicates of the USA, the 'constitution' of the EU (the treaties which give it an authority based on law, not physical coercion[48]) embodies a separation of powers. Enough, perhaps, has been said already about the legislative role of the Council of Ministers, except to note Jacques Delors' assertion in 1988 to Members of the European Parliament that, by 1998, about 80 per cent of economic legislation and, possibly, fiscal and social legislation would emanate from Europe rather than from national institutions. This would appear to merit the continuation of renewed interest in the neo-functionalist view (discredited until the early 1990s) that the 'spill-over effects' of small steps towards integration would eventually lead to 'ever closer union'.

As noted earlier, the Commission is responsible for making legislative proposals to the Council. It is also 'centrally involved in EU decision-making at all levels and on all fronts' and, with the ECJ, is the main guardian of the legal framework. Taking into account its responsibilities and powers, it constitutes 'rather more'[49] than would the bureaucracy of a modern state. Nevertheless, like state bureaucracies, the Commission is a rule-bound organization. It is also 'rather less'[50] than a state bureaucracy in that it is small by comparison and relies heavily upon the bureaucracies of the member states to implement EU policy. Since implementation varies according to bureaucratic and political conditions in the member states, the EU sometimes does not fully embody the 'equal protection of the law'[51] on a Union-wide basis.

The system by which permanent staff are appointed to the Commission is twofold. One route reflects the Weberian criterion of competitive recruitment through examination and knowledge of procedures. The other is based upon secondments from national bureaucracies which, on the one hand, could simply encourage bureaucratic standards and criteria at both levels to reinforce each other. On the other, and together with national nominations to commissionerships, this is a channel for the growth of policy outlooks in which, as Laffan[52] puts it, the European becomes embedded in the national and national in the European.

Intermeshing also follows from the powers allocated to the ECJ, and from the elucidation of doctrines of European Community law: the supremacy and unity of EC law, direct applicability and direct effects. The supremacy of EC law and the idea that its unity behoves all national courts and 'emanations of the state' to apply it have, by and large, been accepted in member states, if with varying degrees of enthusiasm[53] – even in the UK where judicial review, except in a limited form, is contrary to the doctrine of parliamentary sovereignty.[54] Direct applicability means that regulations agreed upon in the Council of Ministers are applicable, without further domestic legislation, in the national courts. The principle of 'direct effects' means that plaintiffs in national courts may rely upon unambiguous treaty articles, as they may also do when provisions of directives are clear and when it can be shown that governments have implemented them defectively. In attempting to ensure that nationals of the states of the EU enjoy the 'equal protection of the laws', ECJ jurisprudence periodically pushes EU policies beyond the boundaries to which member states thought they had agreed.[55] It is for these reasons that Rosas is able to make the claim, referred to above, about the trembling foundations of the inter-state system.

It is possible that the authority of the ECJ may have an adverse effect on legitimacy – in the eyes of national political elites if not also of citizens who win cases. There were such signs in the UK in the 1990s over rulings which overturned British legislation designed to prevent quota-hopping in the fishing industry. On the other hand, the states which agreed to grant such powers to a court for the EU remain recognized as legally independent entities – entitled to submit *amicus curiae* briefs in ECJ cases – and they themselves agreed in the Amsterdam Treaty to extend the ECJ's competence in the field of human rights. Thus, it seems that, though central powers have been separated, the exercise of power, authority and responsibility enmesh the centre and its constituent states. This clutch of Pierson's attributes of the state shows a stronger dynamic than did the previous set towards an increasing role for the EU, even though agreement upon the scope of Union activities and the ways in which the centre and states co-operate to achieve objectives remain the prerogatives of the states themselves.

Aspects of territoriality, citizenship/popular legitimacy, taxation

If the defining features of states in international relations theory include the 'monopolistic powers of adjudication within their boundaries',[56] then it can be said that, in respect of the movement of people, this is an aspect of statehood that is increasingly exercised collectively by the centre and constituent parts of the EU. Though, as noted, the powers of adjudication (and implementation) in general may be applied imperfectly because of the centre's reliance on the different systems of its members, the EU as a whole is developing an increasingly comprehensive regime over territorial issues as they relate to commercial purposes and civil rights.

At Amsterdam it was agreed (with exceptions for the UK, Ireland and Denmark) to universalize the provisions of the 1985 Schengen Agreement, initially formed by the EU's six founder members. This eliminates internal border controls, creating for nationals of the member states an internal territory which extends throughout the Union. And it creates a common external border which will be controlled by common policies on immigration, asylum and visas, and the treatment of nationals of countries outside the EU.[57]

Another way in which the traditional territory of states is changing is the space that is now opening up for the inhabitants, and their elected representatives, of sub-state regions and regions straddling the borders of two member states or even of a member state and a non-member state. These bring about closer socio-economic links between regions and the centre and directly with one another. In the last ten years, this has developed most obviously among those regions eligible for structural funds, the securing and spending of which entail the involvement of the 'social, local and regional partners'. Many regions have established offices in Brussels to circumvent problems in flows of information from the centre via national capitals.[58] Since the Maastricht Treaty, regions have a direct presence in the EU's policy structures in the form of the Committee of the Regions. They by no means supplant governments; the latter are also among the 'partners' in structural fund allocations; the Committee of Regions is very weak in comparison to the Council of Ministers; and different domestic constitutions mean that not all regions have political and administrative infrastructures which enable them to be major players in this new regime.[59] Even so, there is sufficient change in the territorial parameters of the EU's policy-making process for many writers to speak of what is now called 'multi-level governance'.[60]

Although forms of governance are changing, links between citizens and the EU remain indirect because nationality rules and the status of regions (and, hence, who has rights) continue to be matters of domestic policy. But there is also a direct legal link, established in 1962 by the ECJ when, having ruled that the Treaties of Rome amounted to more than a compact of states, it conferred rights upon the nationals of member states.[61] Though this legal link is slight,[62] the effects of EU membership for 'ordinary' nationals of member states were augmented by various socio-economic policies during the 1970s and early 1980s. The Maastricht Treaty introduced some limited political rights. These are: the rights of EU citizens resident in a country where they are not nationals to vote and stand for office in municipal and European parliamentary elections; the right to be assisted outside the EU by the diplomatic and consular services of any member state; and a number of rights relating to access to information and redress of grievance. In both Maastricht and Amsterdam Treaties, the capacity of the European Parliament to exercise powers on behalf of their voters has been strengthened: both treaties refer to the need to improve the effectiveness of national parliaments in their scrutiny of EU initiatives; and the Amsterdam Treaty slightly strengthens the Committee of the Regions, as well as proclaiming, as mentioned earlier, EU adherence to human rights principles and the means of securing of them.

As in the case of the direct legal link, it can be argued that the EU's socio-economic policies and rights are slight, even cosmetic, having been designed to create a popular legitimacy for the EU.[63] It could be said that even this limited objective had failed in that, particularly during the 1990s, popular support for the EU has weakened. But this does not mean that integration or closer co-operation *per se* is regarded as illegitimate. Sinnott[64] finds that people discern distinctions between national or transnational issues and, hence, can identify where they believe there is a legitimate EU competence. But not all issues where EU action is seen as legitimate are regarded as salient, and legitimacy in some cases is undermined by lack of confidence in the effectiveness of Community intervention.

Such perceptions may relate to the obverse of Pierson's point [65] that taxation 'is still a touchstone of the politics of the modern state' – less now to finance wars and more to fund socio-economic policies. The EU has no powers directly to tax its citizens – a lack which may help to explain low salience. Nor do either its small budget (similar to that of a medium-sized state ministry) or its constitution give it more than a very small directly redistributive role in social policy – which may contribute to impressions of ineffectiveness. The harmonization of national taxation systems, let alone the introduction of a Union taxation system comparable to that of the USA, will be very difficult even for 'core' members,[66] despite EMU pressures to 'spill-over' into this sphere.

On the other hand, many observers argue that the EU elements of citizenship and regional representation are important, not just for their current substance, but because they constitute a break with conventional paradigms and practices. For example 'place', as well as nationality, has become a 'trigger' for the exercise of entitlements.[67] And as Chryssochoou,[68] drawing on O'Keefe, says, they contain an expansionary dynamic – as can be seen in the Treaty of Amsterdam compared to that of Maastricht.

The coexistence of developments which are 'neither one thing nor another' with discrepant interpretations of those developments flow from what was noted at the outset – that we have only the concepts of the familiar with which to speak of the unfamiliar. What is unfamiliar is a wider issue than the EU.

IV

In conclusion, it should be recognized that the question of whether the EU is becoming a state at the expense of the status of its constituent parts cannot be explored in isolation from what is going on in the world at large. Though some scepticism is expressed about the notion of globalization,[69] there is a widespread anti-Realist view that the core duties of state are taking a new form and that the means of achieving them are correspondingly different.[70] Economic prosperity – one of the bases of domestic legitimacy – no longer lies in the defence of national economies through the control of territory in order to achieve domination. Borders are incapable of resisting the 'ripple' effects of one state's economic and fiscal decisions upon those of others. Borders mean little to those companies which, because of technological advances, can transfer operations between countries almost with a strike on the keyboard. Instead, states have to co-operate to stabilize the mutual effects of economic and fiscal policy-making and open their borders in the sense of making themselves attractive to inward investors. All this has profound implications for the meaning of sovereignty and other once-defining characteristics of statehood. Sovereignty, in its old senses, is increasingly rejected in favour of words such as 'authority', 'power' or 'capacity to act'.[71] Territorial and foreign policies are becoming more socio-economic than militarily strategic; and foreign policy, no longer separable from domestic politics and the direct interests of citizens, has come into closer alignment with the EU's 'external policy' or 'economic diplomacy'.

The ways in which its member states have caused the EU to develop are their responses to growing interdependence and globalization in the second half of the twentieth century. The states themselves remain important actors, albeit with new and evolving characteristics. But the collective entity which they have created is also subject to global forces. To the extent that we do not yet know how states will continue to evolve or how, collectively, they will manage their Union's capacity to cope with globalization, it is not possible to say whether they are being superseded by a 'super-state'. Perhaps the most that can be said is that the necessity of 'a supranational authority'[72] is not acknowledged as an imperative by governments in the EU, but that states, important as they are as 'societal units', will have increasingly to share their importance with 'both regions and blocks of states'.[73]

Notes

1 Part of this chapter draws upon an article published in a special edition of *Publius: The Journal of Federalism*, 26, 4 (dated Fall 1996 but published at the end of 1997).

2 B. Laffan, 'The European Union: a Distinctive Model of Internationalization?', Paper presented at the Annual Conference of the Political Studies Association of Ireland (October 1997).

3 A. Landau and R. Whitman (eds), *Rethinking the European Union: Institutions, Interests and Identities* (Basingstoke: Macmillan, 1997), p. 172.

4 A. Kazancigil, 'A Prospective View on the European Nation State and Unification', in J. Iivonen (ed.) *The Future of the Nation State in Europe* (Aldershot: Edward Elgar, 1993), pp. 117–19.

5 *Manfred Brunner and others* v. *The European Union Treaty*; Cases 2 BvR 2134/92 and 2159/92 [1994] 1 CMLR 57. See R. Harmsen, 'Integration as Adaptation: National Courts and the Politics of Community Law', Paper presented at the Annual Conference of the Political Studies Association of Ireland (October 1994), p. 21.

6 C. Church, 'Explorations in Ambiguity: the Paradoxical Relationships between Swiss Federalism and European Integration', in P. King and A. Bosco (eds) *A Constitution for Europe: a Comparative Study of Federal Constitutions and Plans for the United States of Europe* (London: Lothian Foundation Press, 1991), p. 141.

7 E. Gellner, 'Nationalism and the Development of European Societies', in Iivonen (ed.) *The Future of the Nation State in Europe*, pp. 28–30.

8 G. Arrighi, 'The Three Hegemonies of Historical Capitalism', in Iivonen (ed.) *The Future of the Nation State in Europe*, pp. 81–4.

9 A. Rosas, 'The Decline of Sovereignty: Legal Perspectives', in Iivonen (ed.) *The Future of the Nation State in Europe*, pp. 145–6.

10 Ibid., pp. 149–50.

11 E. Allardt, 'The Nation State and Nationalism with Different Forms of Technology', in Iivonen (ed.) *The Future of the Nation State in Europe*, p. 100.

12 Ibid., p. 99.

13 A. Kemilainen, 'Patriotism and Nationalism', in Iivonen (ed.) *The Future of the Nation State in Europe*, p. 47.

14 Kazancigil, 'A Prospective View', p. 128.

15 E. Meehan, 'European Integration and Citizens' Rights: a Comparative Perspective', *Publius: The Journal of Federalism*, 26, 4 (Fall 1996), pp. 99–121.

16 C. Bonwick, 'Giving Life to the American Constitution', in King and Bosco (eds) *A Constitution for Europe*, p. 354.

17 A. S. Milward, *The European Rescue of the Nation–State* (London: Routledge, 1992).

18 I. Kramnick (ed.) *The Federalist Papers* (London: Penguin, 1987 [1788]).
19 M. Burgess, *Federalism and European Union: Political Ideas, Influences and Strategies in the European Community, 1972–87* (London: Routledge, 1989).
20 A. Duff (ed.) *The Treaty of Amsterdam: Text and Commentary* (London: The Federal Trust and Sweet & Maxwell, 1997), p. 195.
21 P. Marshall, 'The Ratification of the United States', in King and Bosco (eds) *A Constitution for Europe*, pp. 343–52.
22 Quoted in A. Wiener, *'European' Citizenship Practice: Building Institutions of a Non-State* (Boulder, CO: Westview Press, 1998), p. 272.
23 H. J. Storing (ed.) *The Anti-Federalist Writings by the Opponents of the Constitution. An Abridgement, by Murray Dry, of the Complete Anti-Federalist, Brutus IV* (Chicago: University of Chicago Press, 1985).
24 Ibid., *Federalist Farmer XVII* and *Brutus XI–XIII, XV*.
25 And, by and large, in countries other than the UK and Ireland, the powers of subordinate levels of domestic government; see A. Duff (ed.) *Subsidiarity with the European Community* (London: The Federal Trust, 1993), p. 19; and *The Treaty of Amsterdam*, pp. 96–7.
26 The British dislike of the term 'federal' (witness their success in having it deleted from the draft Maastricht Treaty) had an American equivalent. To Americans, it was the term 'national' that implied centralization and which had to be resisted in favour of 'Union' powers so as to ensure that the Constitution would be ratified. 'National' referred to the state level as can be seen in the references in the Constitution to international affairs, meaning inter-state affairs such as commerce. It has been argued that any sense of belonging to an American nation was 'an unexpected, impromptu, artificial and, therefore, extremely fragile creation of the Revolution' (Marshall, 'The Ratification of the United States', p. 352, quoting John Murrin) and, as such, was not consolidated as an identification additional to that of belonging to a state until well into the next century.
27 S. H. Beer, *To Make a Nation: the Rediscovery of American Federalism* (Cambridge, MA: Belknap Press, 1993); Bonwick, 'Giving Life to the American Constitution'; P. J. Parish, 'The Changing Character of American Federalism in the Nineteenth Century', in King and Bosco (eds) *A Constitution for Europe*.
28 Kramnick (ed.) *The Federalist Papers, Federalist Paper X*.
29 Parish, 'The Changing Character of American Federalism', p. 362.
30 Storing (ed.) *The Anti Federalist Writings, Brutus I*.
31 Bonwick, 'Giving Life to the American Constitution', pp. 356–7.
32 A. Adonis, 'Subsidiarity: Theory of a New Federalism?', in King and Bosco (eds) *A Constitution for Europe*, pp. 63–73.
33 Reluctance on the part of most states other than the UK; Duff (ed.), *The Treaty of Amsterdam*, pp. 185–97.
34 Laffan, 'The European Union', p. 15.
35 C. Pierson, *The Modern State* (London: Routledge, 1996), p. 8.
36 Ibid., pp. 8–12; J. Hall and G. Ikenberry, *The State* (Milton Keynes: Open University Press, 1989).

37 R. Whitman, 'The International Identity of the European Union: Instruments as Identity', in Landau and Whitman (eds) *Rethinking the European Union*, p. 56.
38 Duff (ed.) *The Treaty of Amsterdam*, p. 44.
39 Ibid., pp. 42–5.
40 Ibid., p. 124.
41 Ibid.
42 Ibid., p. 125.
43 Whitman, 'The International Identity of the European Union', p. 56.
44 A. Landau in Landau and Whitman (eds) *Rethinking the European Union*, p. 8.
45 Duchene, 1972, quoted by Landau, ibid., p. 8.
46 Quoted by Whitman, 'The International Identity of the European Union', p. 59.
47 Pierson, *The Modern State*, pp. 14–17.
48 Ibid, pp. 22–7.
49 N. Nugent, *The Government and Politics of the European Union* (Basingstoke: Macmillan, 1994 edn), pp. 85, 116–18.
50 Ibid., p. 85.
51 An element of Pierson's 'Rule of Law' and 'impersonal rule'; see Pierson, *The Modern State*, pp. 19–20.
52 Laffan, 'The European Union', p. 25.
53 Harmsen, 'Integration as Adaptation'.
54 M. T. Fay and E. Meehan, 'British Decline and European Integration', in R. English and M. Kenny (eds) *Rethinking British Decline* (Basingstoke: Macmillan, forthcoming).
55 E. Meehan, *Citizenship and the European Community* (London: Sage, 1993).
56 Pierson, *The Modern State*, p. 13.
57 From the time of Schengen, civil libertarians have been seriously concerned that expanding the freedoms of nationals of the member states of the EU increases the 'closure' effects of citizenship on non-EU nationals ('third-country migrants') – and does so 'behind closed doors'. See D. Curtin and H. Meijers, 'The Principles of Open Government in Schengen and European Democratic Retrogression', *Common Market Law Review*, 32, 2 (1995), pp. 391–442. They were also concerned about ethnic-minority EU nationals who might too readily be assumed to be from outside and, hence, subject to the random non-border checks that were to compensate for the absence of border controls. Whether agreed by convention or, as now, elaborated as common policy, to traverse legally the EU's external border probably will become harder as countries with more relaxed policies are pressed to accept the rules of entry of countries with stricter regulations. But the Amsterdam Treaty does introduce free movement and improved conditions for lawfully resident 'third-country migrants'. And it has been agreed that, over a period, such policies will be made subject to those processes of more open discussion, scrutiny and review that characterize the 'First Pillar', but not the 'Third'.

58 S. Mazey and J. Mitchell, 'Europe of the Regions. Territorial Interests and European Integration: the Scottish Experience', in S. Mazey and J. Richardson (eds) *Lobbying in the European Community* (Oxford: Oxford University Press, 1993).

59 M. Dunford and R. Hudson, *Successful European Regions: Northern Ireland Learning from Others* (Belfast: Northern Ireland Economic Council, 1996).

60 L. Hooghe (ed.) *Cohesion Policy and European Integration: Building Multi-Level Governance* (Oxford: Oxford University Press, 1996).

61 *Van Gend en Loos* v. *Nederlandse Administratie der Belastingen*, Case No. 26/62 [1962] ECR 1.

62 S. O'Leary, 'The Relationship between Community Citizenship and the Fundamental Rights in Community Law', *Common Market Law Review*, 32, 2 (1995), pp. 519–44.

63 Meehan, *Citizenship and the European Community*; O'Leary, 'The Relationship between Community Citizenship and the Fundamental Rights'; C. Closa, 'Citizenship of the Union and Nationality of the Member States', *Common Market Law Review*, 32, 2 (1995), pp. 487–518.

64 R. Sinnott, 'Policy, Subsidiarity, and Legitimacy', in O. Niedermayer and R. Sinnott (eds) *Public Opinion and Internationalized Governance* (Oxford: Oxford University Press, 1995).

65 Pierson, *The Modern State*, pp. 30–4.

66 Duff (ed.) *The Treaty of Amsterdam*, p. 195.

67 A. Wiener, 'Building Institutions: the Developing Practice of European Citizenship', PhD thesis (Carleton University, Ottawa, 1995).

68 D. Chryssochoou, 'Democratic Theory and European Integration: the Challenge to Conceptual Innovation', in H. Smith (ed.) *New Thinking in Politics and International Relations*, Kent Papers in Politics and International Relations, Series 5, No. S2 (University of Kent at Canterbury, 1996).

69 K. Armingeon, 'The Capacity to Act: European National Governments and the European Commission', in Landau and Whitman (eds) *Rethinking the European Union*, pp. 99–109, for example, sees no impact on the domestic policies and structures of states and notes that interdependence does not equalize the conditions of unequal states.

70 Pierson, *The Modern State*, especially Ch. 6.

71 M. Newman, *Democracy, Sovereignty and the European Union* (London: Hurst & Co., 1996).

72 Gellner, 'Nationalism and the Development of European Societies', p. 28.

73 Allardt, 'The Nation State and Nationalism', p. 96.

State and public security

Charles Townshend

In December 1992, a few years after the Cold War had ended – a development that took the British intelligence community by surprise – the first reading of a bill to restore the right to trade union membership to workers at the Government Communications HQ at Cheltenham revived an issue which many cynics thought had long since been successfully laid to rest. The specific point raised in debate by Rupert Allason – confirming his maverick status – was the charge that a break in GCHQ operations during the imposition of martial law in Poland in December 1981 had created a real threat to national security. Behind the substantive question of whether an actual break did occur, there looms the more problematical question of the exact bearing on the security of the United Kingdom of General Jaruzelski's troop movements around Warsaw. The way in which this debate was reported adds a further issue. The *Independent*'s parliamentary column characteristically tagged it 'an echo from Cold War history', with the clear implication that – whether or not it was vital then – such information now would not be so.

This kind of story reminds us how rarely security issues are mentioned, let alone discussed, in British politics, and how difficult it is to determine what is to be covered by what may be called the security blanket. One or two parliamentary statements may suffice to establish how straight is the track which we as members of the public may expect to take through this region. In relation to the Security Service, the Home Secretary, Henry Brooke, said in 1963 that 'the number of parliamentary questions that could be put to me with any hope of an answer being properly given is very limited'. The Prime Minister then said that while the Home Secretary 'is the minister who can most appropriately answer for the Security Service organization in parliament... I must make it clear that the Prime

Minister must be ready to answer questions if he himself judges that they involve the security of the State.' A question put twenty years later may stand for the rest. When Ian Wrigglesworth, the SDP home affairs spokesman, asked the Prime Minister in 1983 what parliamentary questions on security matters *she* was prepared to answer, the reply was: 'I propose to continue my practice, which has always been the practice of my predecessors, not to answer questions on security or intelligence matters.'[1]

Superficially, at least, things are a little more transparent in some advanced countries. To take an example which might not be considered too exotic in the UK, Canada constituted its Security Intelligence Service as a federal agency in 1984 by statute (the Security Intelligence Service Act), a law which also provided for the creation of a Security Intelligence Review Committee (SIRC) to monitor the parallel protection of national security and of civil liberties. The recognition that there was potential for conflict between two of the several possible senses of 'security' is possibly striking from a British viewpoint, and the SIRC certainly gestures towards a kind of discussion which is practically inconceivable here. On the 'peace dividend', for instance: has the end of the Cold War radically altered the nature of the threats to security which underpinned the apparatus of the great game? Has it maybe even reduced them, so that the security apparatus itself could be reduced? The Director of the Canadian Security Intelligence Service set up a task force to assess the implications of changes in the 'threat environment' for the mandate of the service. The conclusion was that the new environment is 'diverse, volatile and complex', and that national security and public safety could be compromised if major cuts were made in the service's resources.[2] We might, without undue cynicism, have seen that conclusion coming. No doubt it is a good thing for such issues to be even partly spelt out, but in the end the contours of the apparently open debate conducted in the SIRC do not seem very much more flexible than those so breezily flourished by Henry Brooke.[3]

In particular the almost casual linkage of 'national security and public safety' indicates either a deliberate relapse into obfuscation or a lack of interest in precision of definition, both of which alternatives will be entirely familiar to a British audience. What I want to do here is to think about the feasibility and merits of greater precision in this vital issue. We might start from the evident ambiguity of the adjective 'public' in the terms 'public security' and 'public safety', setting aside for the moment the question whether the two nouns are synonyms. The more recent coinage 'national security' may seem less problematic on the face of things because, however perversely in the view of historians and social scientists, the word 'national' in this context is generally assumed to refer to the state rather than to the people. Still, it has always been a fundamental tenet of nationalist thinking that there can be no sensible distinction between the two; and the edition of the *Encyclopedia of Social Science* published during the Cold-War era defined national security in fairly broad terms, as the protection of 'internal values' against (external) threats.[4]

Clearly, 'public' can refer to both an abstraction, the public thing – *respublica* – and a concrete entity, the people living in an actual polity. No state is likely to have an interest in pointing up possible contradictions between these meanings, so if it is to be done it is up to the public to do so. Where legitimacy is high, or disaffection is low, people are unlikely to seek out such problems, and it is no doubt a reflection of the jaundiced nature of our *fin de siècle* that it is only recently that academic commentators have begun to dig away at this faultline with anything like earnest endeavour.[5] Benjamin Constant noted, at the dawning of the liberal era: 'Je crois que la surete publique est surtout compromise, quand les citoyens voient dans l'autorite un peril au lieu d'une sauvegarde. [I think that public security is compromised above all when citizens see in authority a danger rather than a safeguard.]'

The grounds for such suspicion have no doubt shifted. The primary reason for contemporary suspicion is ethnicity: where the nineteenth-century nationalist project of homogenizing the identity of all citizens of the 'nation state' can be seen to have failed – and this is almost everywhere – ethnic differences have sharply etched the limits of consensus and legitimacy. Cynthia Enloe's interesting if erratic study *Ethnic Soldiers* was an early attempt to point the distinction between 'state security' and 'citizen security', and Barry Buzan, in *People, States and Fear*, has constructed a more systematic elaboration of this tension, using the adjectives 'national' and 'individual' (or, occasionally, 'personal'). He concluded that 'the grounds for disharmony between individual and national security represent a permanent contradiction', noting along the way that this was not just a theoretical issue: 'for perhaps a majority of the world's people, threats *from* the state are among the major sources of insecurity in their lives'.[6]

That this is the case may say something about the general success rate of states in their project of securing civil peace. The elemental task of the state is to stifle the perpetual war which would inevitably characterize the Hobbesian state of nature. 'The office of the sovereign', as Hobbes said, 'consisteth in the procuration of the safety of the people.' But he added, 'by safety here is not meant a bare preservation, but also all other contentments of life which every man by lawfull industry without danger or hurt to the commonwealth shall acquire to himself.' Thus protection of life and property is the midwife of society: as Locke confirmed, 'the great and chief end of men's putting themselves under government is the preservation of their property'.

I

In the seventeenth and even the eighteenth century this was a live agenda. Fear of popular turbulence vied with fear of an overmighty sovereign to produce a balanced constitution. In the nineteenth century, however, insecurity and the fear of violence were brought under unprecedented control. Liberal political philosophy was able to advance far beyond this elementary realism. 'We do not in this country,' the rising Liberal star R.B. Haldane remarked in the 1880s, 'live on an island where all that is wanted is a society whose function is fulfilled when the lives and property of its members are protected from wild beasts and robbers.'[7] Whereas for Hobbes the fragility of peace is a constant preoccupation, in Bosanquet's *Philosophical Theory of the State* (1899) security scarcely appears as an issue. When it eventually nudges its way into the text, it is in a characteristically oblique way:

> Hegel observes that a man thinks it a matter of course that he goes back to his house after nightfall in security. He does not reflect what he owes to it. Yet this very naturalness, so to speak, of living in a social order is perhaps the most important foundation which the State can furnish to the better life... Speaking broadly, the members of a civilized community have seen nothing but order in their lives, and could not accommodate their action to anything else.[8]

It may be thought that the ambiguity of the term 'public security' is a necessary one, deriving from the dependence of internal peace on the maintenance of sovereign power, and that since the state is the only plausible guarantor of this, the security of the state is functionally identical with the security of the people. This is of course the state's own argument, nowadays as it was in the France of Louis VI, as G.M. Spiegel has shown.[9] The distinction on which Buzan rests some weight seems to hold equally well whether the state is minimalist or maximalist. Buzan suggests that minimal states are characterized by 'a low level of disharmony between state and individual interests', whereas in the maximal state, in which 'the state has to be viewed either as the source of all value or, at a minimum, as the necessary precondition for the realisation of any value, the preservation of the state, and the consequent pursuit of state interest, supersede the individual values from which they notionally derive'. Thus 'internal security becomes a natural and expected dimension, and there is no necessary striving to harmonize state and individual interests'.[10] This logic seems flawed, however. The most archetypical of maximal conceptions of the state – the supercharged Hegelian *Volkisch* nation state hymned in the works of Treitschke – actually presupposes a higher level of social harmony (*Volksgemeinschaft*) than does its opposite, the Manchester-school's minimalist 'nightwatchman-state'. The Treitschkean state 'does not ask primarily for opinion, but demands obedience' because it knows that it expresses the inner unity of the *Volk*.[11] This is not liberal democracy (Treitschke impatiently snorted: 'it is a false conception of liberty to seek for liberty not in the State, but from the State'), but neither is it a blueprint for a 'police state' or a 'security state' in the purely coercive sense.

Still, it does seem likely that in practice the maximalist state – which, as Buzan notes, seems to offer a greater correspondence with what we generally find in the real world – will tread on a multiplicity of individual toes, not so much through oppressiveness as because its project is so extensive. It will mess up the lives of some of its citizens, bulldoze their homes or conscript their children; but it will not necessarily need or use a powerful security apparatus to do this.[12] The power of the security service, and the scope of its activities, are likely to relate in some way to the kinds of danger perceived by the state. This is another way of putting the old maxim that the level of freedom within a state is inversely proportional to the level of threat to its stability – only that when that maxim was coined, the threats were assumed to be external ones. The burgeoning power of the late-nineteenth-century state appeared to snuff out the likelihood of violent internal challenge (as Friedrich Engels gloomily recognized when he argued that modern weapons had eliminated the prospects of insurrection). But, in the twentieth century, the trajectory has changed again.

Security is a fragile and tenuous state of life. Even the best liberals can have Hobbesian anxieties in this respect. Norman Angell chillingly evoked the fragility of civilization as 'a brief gleam in the long night of fear'. Although insecurity is a negative word, it is security that is surely the negative quality: no definite criteria can be established for it, only the absence of insecurity or fear. Security is always vulnerable, always under threat, though the threat environment changes. Reading that environment, assessing dangers, is a crucial task for those who take responsibility for public safety. But because security is a subjective condition, with no necessary relation to objectively measurable safety, as Buzan warns, it can never be complete.[13] If pushed too far, the search for greater objective security can lead to paranoia, a dramatic increase in subjective insecurity.

The special dangers generated by the twentieth century seem to have screwed up this cruel irony to a new pitch of intensity. The new dangers were fuelled by ideology, but were also a product of technology or methodology: in the international sphere, total war, mechanization, air power, comunications and information technology; in the domestic sphere, industrial action, political violence, terrorism, insurgency and, above – or rather beneath – all, subversion.

II

These problems may be usefully related to the experience of the modern British state over the past century. A hundred years ago the UK was on a cusp, as it were, between minimal and maximal states. The image of the state in British political culture remained minimal, but the extent of state activity was already vast and growing rapidly. Britain was creating a maximal state by stealth, at least according to the critiques of jurists such as A. V. Dicey (opposing collectivism) and C. K. Allen (delegated legislation): a maximal state in minimalist clothing, or, to put it less vulpinely, one still equipped with a minimalist thinking apparatus. The word 'state' itself', though respectfully capitalized in most political writing, was never less favoured by the authorities than during this phase of exponential growth. This state had a low profile; it had no immoderate fear of either internal or external enemies. Prime Minister Gladstone's appalled reaction when, at the height of the Irish–American Clan na Gael terrorist campaign of the 1880s, his Home Secretary suggested that he should receive full-time police protection, helps us to measure the distance we have travelled since then (as, in a different way, does the fact that he was almost as shocked by a proposal to fly the Union's flag over the Houses of Parliament). Over the course of a century Britain has, like most states, become more security-minded. Whatever Gladstone's reservations, the Irish–American terrorist campaign led to the creation of the first permanent security police, the Special Branch.

Although the USA did not discover what Daniel Yergin calls 'the gospel of national security' until after the Second World War, Britain had dreamed up its own cold-war spy scares about Germany before the First, and begun the elaboration of its far-reaching Official Secrecy legislation.[14] (We should note, in passing, that the framers of the Official Secrets Act did set at its heart 'the safety of the state'.) The Great War permanently heightened the pitch of paranoia.[15] At the height of the war, in a strange but undoubtedly significant judgment concerning a neutral ship, the *Zamora*, the House of Lords demonstrated how terminology could evolve. Not only did 'war' give way to 'defence of the realm' as a description of the prerogative power (to requisition cargo), but the term 'national security' appeared – for the first time, it seems. The shifts are striking, in retrospect, but were never explained.[16] The national government of the 1930s discovered the burgeoning threat of 'incitement to disaffection', and fundamentally recast the law of public meeting to counter it. At last, after 1945, the existence of the 'Security Service' was acknowledged. Unlike the CIA and FBI, however, its mission and legal status remained shadowy. D. G .T. Williams, the first jurist to make a serious study of 'the problem of security in democracy' (one which, until Lustgarten and Leigh's recent work, has had sadly few emulators), tolerantly accepted that 'the security of the state has to be ensured, and it is hence difficult to divorce counter-espionage proper from countering sabotage and subversion'.[17] While Lord Denning stoutly emphasized, in the wake of the Profumo affair, that the operations of the Security Service 'are to be used for one purpose, and one purpose only, *the Defence of the Realm,*' he could only go on to echo the official remit provided by a Committee of Privy Councillors in 1957:

> The Security Service is part of the defence system of the country, and its supreme task is the defence of the Realm, and this necessarily involves protection from espionage, from sabotage, and indeed from every kind of action that threatens the security of the State.

The Committee's historical inquiries into such security powers as the interception of communications (from letter-opening to telephone-tapping) could produce only 'long usage' as their basis. This is, it must be concluded, characteristic of the whole system. Britain has, we may suggest, created a space-age security system under a dark-age law.

A superficially dramatic development has taken place since the passage of the Security Service Act in December 1989, which not only announced the existence of the eponymous organization, but defined its functions (both to protect national security and to safeguard the economic well-being of the UK), and set out the responsibilities of that once most shadowy of public figures, its Director General. The newly self-publicizing Security Service was equipped with a trademark logo (a griffin ringed by roses and portcullises) and a motto – *Regnum Defende* (deliberately echoing Maxwell Fyfe's 1952 'Defence of the Realm' directive). In 1994 it was spectacularly rehoused in an extremely showy building on the Thames riverfront, as if to rival the South Bank complex as an assertion of national culture. A glossy HMSO booklet issued in 1993 contained a remarkable signed assurance by Michael Howard, the Home Secretary, that it was government policy 'to be as open as possible about the the Security Service'.[18] It contained a still more remarkable open letter by Stella Rimington, the Director General, acknowledging that many of the threats that had supplied the service with its traditional role and raison d'être had receded (subversion and espionage in particular), but pointing out that others were continuing (terrorism) or even growing (proliferation of nuclear, chemical and biological weapons). The Director General evidently believed it important to reassure the public that the service was not looking to find a new role in countering crime, or in surveillance of the public. The first of these solemn undertakings, at least, was to be blithely overthrown in a couple of years. But the bottom line was accountability, and it was made quite clear that although the government was now happy to admit the existence of the SS, its operations would remain a closed book. ('It is difficult to

comment on allegations about the Service without revealing ...
information that might compromise past [sic], present and future
operations...'[19]). The service remained 'self-tasking', as one
commentator sharply noted, since it still defined the threats to
national security.[20] Amid all the verbal and symbolic trappings of
modern corporate culture, the concept of 'performance indicator'
was conspicuously lacking.

III

Despite the tendency of modern security agencies to identify a
diverse and ever-changing 'threat environment' – Canada's SIS has
included both international crime and industrial espionage among
the threats to public security – it probably remains true that military
or quasi-military threats remain the key indices of insecurity.
Certainly the crucial catalyst to the creation of a security-minded
state in Britain was total war. It was the Great War that brought the
most celebrated emergency statute, the Defence of the Realm Act
(as the Napoleonic Wars had induced its nominal ancestor), with its
battery of regulations which by the end of the war bulked almost as
large as the complete Indian Penal Code. This self-contained legal
system was entirely dependent upon that single clause of the
enabling Act – giving 'power...to issue regulations...for securing the
public safety and the defence of the Realm' (the distinction implicit
in the use of two concepts was never to be elaborated). The powers
were not granted to the government but assumed by 'His Majesty in
Council' – the decorous British euphemism for the state. The powers
had the overwhelming approbation of a public hungry for resolute
action against any manifestation of the hydra-headed German
menace. In consequence, they were not abused. A key element in the
well-known argument about war emergency powers, adduced by
Clinton Rossiter in the light of the two world wars, was that they
had been exercised with restraint and moderation in keeping with
liberal political culture.[21] Thus Britain had pulled off the difficult
trick of concentrating absolute power without any long-term
degradation of civil liberty.

The same achievement, on this view, marked the Second World
War. The 1939 Emergency Powers (Defence) Act was offered as a
measure still more radical and comprehensive than DORA, and
even so required to be bolstered less than a year into the war by
extended powers. Both the second EPA and the Treachery Act 1940

expressed the determination to root out internal weakness and 'curb activities of an anti-war character', whether on the part of enemy aliens and sympathizers or of 'people actuated by "internationalist" affiliations or by disinterested opposition to the war'.[22] (A nice Freudian slip appears in the draft conclusions of a Home Office discussion in June 1940 of the possibility of declaring martial law in the event of a German invasion: the military 'would be justified without special power in dealing with spies or other persons actively assisting the enemy, and even in shooting such persons without trial were it necessary to do so for the safety of the regime' – the last word expunged in favour of 'realm'.[23]) The grant of these wide powers was not altogether unopposed in parliament, but their use – e.g. to intern Oswald Mosley and his supporters without trial – was generally undisputed. One leading case indicated the possible lines of counter-argument: in Liversidge v. Anderson, Lord Atkin's dissenting judgment protested 'against a strained construction put on words with the effect of giving an uncontrolled power of imprisonment to the minister'.[24] Otherwise the issue of parliamentary or judicial scrutiny of actions taken under the mantle of national security barely intruded.

So far, so good. The two total wars are, we may agree, the most obvious accelerators of the growth of security laws and machinery: too obvious, perhaps. A widespread assumption about state security powers, not made explicit by Rossiter but strongly reinforced by his work, is that since the world wars were the ultimate test of national security, drawing forth virtually dictatorial powers, without essential damage to the constitution, it is unlikely that lesser emergencies have done, or will do, any serious damage. However, a divergent view is possible. The very extremity of total war created an environment in which the arbitrary exercise of power, by virtue of being openly declared, retained sufficient transparency to avoid a fatal rupture of traditional beliefs in accountability. However much they might grumble, people generally endorsed these powers. Whatever else might need to be done, concealment was not necessary.[25] Less extreme emergencies, on the other hand, commonly do not permit such free exercise of executive power, and may paradoxically drive the authorities to strain the law beyond its limits; such actions could pose more substantial threats to the prospects of return to normality. Is there a case for saying that inadequate emergency powers may be more dangerous than ample ones?

Threats to public security short of actual war have multiplied in this century, in part because the category of formal war has become more exclusive, and in part because states have become more sensitized to the possibly dangerous implications of once harmless (or even healthful) manifestations of public opinion, like public meetings, processions and demonstrations.[26] On the one hand, the extension of belligerent rights, in such laudable attempts to regulate the violence of war as the Hague and Geneva conventions, inclined states to refuse such rights to rebels lest they concede thereby the legitimacy which rebels claim. 'You do not declare war against rebels', as Lloyd George sermonized to his military men, eager to take the gloves off against the IRA in 1920. (There was also recognition that open-war measures might strain public tolerance even more than the dubious police actions then in full swing.) So rebellion, whether of low or high intensity, would be classified as peace, or at any rate as something other than war.

At the same time, the concept of subversion was constantly extended. Fellow-travellers, fifth-columnists, and moles have burrowed into the grounds for the belief in social cohesion, or at least convergence, which underpinned the 'age of equipoise'. The very success of nineteenth-century social pacification tightened the requirement upon the state to vindicate its monopoly of force, and heightened the jarring impact of civil disorder and violence. Indeed, so extensive are the threats to security, and so great the vulnerability of the complex modern 'open society' to its enemies, that it may seem surprising that this country still lacks constitutional provision for a formal state of emergency. The nearest approach to this is the package of powers available to preserve the 'life of the community' in face not of its declared enemies but of its fellow-citizens engaged in formally legal industrial action.[27] An oblique form of declaration of political emergency has surfaced at times, through derogation from international human rights' conventions on grounds of 'emergency threatening the life of the nation'. 'State of siege' remains something for foreigners, however, and this may be taken as evidence of the successful preservation of the essence of the 'British way' – or, possibly, not.

IV

The military threat which has come to dominate state anxiety since the Second World War is insurgency, a label that may be preferred to such others as terrorism, or guerrilla warfare, or low-intensity conflict, for various reasons, but partly because it has not been used in the state's own laws or instruments. What's in a name? Not necessarily very much; as we are tirelessly reminded, one woman's terrorist is another woman's freedom fighter. In this case, though, the non-naming of a phenomenon provides useful insight to the way public security is defined and defended. In the middle of a particularly inchoate insurgency in Palestine 'between the wars', one sharp observer suggested that the government's effort to restore (or create) public security was fatally hamstrung by its inability to see what it was up against. He proposed his own name, sub-war, for the situation, in the hope of alerting the powers that be to the full seriousness of the threat. It did not catch on.

Insurgency, which has been defined by a recent analyst as 'the armed expression of organic, internal political disaffiliation'[28] – and which I am taking to mean systematic violence set within a formal political challenge to the state's legitimacy – is especially important because it exploits that open-textured complexity which is the salient characteristic of modern societies. Britain had to learn the hard way that modern rebellions are worlds away from the Duke of Monmouth's or Bonnie Prince Charlie's. They may spend months or even years apparently not getting anywhere, and not justifying anything beyond mild police control. By the time the police come under visible pressure, it may already be too late for anything short of full-scale military intervention. The first sign of a breakdown of public security, in either sense, may be a rather vague malfunction of the law enforcement system. Austen Chamberlain, as Secretary of State for India, put this with unusual clarity to the Governor of Bengal in 1915:

> Although these acts of lawlessness may not be a serious menace to the state, they do seem to me a very real danger to society, and the worst of it is that the longer they continue the less will be your chance of securing the active cooperation of the population in the detection and conviction of the criminals. I am quite ready to admit with John Bright, at whose feet I sat as a boy, that 'force is no remedy for a just discontent', but Bright himself never pretended that this was a reason for allowing free play to the forces of disorder.[29]

In light of the late-1980s' Conservative contention that there is no such thing as society, the distinction drawn here is especially interesting. By inviting the authorities to classify minor acts as a kind of latent civil war (a notion which, needless to say, never appears in British official views) it showed that a quintessentially English statesman could think against the grain of the English preference for indefinition – and, some might say, facile optimism. India was perhaps the only place where this could be done. But even if the condition were accurately diagnosed, the problem was to find an appropriate remedy for this cumulative corrosion. The danger of error was all too clearly shown at Amritsar in 1919, just the kind of thing that Chamberlain (with strong family memories of miltary excesses in South Africa) dreaded.

Both diagnosis and action came more easily in India than in Ireland, where Britain faced after the Great War the first true insurgency in the modern sense. When Sinn Fein issued its unilateral declaration of independence in January 1919, Britain was unusually well-equipped with internal security powers. The purpose-built Crimes Act of 1887 was supplemented by the vast reach of the Defence of the Realm Act; on top of which the proclamation of martial law in April 1916 had never been publicly rescinded. The reluctance of the government to invoke these powers is in retrospect very striking: martial law was deliberately abjured; DORA was used with extreme caution; the Crimes Act's powers were hardly stretched. It took eight months of agonizing over the problem to reach the (no doubt mistaken) decision to proclaim Sinn Fein a 'dangerous association'. In this period the tempo of armed action by the Irish Volunteers was increasing, but it was still possible to take a sanguine view. The need to believe in the chance of a 'return to constitutionalism' was reinforced by an ingrained hostility to military intervention. The resulting drift permitted the danger to society of 1918 to become the unambiguous menace to the state of 1920, but even the more draconian measures eventually adopted, the Restoration of Order Act in August 1920 and the declaration of martial law in eight south-eastern counties at the end of the year, were attempts to avert rather than to assert anything which might be recognizable as a state of war. So, yet more fatefully, was the determination to reinforce the police rather than the military forces. The tale of the Black-and-Tans is a cautionary one, not only for Anglo-Irish relations, but also for the long-term fate of the British constitution. The Tans became something that could not be recognized or utilized as either a police or a military force. The archaic title 'Crown forces', still in use then, disguised a modern 'security force' whose distinctive mode of operation was just a little beyond the fringes of strict legality. The covert aspect of these operations, ultimately destructive of legitimacy, was necessitated by the state's insistence on preserving as far as it could the fiction of normality.

No state has been more alert than the British to the symbiotic relationship between consensual policing and public security. The corrosive power of modern insurgency has, however, repeatedly impaled it on the horns of a deadly dilemma: whether to disarm and 'normalize' the police with the attendant risk to their lives, in the hope of generating enough public support to overcome the weakness of law enforcement, or whether to increase their military effectiveness in order to reduce the need for public support (or, in the strongest version, to try to coerce public co-operation by such methods as collective punishment). Adoption of the latter course has not always been a foregone conclusion, but it *has* always been the conclusion. A rare counter-example, such as the 1922 Irish provisional government's extraordinary decision to create an unarmed police force in the midst of civil war, was possible just because the counter-insurgency was being conducted as open war. What follows from militarization of the police is the open or tacit – and of course temporary – abandonment of other criteria of ordinary legality.

To come rather closer to home: the decision to commit troops to aid the civil power in Northern Ireland in 1969, surely one of the century's more momentous political acts, provides a stark illustration of the obscurity of traditional thinking in a modern crisis. The 1968 *Manual of Military Law* was the latest in a long line of attempts to clarify the unwritten law of emergency to render it usable on the street. It offered this distinction between riot and insurrection:

> a riot has in view some enterprise of a private nature, while an insurrection savours of high treason, and contemplates some enterprise of a general and public nature. An insurrection, in short, involves an intention to 'levy war against the Queen', as it is technically called...

Pushing as best we can through the veil of semi-Elizabethan legal language, we see how far we have outstripped everyday semantics. A riot is 'private', while the public nature of war is revealed in savouring and contemplation; later on, the appearance of logical clarity given by the simple dualism is quickly obscured by the recognition of another category, 'riots which savour of rebellion'.[30] The question was, what kinds of riot were happening in northern cities? The Northern Ireland government argued that they were a local matter, though – contradictorily – the disturbances were an assault on the state rather than a mere civil rights campaign. The British government thought that the disturbances were a national-public security issue, yet not – equally contradictorily – a direct challenge to the state. The law could not help to resolve such inconsistencies. Troops were committed, but under strict controls which, in the view of some commanders, prevented them from achieving the decisive impact which alone would have permitted them to be withdrawn again.[31] Pressure was never to be lifted from the police for long enough to permit a sustained attempt at 'normalization'.

The question implicit in this is whether, in the longer term, underreaction may be more destructive than overreaction of the values which constitute the substance of national security. To give a positive answer is admittedly risky. The state is not to be lightly invited to cast the blanket of public security more widely than it already does. The sketch of effective counter-insurgency offered by General Kitson a quarter-century ago struck many people as fairly alarming. But one important fact about Kitson's work was that it was published: it invited public debate.[32] His work may carry many of the presumed foibles of the military mind, but it could not coherently be described as sinister: he was frank in word as in name. In this it was very different from most of what has been done in the name of public security since then.

The argument against underreaction nonetheless remains hard to stabilize. It is easy to be perceptive and judicious after the event. Such hindsighted wisdom may be found, for instance, in the reprimand which the Permanent Mandates Commission of the League of Nations handed out to Britain for its failure to react vigorously enough to the Arab Higher Committee strike in Palestine in 1936. The Commission held British vacillation responsible for the drastic deterioration of the situation, but one cannot be wholly confident that the League itself would have been any more decisive in drawing that particular line in the sand.

The argument must – obviously enough – be for neither inadequate nor excessive force, but for correct action appropriate to the threat. The irony here is that this is precisely the spirit underpinning the English common-law doctrine of necessary force. Force must be met with exactly the degree of force necessary to defeat it. If anything, this doctrine has become semantically stricter in modern times: being habitually referred to as 'the principle of minimum force' rather than *necessary* force.[33] Yet it is harder than ever to utilize; the problem remains one of calibrating the threat and the degree. Traditionally, the appropriate level of force was justiciable: it could be assessed in a court of law. This was an inefficient retrospective check, but once even that check has disappeared, as it now largely has, it is not clear what we are left with. There must be a danger that a perpetual diet of concealment will finally deaden the vigilance which the old idea of 'public opinion' presumed.

It would be rash to predict what, if anything, it will be for which history remembers Sir Patrick Mayhew, but constitutional history should always hark back to his classical invocation of 'the public interest' in January 1988 when, as Attorney General, he announced that the findings of the Stalker–Sampson inquiry into illegal police action in Northern Ireland (the so-called 'shoot to kill' policy, and collusion with loyalist paramilitaries) would not be published. Once again, setting aside the significance of this moment in Anglo-Irish relations, the point here is the process by which the state determines that it has less to lose than to gain by concealment. The fact that the announcement, which was heard with disbelief or outrage in Ireland, was received in Britain with indifference or resignation, underlines the abandonment of any idea of public scrutiny of this process.

The security blanket has come to obliterate the very possibility of public discussion or evaluation of danger, and hence of shared commitment to maintain public security. (A.J.P. Taylor pinned the attitude of the British authorities with barbed accuracy: 'not in front of the children' – the citizenry, of course, being the children.) Secrecy remains at the heart of the matter. Control of information has become the key to state security: this is why the GCHQ story is relevant. The information handled there is picked up on the air. It is in that sense freely available, originally. It is not the quality of the information itself, but the fact that the state has it, that renders it secret, sensitive, and vital to national security. There is no limit to what the state wants to know, and it does not wish others to know how much it knows. Information floods in to it, but emerges like blood from a stone. Yet, as the philosopher Sissela Bok points out, secrecy here creates 'public ignorance about what should be the public's business above all else'. The public – that is, the people – is asked to take on faith the need for secrecy on the ground that an open debate of the reasons for such a need might endanger national security. She wonders whether 'democratic processes *can* persist' in face of this duplicity.[34]

Bok frankly admits bafflement on this issue. But an argument that greater transparency might actually strengthen rather than threaten public security can be made, on the basis of a tradition of democratic thinking, though one which has admittedly lost its former grip on the public mind. This is the belief that liberty is, first of all, the central pillar of the values which constitute the public sphere whose security is at stake, and, second, a practical vehicle for mobilizing public energy in defence of it – of the realm, if you like. *Regnum Defende* – but *Ruant Coeli, Fiat Justitia*. A utopian doctrine, surely, but the aspiration it articulates formed a vital nerve in what used to be called our body politic. And there is a Machiavellian rider which cannot be safely sidelined by even the most executive-minded: strict legalism is one of the few reliable weapons which lawfully constituted authority can wield in its struggle for legitimacy. History suggests that it sets it aside at its own peril as well as at ours.

Notes

1 *House of Commons Debates*, 6th series, vol. 47 c.496, 4 November 1983.
2 Security Intelligence Review Committee *Annual Report, 1992–1993*, Ch. 2. 'The Canadian Security Intelligence Service's unique mandate and set of skills to investigate, analyze and forewarn continue to be integral to the maintenance of national security and public safety' (Canadian Security Intelligence Service, *Public Report 1992*, p.1).
3 Indeed, by 1996 the argument about Canadian security had been almost entirely globalized: 'national security and public safety depend on the existence of a stable security environment' (CSIS, *Public Report, 1996*). In place of any direct threats to the security of Canada, there was a 'volatile environment' in which 'persistent threats must be dealt with and new ones emerge almost daily' (Solicitor General, 'Statement on National Security', House of Commons, Ottawa, 14 May 1996).

4 Cynthia Enloe, *Ethnic Soldiers* (Harmondsworth: Penguin, 1980), advanced the argument that national (i.e. citizen's) security should be distinguished from state security.

5 This neglect has at last been remedied in the probing and subtle opening chapter of L. Lustgarten and I. Leigh, *In From the Cold. National Security and Parliamentary Democracy* (Oxford: Clarendon Press, 1994).

6 B. Buzan, *People, States and Fear: an Agenda for International Security Studies in the Post-Cold War Era* (London: Routledge, 1983 [1973]), pp. 26, 33.

7 'The Liberal Creed', *Contemporary Review*, vol. LIV (October 1888), p. 465.

8 B. Bosanquet, *The Philosophical Theory of the State* (London: Macmillan, 1923 edn), p. 190

9 G. M. Spiegel, ' "Defence of the Realm": Evolution of a Capetian Propaganda Slogan', *Journal of Medieval History*, vol. 3 (1977), p. 119. Cf. the Committee of Privy Councillors in 1957: 'It is upon the security of the State that citizens rely for the enjoyment of their freedom.'

10 Buzan, *People, States and Fear*, pp. 22, 24.

11 Though Treitschke like many nationalists had it both ways; he insisted that the state was a work of art, and that statesmen do not need nationality to construct effective political communities, yet he also insisted on the essential difference of nations. See H. W. C. Davis (ed.) *The Political Thought of Heinrich von Treitschke* (London: Constable, 1914), Ch. IX.

12 Buzan implies that the size of the security apparatus ('disproportionate', 'massive') is an indicator of maximal states, but size must be less relevant than procedure here: it is the reach and activity, rather than the number, of the security forces which really affect the quality of life.

13 Adding that 'indeed few would relish for more than a short time the flatness and predictability of life in which it was complete' (*People, States and Fear*, p. 19).

14 J. Jacob, 'Some Reflections on Governmental Secrecy', *Public Law* (1974); J. Michael, *The Politics of Secrecy* (London: NCCL, 1979); K. G. Robertson, *Public Secrets* (London: Macmillan, 1982).

15 Cf N. Hiley, 'Counter-Espionage and Security in Great Britain during the First World War', *English Historical Review*, July 1986, pp. 635ff.; D. Englander, 'Military Intelligence and the Defence of the Realm: the Surveillance of Soldiers and Civilians in Britain during the First World War', *Bulletin of the Society for the Study of Labour History*, vol. 57 (1987), pp. 24–32.

16 *The Zamora* [1916] 2 AC 77; Lustgarten and Leigh, *In From the Cold*, p. 326, note that the term was treated as something distinct from defence, and apparently wider, but 'it is impossible to deduce what the distinction was intended to convey'.

17 *Not in the Public Interest. The Problem of Security in Democracy* (London: Hutchinson, 1965), p. 140.

18 It would be remarkable, no doubt, to the authors of the recent 'Democratic Audit of the United Kingdom', in F. Klug *et al.*, *The Three Pillars of Liberty. Political Rights and Freedoms in the United Kingdom* (London: Routledge, 1996); cf pp.141–64.

19 Home Office, *The Security Service* (London: HMSO, 1993), p. 4.

20 M. Urban, *UK Eyes Alpha. Inside British Intelligence* (London: Faber, 1996), p.291. Urban politely raised the question 'whether national security is under the kind of threat today which justifies a staff several times that which the MI5 had on the eve of the Second World War', noting that there was no way of discussing this issue.

21 C. Rossiter, *Constitutional Dictatorship. Crisis Government in the Modern Democracies* (Princeton: Princeton University Press, 1948).

22 Ad Hoc Committee on DORR18B; see N. Stammers, *Civil Liberties in Britain during the Second World War* (London: Croom Helm, 1983), p. 8.

23 Home Office Departmental Conference, 26 June 1940. PRO HO 45 20245.

24 Atkin suggested that the only authority which might justify the 'method of construction' suggested by the Home Office was Humpty Dumpty. *Liversidge* v. *Anderson* [1942] AC 206. R.F.V. Heuston, '*Liversidge* v. *Anderson* in Retrospect', *Law Quarterly Review*, vol. 86 (1970), p. 86.

25 But cf Simpson's investigation into the DR18B detention orders [A. W. B. Simpson, *In the Highest Degree. Odious Detention Withtout Trial in Wartime Britain* (Oxford: Clarendon, 1992)], which strongly suggests a (wholly unnecessary?) cover-up.

26 Lustgarten and Leigh, *In From the Cold*, provide the most extensive and careful analysis of the slippage in security terms since 1945; e.g their finely nuanced discussion of subversion, pp. 395–405.

27 A subject dissected in the pioneering study by K. Jeffery and P. Hennessy, *States of Emergency* (London: RKP, 1983).

28 L. Cable, 'Reinventing the Round Wheel: Insurgency, Counter-Insurgency, and Peacekeeping Post-Cold War', *Small Wars and Insurgencies*, 4, 2 (1993), p. 229.

29 Secretary of State for India to Governor of Bengal, 17 December 1915. University of Birmingham Library, Austen Chamberlain Papers 63/4/4.

30 *Manual of Military Law* (London: HMSO, 1968), Part II, V.

31 See R. Evelegh, *Peace-Keeping in a Democratic Society* (London: Hurst, 1978); S. Deakin, 'Security Policy and the Use of the Military: Military Aid to the Civil Power, Northern Ireland 1969', *Small Wars and Insurgencies*, 4, 2 (1993), pp. 211–27.

32 F. Kitson, *Low Intensity Operations. Subversion, Insurgency and Peacekeeping* (London: Faber, 1971).

33 As for instance in the discussion of plastic bullets or 'baton rounds': *House of Lords Debates*, 5th series, vol. 424 (20 October 1981), c. 689.

34 S. Bok, *Secrets. On the Ethics of Concealment and Revelation* (New York: Random House, 1983), p. 202.

Chapter 8

The state and pro-state terrorism in Ireland

Steve Bruce

I

This essay argues that many of the characteristics of loyalist paramilitarism in Northern Ireland are a consequence of its relationship to the state. Much about the Ulster Defence Association (UDA) and Ulster Volunteer Force (UVF) is a result of the organizations' pursuit of pro-state, rather than the more usual anti-state, terrorism.

John A. Hall has suggested reasonably that 'the state' can usefully be defined by three elements. First, the state is 'a set of institutions which possess the means of violence and coercion'. The state staffs such institutions with its own personnel, and their continuity distinguishes the state from the transient governments and administrations that operate the state. Second, these institutions normally govern a specific territory, which is usually a society. Third, the state monopolizes rule-making within its territory. 'This tends towards the creation of a common political culture shared by all citizens. Differently put, the historical record witnesses an increasing merging of nation and state. Sometimes national sentiment is created by the state, but sometimes the national principle can call into existence new states.'[1]

A recent study of the Northern Ireland conflict conveys its central thesis in its title: *Mirror Hate: the Convergent Ideology of Northern Ireland Paramilitaries, 1966–1992*.[2] In describing various aspects of the Irish conflict, it stresses the extent to which Irish nationalism and Ulster unionism, and republicanism and loyalism, and republican terror and loyalist terror, have borrowed from each other and have been similarly influenced by the structure of conflict to become 'mirror images'. Clearly there are common features, and it is useful to be reminded of the similarities, but the mirror-image idea neglects the most important fact about any political conflict in a modern society, and that is the power of the state. Whatever similarities may be shared by political parties, social movements, and terrorist organizations, that some of these represent social groups which dominate the state apparatus (or ideologies which are embodied in and protected by the state) while others are dissidents, is a social fact with enormous implications.

II

What is the purpose of pro-state terror? Let us assume the existence of a relatively stable state. Arraigned against it may be dissident organizations which contest, on separate or linked grounds, some or all of the above constitutive elements of the state. Some groups challenge the state's monopoly of violence (for example, by wishing to police their own areas). Others challenge the territorial integrity of the state (the agenda of the secessionist movement). Others defy the tendency of the modern state to produce a common political culture. The Provisional Irish Republican Army (hereafter IRA) is a typical anti-state terror organization in that it denies the UK state's legitimate monopoly over coercion, denies the status of Northern Ireland as part of the UK, and defies the homogenizing tendencies of the state, seeking instead to create an alternative culture. The second and third of these it shares with such non-violent Irish nationalist movements as the Social Democratic and Labour party (SDLP).

The existence of such groups, and even just the possibility that they might exist, raises the issue of the stability of the state and creates the possibility of pro-state terrorism. The pro-state terrorist movement has as its most abstract goal the maintenance of the state. When those who support or are 'loyal' to the state suspect that its personnel are not sufficiently robust in the defence of the institutions they man, they may use force to stiffen the resolve of the legitimate defenders of the state and they may try to do the state's job for it by challenging its monopoly of the legitimate use of force.

Making the state more robust could take two forms: the imitation of dissidence and the simple conditional threat. The former tactic is attractive because it allows people to draw on the widely used vocabulary of equity. For example, from the start of the serious communal violence in early 1970 to Operation Motorman in July

1972, the government tacitly accepted the barriers which made parts of nationalist Belfast and Londonderry 'no-go' areas for the crown forces. This was a major affront to loyalists in these cities. On one level it was simply 'unfair' that the rebels should be relatively immune to policing while the good law-abiding loyalists were vulnerable to raids on their pubs and clubs. More specifically it was unfair in the facilities that it permitted, respectively, to rebels and loyalists in preparing for the use of force in pursuit of their politics. By permitting nationalist 'no-go' areas, the government was allowing the enemies of the state to arm, train and mount operations. The loyal defenders of the state were denied the same opportunities. Well, actually they were not: the policing of loyalist areas was not that successful. Gusty Spence, the founder of the 1966 UVF and one of the best-known faces of the Troubles, was 'on the run' from prison in the Shankill area of Belfast for four months in the summer of 1972. Nonetheless, working-class Protestants contrasted their circumstances with the apparent liberty of nationalist areas and felt themselves relatively deprived. At its most abstract, the no-go area was the ultimate threat to unionism because it was secession on a small scale. The citizens of Free Derry could be British enough to claim their welfare benefits but, when it suited them, they could act as if they had already left the United Kingdom.

Loyalists called for the removal of nationalist barricades, and when that was not done they erected their own. In some streets of north and west Belfast the barriers were protective, an obstacle to the drive-by shooting, but they were introduced also in areas where there was little threat from republicans (south-east Antrim, for example) and where the main point was to dramatize the complaint against nationalist no-go areas. Barricades were set up for weekends and taken down on Monday morning to allow people to go to work. The Monkstown UDA even promised to return hijacked cars when the barricades were dismantled. Unlike those erected by nationalists, the loyalist barricades had little effect in hindering the government, but they gave a cheap and easy way of embarrassing it by repeatedly drawing attention to the state's failure to enforce the run of its writ. This imitation of dissidence had an additional element in that it looked ahead to the response of the crown forces. If all barricades were removed, the battle would have been won. If the army and police took the easy option of removing just the loyalist barricades, that further proved what many loyalists took to be the case: that the state was soft on the IRA.

A second general device for stiffening the state's resolve is the simple threat: if the government will not stop the IRA, we will kill Catholics. Naturally, it was rarely put as bluntly as that, at least not in public. Instead, unionist politicians and the spokesmen for the loyalist paramilitaries would look mournful, dolefully announce that they deplored all such actions, and then add words to the effect that 'so long as the IRA can bomb our streets and clubs and shops, unfortunate though it is, some young men will react by taking revenge'.

Pro-state terrorism always has two very different audiences and purposes. Some operators articulated their motives in terms of reducing Catholic support for the IRA. Typical was the UDA man who gave me the following explanation for loyalist terror:

> The point? To make the bastards pay. If they're going to let their people blast our pubs, our shops, dismember our people, then they're going to pay the same price, a bigger price. That's what they understand. The only thing that would stop them was us giving it back to them. In [an area of Belfast] they run amok until we gave them a good slapping and then there was not a squeak from them for two years.[3]

In straight-forward retaliation, the target for the violence and the target for the message are the same: loyalists hoped to undermine support for the IRA by attacking Catholics. It is as likely that loyalist terror increased republican support but doubts about the 'in order to' reason for murder were offset by the 'because' explanation. If nothing else, revenge was cathartic. But alongside the desire for retaliation was the aim of using one target – the Catholic community – to influence a very different audience: the British government. In essence this is hostage-taking: do what we want, or the little guy gets it. It differs from much hostage-taking only in that the supposed lever is not sympathy for the victim so much as the state's supposed sense of obligation. It may sound slightly perverse when set out in these terms, but the logic is this. The state has an obligation to maintain its monopoly of coercion and thus to protect its citizens from the political violence of others. By failing to crush the IRA (on occasions, indeed, by being apparently willing to concede its main demands) the state is failing to protect loyal

Protestant citizens from murdering republican scum. We will draw attention to its failures by murdering some Catholics. This will create powerful pressure from Catholics for more effective policing. This will (a) expose the hypocrisy of Catholic leaders; (b) expose the hypocrisy of the state (when it acts to protect Catholic victims in a way it never did to protect Protestants); or (c) embarrass the state into acting effectively to protect all its citizens. The third is the preferred goal, but the other two will do as compensation.

Although much of the pro-state terror group's effort is taken up with such efforts to encourage or coerce the state into action, it may also simply substitute itself for the state. Most such cases can be interpreted in two ways. The critics see it as usurpation. The proponents see themselves as exercising their rights to withdraw from their contract with the state when the state has failed to live up to its obligations. In interviews with loyalist paramilitaries I routinely asked how and why they got involved. Almost all the replies contained something along the lines of the following:

> Because I had to. People was getting killed left, right and centre and nothing was done. Nothing. The Royal Ulster Constabulary was a joke. The border was a joke. Republicans was doing what they liked. I was up in the [a bar] and this wee fella says to me: 'There this team here that's gonna do something' and was I on side, and I says 'I'm in'. If the police and the army had been doing what they should have been doing, I'd have never left the fuckin' bar. [4]

That man retired from active service in the UDA in the late 1970s because he felt that the crown forces were by then doing 'what they should have been doing'.

Political action may be confined to conventional electoral politics. It may extend to extra-electoral but nonetheless legal means: street demonstrations, economic boycotts, dramatic temporary abstention from activities which are seen to legitimize the state. It may go further, to illegal but non-violent activities: rent or tax strikes, for example. It may take the form of terrorism (by which I mean simply the illegal use of violence for political ends). Those members of the minority population who move to the second and third stages explain their actions as a reluctant response to the failure of the state. Likewise, the pro-state terror group generally presents itself as having arrived at this final position after exhausting the more acceptable alternatives. From the ease and speed with which both pro- and anti-state groups struck violent and antagonistic positions, the outsider may reasonably conclude that there is a large amount of self-serving disingenuity in such protestations of innocence. The trial of the non-violent alternatives seems more theoretical than actual, and extremely brief. Often it is truncated by the assertion of some ethnic stereotype, such as 'You cannot trust that sort anyway', or by the logic of the (doubtless apocryphal) rugby-team captain's instruction that his players should get their retaliation in first.

To make explicit what has been implicit in the above, the three principle actors – the state, dissident terrorists and pro-state terrorists – can be represented as the three points of a triangle. Around these last two can be drawn wider circles to represent the nationalist and unionist constituencies. This simplifies, of course, because it assumes an unwarranted degree of homogeneity in the last two actors and the homogeneity of even the state may on occasions be questioned.

Each corner has three sets of relations to contemplate: two involving itself directly, and the third frequently forming a benchmark for comparisons. Thus the pro-state terror group relates directly to nationalists and to the state, but its thinking about those links is influenced by its views of the links between nationalists and the state.

That implicit comparative dimension is often over-looked, but is profoundly important. We are now well-acquainted with the proposition in studies of poverty that what matters is not so much poverty measured in some absolute sense, but relative poverty. The extent to which people feel poor is a matter largely of the comparisons they make with their past circumstances, their imagined future, and with the present circumstances of some other group. This is especially important in ethnic conflicts, which of their nature are zero-sum. When unionists are trying to decide how good or bad they ought to feel about their circumstances, they often compare their position with what they take to be the position of nationalists: 'If they appear to be making progress, then we must be losing.' The triangle is also useful in reminding us that what many loyalists wanted was for the state to elevate them and their culture at the expense of nationalists (but see below for a very different kind of loyalism).

III

What of support for pro-state terror? The triangular nature of the
links between nationalists, unionists and the state allows us to
understand the changing unionist demand for vigilante activity. In
1912 there was a popular unionist response to the impending home-
rule legislation, and a large and popular militia – the original Ulster
Volunteer Force – was founded. Rebellion was averted by the onset
of the 1914–18 War and the post-war compromise of partitioning
the island of Ireland. In the 1920s, when there was again a
widespread perception that the British response to armed force
republicanism would not be sufficient to guarantee the partition
settlement, unionists again responded with support for a militia.
The UVF was re-activated and incorporated into the state's forces as
the B Special Constabulary. There was no such popular response to
the republican campaign of the late 1950s because, with local
security firmly in the hands of the Unionist Party, most unionists
were happy to leave the crushing of republicanism to the state.

The third UVF, of 1966, was formed by a very small group of
loyalists who took seriously Prime Minister Terence O'Neill's liberal
rhetoric and believed that such appeasement of rebels would only
encourage a return to republican violence. Date coincidence led
Augustus 'Gusty' Spence, leading Shankill Road Protestant, to
believe that the IRA would stage an uprising at the Belfast City Hall
at Easter 1966, fifty years after the original in Dublin. The
perception that Ulster was under threat was not widely shared, and
it was not until the serious violence of 1969 and after that the UVF
recruited large numbers of activists and various local area vigilante
groups merged into the Ulster Defence Association (UDA). Now
loyalists were reacting to nationalist agitation and republican
violence *and* to the shift of power from Stormont to London.
Rightly, as it turned out, there was a widespread sense that the
regime which administered Northern Ireland directly from
Westminster would be prepared to make considerable concessions to
Irish nationalism, even to the extent of being willing to give away
the province.

Disentangling the pattern of loyalist violence is made complex
because each of the main stimulants – what nationalists/republicans
were doing and what the state was doing – had short cycles, based
on responses to particular incidents, and longer cycles, based on
more general moods. Nonetheless we can see the operation of both

sources of motivation very clearly if we graph together republican and loyalist murder rates.

When the 1966 UVF killed three people – one by accident – there was very little public support for its actions and little opposition to it being banned. Of the sixteen people who died in 1969, the majority were killed by the security forces during riots and demonstrations, most of them deliberately staged to provoke an over-reaction. Republicans killed three people; loyalists killed one. There was also one loyalist 'own-goal': Thomas McDowell burnt himself while planting a bomb at a power installation in the Republic. In 1970, twenty-four people were killed. In two cases the assailant is unknown and eight (six IRA men and two Catholic civilians) were killed in three IRA own-goals. The British Army killed five people; three during street demonstrations. Of the paramilitary killings, the IRA killed five Protestants and loyalists killed one Catholic and one Protestant. In 1971, republicans murdered eighty-five people. Until 4 December, when the UVF planted a bomb in McGurk's Bar in Belfast and killed 16 people, loyalists had killed only one person.

As we see very clearly in the graphs in Figure 8.1, the loyalist curve follows behind the rising republican line. But it also rises with political instability. The years from 1972 to 1976, which saw the British government negotiating with the IRA, the closing of Stormont, a constitutional convention, and the Sunningdale Agreement with its power-sharing executive, were also the peak years for loyalist killing: an average of 100 victims in each of those years. In September 1976 Roy Mason became Secretary of State for Northern Ireland. After a very brief and unconvincing flirtation with potential political innovations, he abandoned the search for political solutions and concentrated on security policy and economic development. The re-formed and massively expanded RUC began to be effective in its responses to the IRA. Many of those in the broad mass of UVF and UDA membership retired, and even those in the core of both organizations reduced their killings to the extent that, through the late 1970s and early 1980s, both UVF and UDA seemed to continue themselves on a care-and-maintenance basis. For 1977–85 loyalists average only 11 murders per year, and a quarter of the total of 101 occurred in the first year of that period.

The decline in loyalist activity is explained partly by RUC success against the UDA and UVF, but many loyalists were being locked up in the early 1970s. The difference between the two periods is that at

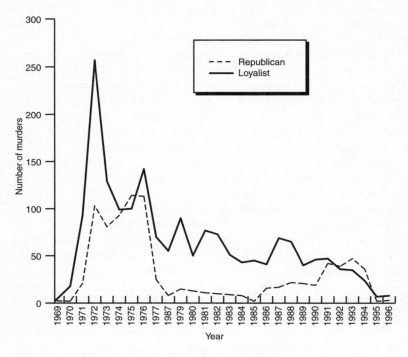

Figure 8.1 Republican and loyalist murders 1969–93

the start of the Troubles loyalist demand for terrorist activity was so great that those removed were readily replaced.

The interesting feature of the 1977–85 period is that, although there were spasmodic increases in demand for a loyalist terror response to IRA atrocities, the loyalist rate remained low, while the IRA's was considerably higher: an average of some 60 deaths a year. Quite why the UDA and UVF were so reticent is not obvious, although I have already mentioned the low incidence of dramatic political initiatives and the calming effect this had on unionist perceptions of their precarious position. Detailed interviewing of activists suggests a number of different elements to an overall explanation. Some (but by no means all) loyalist 'operators' came to question the wisdom of sectarian killings. Even those who had no moral objection to killing innocent Catholics – and it has to be recognized that there are very large numbers of people in both ethnic camps who are sufficiently hardened with hatred that they see nothing terribly wrong with 'another one of them getting slapped' – can sometimes wonder about the long-term effectiveness, catharsis apart, of more murders. Hence there was growing pressure among some sections for a more selective campaign directed at republican leaders, an option made easier by the emergence of Sinn Fein as a political force and a source of identifiable 'legitimate' targets. Others felt that the UDA and UVF had done enough in the early 1970s to prove that they were a potent source of terror and hence could continue to enjoy the influence that gave them, without so often running the risks of being killed or imprisoned. Keeping the organizations alive and committing the occasional murder brought as much benefit.

To an extent, although this should not be exaggerated, there was a tension between what the UDA and UVF had to do to acquire a voice (kill lots of people) and what they had to do to make that voice heard. In the late 1970s and early 1980s, when Glen Barr and others were developing and promoting the UDA's programme for negotiated independence, they had an interest in making sure that their political efforts were not frequently embarrassed by the UDA engaging in sectarian attacks. The clash between the two roles the organization was then pursuing was neatly illustrated by a bitter row between one of the more politically minded leaders and the overall military commander. The spokesman had agreed to take part in a BBC discussion which would also feature Irish republican Bernadette McAliskey. As he parked his car near the BBC he saw the military commander, apparently on a scouting mission, and accused him of betraying an important principle by using the debate as an opportunity to watch McAliskey for a future assassination attempt.

There was a tension also between racketeering and terrorism. There were people in both the UVF and the UDA who used their positions to enrich themselves. In some units, racketeering to raise necessary funds for the organizations was gradually displaced by racketeering for personal profit. Such groups were reluctant to jeopardize their incomes and lifestyles by provoking too strong a police interest in their activities, and were thus happy to go along with those who had less selfish interests in reducing the terror.

However, all of these personal motivational considerations were effective only within the bigger environmental change. Mao Tse Tung's fish-and-river analogy contains a large element of truth. The UDA came into being and the UVF grew from its diminutive

1966–1970 size because there was widespread demand within the Protestant working class for some sort of response to republican violence and government treachery. As that demand fell away, so the organizations shrunk.

As with the scaling-down, the increase in loyalist terror in the late 1980s had diverse causes. At the organizational level, one important factor was the removal of a generation of the UDA's leadership. In December 1987 John McMichael, the political spokesman and some-time military commander, was murdered by the IRA. Two weeks after McMichael's death, the north-Belfast brigadier was arrested in possession of the UDA's share of a vast combined loyalist weapons' purchase. The mid-Ulster brigadier was arrested for extortion. Andy Tyrie, the supreme commander for sixteen years, was ousted. The new leadership, composed of men who had been active in the organization since its foundation, was removed by the Stevens enquiry into the passing of classified security intelligence from the Ulster Defence Regiment and the British Army to the UDA. A second tier was removed by three extortion cases. The overall result of these successions was the promotion of a younger and considerably more aggressive leadership and a marked increase in UDA murders.

However, that the UVF, which experienced very little change in its senior leadership in this period, also stepped up its murder rate suggests that the main explanation of the loyalist return to terror is to be found elsewhere than in the succession of generations in the loyalist paramilitary organizations. Rather it must be sought in the wider political climate. The escalation of loyalist violence in the late 1980s was a response to the Anglo-Irish Inter-Governmental Agreement of November 1985. More important than any detail of that inter-state accord was the general principle it represented. For the first time, Britain was moderating the traditional state's claim to monopoly control of territory.[5] It was in effect saying that whatever the constitutional future of Northern Ireland (and it might not in any short term be much changed) the problem was one which would be addressed in consultation with the Irish Republic. The guarantee that Northern Ireland would remain British so long as the greater number of its citizens wished it to was no longer solely a British guarantee: it was a British and Irish guarantee, and although one might see that as strengthening the promise, it also represented a fundamental and unprecedented weakening of Northern Ireland's Britishness. Once the basic principle of state sovereignty was compromised, who knew where the compromises might end? If Northern Ireland was not British in the way that Scotland or Wales was British, then all guarantees were shallow.

Worse, the reassurance given privately by British officials only heightened the uncertainty. They sought to comfort concerned unionists by repeating the bar-room wisdom of political insiders: Dublin is not really interested in a united Ireland; nationalist rhetoric from Irish political parties is intended only to placate their wilder 'home boys'; the claims in the Republic's Constitution to the whole territory of the island of Ireland are archaic survivals; and sophisticated people know that a modicum of formal involvement in the affairs of Northern Ireland will fully satisfy Dublin's desires.

This was a mistake in two ways. First, there are a lot of evangelical Christians in Northern Ireland. They can happily believe that sophisticated people say one thing in private and another in public, but they do not want to be governed by such people. Second, the general principle that governments do not really mean what they say is one that cuts both ways: it could be that Dublin is really less green than it sounds but it could also mean that Dublin is far greener than it appears when chumming up naive British civil servants.

Either way, the bluff was called by Chris and Michael McGimpsey, who argued through the Dublin courts that the intergovernmental accord was unconstitutional in that, by accepting the status quo of Northern Ireland as part of the United Kingdom, it denied the territorial claims of Articles 2 and 3 of the Republic's Constitution. The Supreme Court ruled that the articles were not merely 'aspirational' but were a 'claim of legal right' and a 'constitutional imperative'. As Robert McCartney QC, now MP for North Down, put it:

> The Supreme Court is to be congratulated for its clear and unambiguous exposition of an issue which British and Irish politicians have attempted to hide for many years ... What the Supreme Court's decision has now made clear beyond argument is that Article 2 of the Irish Constitution assigned to the Irish government a constitutional imperative to work towards the making good, in fact as well as in law, of the Republic's claim to the territory of Northern Ireland.[6]

It may well be that the Anglo-Irish accord gave little of practical value to northern nationalists but it certainly deepened unionist fears for their own future. The regular meetings of Dublin and London politicians and officials regularly gave symbolic offence to unionists and strengthened the resolve of the armed men, who drew one obvious conclusion from the accord and the decade of political manoeuvring that followed. In March 1972, the British government had given in to republican violence and closed the Northern Ireland parliament. In November 1985, the British government had given in to republican violence and accepted a fundamental weakening of the constitutional position of Northern Ireland. The mainstream Unionist parties initiated a series of protests – rallies, marches, resignations of Westminster seats and by-elections, boycotting of government ministers – and the men in balaclavas went back to work.

IV

To the two contrasting types of terror – anti-state and pro-state – we need to add a third: state terror. Clearly it is possible for the agents of the state to engage in terrorism. However, the distinction between pro-state and state terror is a vital one. Republicans in Northern Ireland routinely argue that there is no significant difference between the UDA and UVF and the crown forces. It is all state terror. They do not see a triangle of relationships. Rather they see themselves as the legitimate agents of a people oppressed by the state-and-loyalists.

This claim is both theoretical and empirical. At the theoretical level it remains the case that, for all that republican thinking has become more nuanced since the rise of Sinn Fein, there is still the bedrock assumption that Ulster unionist, Protestant and loyalist identities are shallow entities depending for their continued existence on state support and patronage. Without the privileges accorded to Protestants by the UK state, Ulster Protestants would recognize themselves as Irish and settle down to a happy future in a united Ireland. The mundane correlate of that abstract assumption is the belief that loyalist paramilitaries are logistically dependent on the security forces for their capacity to engage successfully in terrorism. Almost every loyalist murder is claimed to have been at least in part the work of British intelligence. The bombings of Dublin and Monaghan in 1974 are just two instances of a claim made so routinely and so quickly that one has to suppose it reflects background belief rather than evidence about the particular event.[7]

At its raciest the claim is that the assassins were actually SAS men. Sometimes it is that the assassins were armed, trained, briefed or aided by the crown forces. At the very least, it is routinely claimed that there was, until the moment of the murder, a heavy security force presence in the area and that the occurrence of the murder after the road checks have moved is proof, not that the assassins had the wit to wait until the coast was clear but that the coast was deliberately cleared for them. On the very rare occasions when a more specific claim cannot be made, it is asserted that, as the crown forces should be happy with the results of the work of the UDA or UVF, they must really be on the same side.

Nothing in my research leads me to that conclusion and it is not one supported by such experienced and disinterested commentators as David McKittrick of the *Independent*. Although they would like to be seen in that light, the UDA and UVF are not branches of the state security apparatus, as the very large number of loyalist vigilantes who have been convicted and punished with lengthy prison sentences demonstrates. Clearly, relations between the state's own forces and the vigilantes who take it upon themselves to bolster the defences of the state can vary in degrees of closeness and warmth. In 1960s Guatemala more than twenty right-wing paramilitary organizations were fully armed and supplied by the army. When Arana was appointed President in the 1970s, many of the terrorists were put on the government pay-roll. But such co-option is not the only possibility. If the state encourages and tolerates the pro-state group, then the latter enjoys many of the advantages of the former; but if the government feels that its own agencies are capable of dealing with the threats to the state, then the pro-state terror group is in competition with the state. I will now briefly look at some of the consequences of that competition.

Recruitment

There is a danger of circularity in saying that the flow of recruits to both pro-state and anti-state terror organizations will vary with the perceived need for such groups: their very success may make more popular their analysis of the situation, which creates the sense of need. But much of that sense of need is not immediately amenable to propaganda work by the terror organizations. For the anti-state group, what helps create a market is the widespread sense among the subordinate population from which it recruits that the state is failing to represent its interests, either in the way that it directly deals with that population (by discrimination, for example) or in the way that it fails to curb the actions of the superordinate population (by failing to prevent the majority from discriminating). For the pro-state group, what helps create a market is the widespread sense that the state is failing to represent its interests, either in the way it directly deals with that population (by being willing to compromise the constitutional position of Northern Ireland, for example) or in the way that it fails to curb the actions of the rebellious population (by failing to prevent murderous attacks on Protestants, for example).

For both pro- and anti-state groups, the actions of the state can heighten or dampen demands for political violence but – and this is a vital difference – the latter enjoys an autonomy which is denied to the former. After all, the anti-state terror group has considerable power to persuade the state to behave badly, to undermine its own legitimacy by breaking its own rules. Indeed that will almost do as a description of the military strategy of the anti-state group.[8] The pro-state group does not have that option. Or, to be precise, the further it goes in destabilizing the state, the further it undermines its own goals. Thus over the course of the Troubles we have seen brief petulant outbursts of UVF and UDA violence directed against agents of the state (for example, in attacks on prison officers), then quickly reined in as the leaders came to appreciate the paradoxical and unpopular nature of such campaigns.

There is also a structural difference in the distribution of opportunities to act on one's beliefs and values. So long as the state acts as robustly against its self-appointed defenders as it does against its enemies, then the price of involvement in both sorts of terrorism is very high. But the pool of those willing to pay that price for pro-state reasons is limited by the fact that there are so many respectable, legitimate and well-rewarded avenues for supporting the state. A Belfast Protestant who wants to 'do something about the IRA' can join the army, the police or the prison service. The UDA man who gave the following account illustrates the point:

> When things started to get bad, I tried to join the Specials but they were being stood down. I put my name down for the UDR [Ulster Defence Regiment] but for some reasons – they never tell you the reason – I was rejected. So I had to look elsewhere. I

got involved with my local vigilantes and just went on from
there.

To exaggerate the differences in quality of those recruited to the
Sinn Fein/IRA and those recruited to the loyalist paramilitaries
would be a mistake, but it is the clear impression of many who have
extensive contacts in both worlds that the republican movement has
within it clever, articulate people who in different circumstances
could easily have moved into professional white-collar work, and
that such a cadre is much smaller on the loyalist side. Data on the
social class, occupational and educational background of convicted
terrorists seems to bear this out.[9]

Alienation and counter-culture

Recruits to terrorism are a sub-set of their populations, and
differences at that level can be traced back to the more general
observation about the extent of alienation from the state. We can see
the point if we consider the relative success of the republican
movement in creating a network of community activities and
institutions which provide wider legitimating contexts for terrorist
activity. Northern Catholics can create Irish-language schools, an
Irish language newspaper, advice centres, concerned citizens' groups,
and a range of community activities, all of which are, to differing
extents, oppositional to the state's provision. Protestants do not
have the same need for such institutions and activities, and those
loyalists who have worked to create a network of community
activities have found it more difficult than have their nationalist
counterparts. Protestant working-class passivity, often seen as a
personality characteristic of Protestants, is actually a feature of the
structure of the conflict.

Isolation, state penetration and resilience

One of the most obvious but little-commented upon facts of the
conflict in Northern Ireland is that the state is far more effective in
punishing loyalists for their crimes than it is in making republicans
similarly amenable. Put in round terms, for every victim of loyalist
violence, at least two loyalists are convicted. For every two victims
of republican terror, only one republican is convicted. Though it

often fails to prevent serious crime, the state finds it easier to punish loyalists than republicans for their deeds.

One does not need to exaggerate the alienation of Northern Irish Catholics to appreciate that there is a much greater social gulf between the population from which the IRA recruits and the agents of the state than there is between the Protestant working class, the army and the RUC. Although the loyalist paramilitaries have on occasion attacked the security forces, they also paint 'Protestant West Belfast Welcomes the British Army' on gable ends in the Shankill.

Though loyalists are almost always wrong in this hope, their expectation of approval from the security forces explains why they find it far harder to remain reticent. The high standards of proof required by the courts explain why a number of notorious loyalist killers have remained free from prosecution; they have had the good sense to say nothing at all when arrested. A large number of loyalist suspects are manipulated into confessing by interrogators who successfully play on the loyalist expectation to be praised. One leading west Belfast man, Johnny Adair, was convicted in September 1995 of the newly introduced offence of directing terrorism:

> Armed with the new law ... the RUC set about using Adair's bravado and big mouth to trap him. In a highly secret operation, an RUC officer was fitted with a concealed microphone. Even the officer's colleagues were unaware of his mission. Over several months, the officer engaged Adair in conversations. Gradually Adair began to boast of his exploits and role as a UDA commanding officer. Finally the trap was sprung.[10]

It is clear that the RUC has managed to recruit many high-ranking IRA men as spies. With far less effort, it has been able to be very well-informed about the loyalists.

Targeting and planning

It is a widely held view that in comparison with much republican violence (especially that of the IRA) loyalist terror has been much less selective and professional. The differences should not be exaggerated. It is easy to remember spectacular successes, such as the bombing of the British Cabinet at a party conference in Brighton or the destruction of the financial heart of the City of

London, and to forget that the IRA pioneered the use of the large anti-civilian car bomb, bombed public houses in Protestant areas, and killed a very large number of civilians (Catholic as well as Protestant). It is easy to remember the work of Lenny Murphy and the Shankill Butchers, or the murders of customers in bars in Greysteel and Loughinisland, and forget the many loyalist assassinations of leading republicans.

Nonetheless a simple comparison of the number of 'uninvolved civilians' murdered by each side does show that, over the period of the Troubles, a greater proportion of the IRA's victims constitute what it would define as legitimate targets than is the case with the UDA and UVF (see Table 8.1).

That difference can be explained largely by the difference in availability of targets, which in turn is related to the difference between anti-state and pro-state terror.

In the first place, there are far more people who can be presented as agents of the state (and hence as legitimate targets for republican

Table 8.1 Victims of republican and loyalist terrorism 1969–93

Status of victim	Republican		Loyalist	
	No.	%	No.	%
1 British Forces	1,064	55	12	1
2 Own activists	91	5	61	7
3 Own activists accidentally killed	102	5	23	3
4 Other side's activists	38	2	60	7
5 Civilians	630	33	765	85
Total	1,925	100	911	100

Source: Adapted from Malcolm Sutton, *An Index of Deaths from the Conflict in Ireland, 1969–1993* (Belfast: Beyond the Pale Publications, 1994).

Notes:
'Activists' here includes members of paramilitary organizations and of closely linked political groups. The total 'Own activists' category includes those shot as informers and the victims of feuds between organizations on the same side.

murder) than there are active opponents of the state who can be similarly seen by pro-state terrorists. Take the number of soldiers. Add the RUC and the RUC Reserve. Add judges, court officials, prison staff and senior civil servants. When the IRA then claims as legitimate targets anyone who has ever been any of these things, along with their relatives, it has an enormous range of targets. Add further all civilians who in any way work with or provide services for these groups (building contractors who work on barracks, caterers who provide meals for soldiers, publicans who do not refuse to serve service personnel), and one has a vast population of targets. It seems hardly unfair to their motives to say that republicans can afford to be precious about their targeting because there are so many legitimate targets that they can entirely satisfy their desires for victims.

Furthermore, the targets of anti-state terror are highly visible. While small units of the security forces can be covert, a large part of the point of the security forces is that they should be seen. Not to exercise their right visibly to patrol is to abnegate their responsibilities. And the physical plant which can represent the state is enormous. Army barracks and camps are large public places. The City of London is a big target. Such premises as could be regarded as equivalents on the republican side are scarce and small. IRA men do not wear uniforms and do not have to make themselves visible.

The issue of targeting is an important one. On both sides there are many people who are so thoroughly hardened as to accept that anyone on the other side 'deserves it'; but there are also many people who accept only reluctantly that a degree of violence is necessary to pursue legitimate political ends and who wish to believe that their terrorists are selective. This section is a vital swing vote which can encourage or constrain the terrorists.

This brings us back to propaganda. Whether or not any action is justified is a matter of competing definitions of the situation. The state attempts to portray terrorists as mindless psychopaths; the terrorists attempt to portray themselves as principled patriots or liberators. In the propaganda battle the anti-state terrorist has an advantage in that his constituency is generally not receptive to the views of the state.

One area in which public perceptions are vital is fund-raising. All terrorist organizations raise money in illegal ways. The willingness of the surrounding population to tolerate such crime depends partly on the nature of the crime. Rackets which involve depriving the

Exchequer of revenues (such as the IRA's use of exemption certificates for building-site workers) bear less pressingly on the tacit supporters of terrorism than do rackets which involve direct threats to small firms and individuals who belong to the community supposedly being defended by the terrorists. But toleration depends also on the perceived need for those defenders and on the perceptions of the integrity of their motives. It was widely known among the Protestant working class of Belfast that such early leaders of the UDA as Charles Harding Smith or Tommy Herron were funding the organization by protection rackets and robbery, but many blind eyes were turned because people believed they needed the UDA. In the early 1980s, when republican violence had been reduced, those people became more critical of the UDA.

The question of the integrity of the terrorists is more obviously amenable to the propaganda work of competing definitions of the situation. Colin Wallace's disinformation unit at Army HQ in Lisburn invented the Ulster Citizen's Army and issued a number of broadsheets under its name which, among other things, accused leading loyalists of profiteering from the Troubles. In the 1980s, the RUC began to have significant success against extortion rackets and made much of the involvement of some paramilitaries in drug-dealing. On both fronts, there was a deliberate policy of arguing that the terrorists were fund-raising to line their own pockets rather than to support their organizations.

There is no doubt that many leading loyalists enriched themselves through their positions. Controlling such people became a major concern for the UDA and UVF, and a number of individuals were sacked, exiled or murdered. In an enterprise which is itself illegal and hence cannot employ standard accounting methods and checks, the accusation of 'dipping' can so readily be made that one has to be sceptical about its application in any particular case. Nonetheless, and this is my main point, there is a structural difference in the vulnerability of anti-state and pro-state terrorists in this matter. Even if the amount of self-serving racketeering were the same on both sides, the greater degree of alienation in the anti-state population would make it far easier for the RUC to blacken the reputation of the UDA and UVF than it would be to damage the standing of the IRA among its actual and potential supporters.

International support

International relations being what they are, the anti-state group always stands a better chance of finding foreign patrons than does the pro-state terror group. A country or a group of people within a country which wishes to damage British interests can support the republican movement; Libya is an example of the former and Noraid of the latter. But any country which wishes to support British interests will do so by supporting the British government and not by funding loyalist paramilitaries.

To summarize: while it is important not to exaggerate the differences between anti-state and pro-state terrorism, it is important also to appreciate that relatively small structural differences can have major consequences.

V

The IRA cease-fire of 1994 changed, for a short time, the nature of the Northern Ireland conflict and shifted the focus from terror to pressure group and party politics.

There is much to be said about loyalist politics, but for my purposes here I will summarize developments in terms of a choice about the legitimation of Ulster unionism. Put briefly, there are two very different types of Ulster unionism: ethnic and civic. Very much the mirror-image of Irish nationalism, ethnic unionism supposes that there is a unionist people, united in culture (English-speaking, Protestant and democratic), in ancestry (descended from Scottish and English settlers), and in adversity (the common victims of Irish nationalism). This people has the right to self-determination. At Partition, the Irish were given three-quarters of the island; the unionists deserved to keep the rest in union with the United Kingdom. This ethnic vision informs the politics of Ian Paisley's Democratic Unionists and a part of the Ulster Unionist Party.

The 'civic' version, presented most cogently by Aughey,[11] draws on the work of such political theorists as Parekh, who identifies concern with territory as the constitutive feature of the modern state.[12] It is possible for a state to comprise simply all those people who inhabit a certain territory, irrespective of their religion, language and ethnicity. To suppose that the state should also be a nation is to accept the logic of nationalism and to miss this other possibility. At least in theory, the British state is multi-national and multi-cultural. Despite the efforts of a handful of 'English nationalists', the British state does not attempt to impose a common culture or promote a single national identity. Given that it has to encompass Wales and Scotland, it could not do so. In contrast, the Irish Republic is sectarian in privileging one religion, one language and one culture. It follows that, while Ulster Catholics will be treated as equal citizens by the United Kingdom, Ulster Protestants would be the victims of discrimination in the Irish Republic. It follows that it is better for everyone if Northern Ireland remains part of the United Kingdom. This argument supplements the argument from numbers. Leaving aside any consideration of ethnicity, the greater number of people in Northern Ireland wish to remain in the United Kingdom. The modern state should accept that decision. The paradox of Ulster politics is that this new civic unionism is most heavily promoted by a liberal section of the Ulster Unionist party and by the Progressive Unionist party and the Ulster Democratic party, which are associated with the UVF and UDA, respectively.

There is no need to rehearse here the details of the evolution of political thought among the loyalist paramilitaries,[13] but a few main points are useful. First, leaders in both the UVF and the UDA, spurred to reflection by their paradoxical position of being imprisoned by the very state they sought to protect, early on questioned the ultra-orthodox unionism which had informed their thinking when they first became involved in terrorism. Spence at the start of the Troubles publicly said that he accepted the nationalist description of Stormont as '50 years of mis-rule', and bitterly observed that the Protestant working class had been as badly treated as had the nationalists. The break with traditional unionism was most dramatic in the UDA's promotion of negotiated independence for Ulster in the late 1970s. Many in both organizations explicitly rejected the ethnic vision of unionism, in good part because they rejected the links between unionism and evangelical religion. In the late 1980s the UDA shifted back from independence to a more straightforward unionist position, but followed the UVF lead in defending this in terms of the equal rights of all citizens, the majority of whom were unionist.

Throughout the Troubles, optimistic commentators have made much of progressive sounds coming from within the UDA and UVF but, so long as the war was being fought on the streets, loyalist politics was really neither here nor there. Even within the two organizations, the political pronouncements were often greeted with indifference, and it was hard for outsiders to reconcile the liberal and tolerant political line with the gross reality of sectarian murder. However, the IRA cease-fire in 1994 radically altered the environment. It was now possible for the ex-UVF men in the PUP and their counterparts in the UDP to be heard.

And what was heard was ameliorative and progressive. At some considerable risks to themselves, leading figures in the PUP and UDP sought at every opportunity to defuse tensions, to insist that negotiations with republicans were necessary for a long-term solution, and to stress that changes were required to make Northern Ireland attractive to the nationalist minority. While they kept stressing the bottom line of the Union, the PUP and UDP set themselves against the approach of the two main unionist parties which was to maximize opposition to British government initiatives and take every opportunity to stall them.

As a result, the UDP and the PUP have been frequently attacked by the UUP and the DUP as being weak on the union and too sympathetic to nationalism. Mainstream unionist politicians have sought to amplify tensions within both organizations and encouraged the more religio-ethnic-minded individuals to criticize their own leadership. This led, in 1996, to the mid-Ulster unit for the UVF being disbanded for denouncing the leaders of the PUP as 'traitors'.[14]

VI

Writing in the late-1990s, it is very difficult to predict Northern Ireland's future. The official British and Irish line is that, though the road is rocky, the present talks' structure offers 'the only game in town' and will eventually bear fruit. The view of many experienced commentators is that community relations are now at an all-time low and that the province is very close to an explosion of violence which will surpass that of the early 1970s. Both views agree that everything hinges on Sinn Fein and the IRA's conclusions about the political value of violence. If the republican movement does escalate its terror campaign, it is difficult to imagine how a loyalist cease-fire can hold. And if substantial parts of the UVF and UDA go back to terrorism, the politics of the PUP and UDP will become irrelevant.

The present tensions within unionism suggest a second possible source of loyalist violence, a route which involves widespread unionist alienation almost accidentally stumbling into terrorism. Though this has passed largely unremarked upon by journalists, it is significant that the alliance which led the protests over banned parades in the summer of 1996 was not based on the UVF and UDA but on radical elements in the Orange Order, the Ulster Unionist Party and the Democratic Unionist Party. This more disruptive expression of religio-ethnic unionism has previously been seen in the more respectable and short-lived paramilitary organizations[15] of the early 1970s and in the Ulster clubs and Ulster Resistance in the period after the 1985 Anglo-Irish accord.

It may well be that the British and Irish governments will manage change sufficiently skilfully as to ensure that no single event galvanizes that diffuse constituency to organized violence. The threat from the UDA and UVF is more apparent and immediate, but the political direction in which the PUP and UDP have led their people will make it difficult for them to go back to terrorism with enthusiasm. Too much effort has been put into maintaining the cease-fire and justifying it to the sceptical for it to be readily abandoned. They may still do it. The cease-fire was predicated on two assumptions: an end to IRA violence and the security of the Union. The first condition fell in February 1996 and government actions in the next year may convince enough people that the second has also fallen.

Whatever the attractions of a return to violence, the paramilitaries may find the alternatives closing down. Ironically the action taken by the UDA and UVF in August 1996 to control its more radical elements may force them out of the political process. The death threats against dissidents are being used by the main unionist parties as an argument against the continued involvement of the paramilitaries in the talks and, if the UVF and UDA actually murder their own rebels, it is hard to see how the British and Irish governments can continue to use the lack of an IRA cease-fire to exclude Sinn Fein while keeping the PUP and UDP involved.

This brings us back to the lack of symmetry between anti-state and pro-state terror. Irish nationalists represented by the SDLP and the Dublin government seem willing to forgive the IRA its violence in order to bring republicans into the political dialogue but, from their position as representatives of the status quo, the main unionist parties are using the requirement of loyalty to the state as a way of trying to exclude those who are prepared to use illegal violence on behalf of the union.

Lending some weight to the hopes of a continuing loyalist cease-fire is the atmosphere among the paramilitary leaders closest to the political representatives. Although there is no logical reason why the civic unionism promoted by the PUP and UDP should be incompatible with terrorism (after all, one could defend the resort to arms by arguing that the state is failing its citizens), it does seem to be psychologically and socially incompatible; the PUP and UDP have been mixing for over two years with people who share their constitutional politics but who abhor violence and are unlikely in any circumstance to be moved to violence. While the paramilitaries presently possess the facilities and the expertise for a renewed terror campaign, they are less convinced than the more traditional unionists that the present political climate requires a resolutely oppositional approach. That many have been involved in terrorism for twenty years prior to the two years of peace perhaps gives them a clear notion of just what will be involved in a return to all-out war. This suggests that in the long run, and under the right circumstances, the greater danger on the unionist side is of more radical elements of the religio-ethnic brand of unionism gradually and inadvertently escalating the tensions within an extremely tense situation.

Notes

1 J. A. Hall, 'State', in J. Krieger (ed.) *The Oxford Companion to Politics of the World* (Oxford: Oxford University Press, 1993), p. 878.
2 R. Davis, *Mirror Hate: the Convergent Ideology of Northern Ireland Paramilitaries, 1966–1992* (Aldershot: Dartmouth, 1994).
3 All quotations which have no specified source are from interviews conducted between 1986 and 1996.
4 Like most juvenile delinquents, many terrorists retired because they felt the pressure of mature family responsibilities. Others withdrew because their previous records made them vulnerable to police pressure and thus they could no longer be trusted by their comrades. Some found that during their time in prison they had been replaced in their organi-zations by younger men. But underlying the varied reasons for drop-ping out of active terrorism was a general pattern of responding to the perceived interaction of republican violence and security force activity. In periods when the IRA scaled back or when the security forces seemed to be getting on top of the IRA, fewer loyalists were active in the UDA and UVF.
5 Dublin's influence on the running of Northern Ireland is now considerable, not because the accord gives great formal powers but because the lack of representative democracy in Northern Ireland exaggerates the impact of informal channels of influence. For example,

Dublin is invited to nominate the great and good to sit on the many quangos that run much of Ulster's life.

6 P. Bew and G. Gillespie, *Northern Ireland: a Chronology of the Troubles, 1968–1993* (Dublin: Gill & Macmillan, 1993), p. 231.

7 See J. B. Bell, *In Dubious Battle: the Dublin and Monaghan Bombings, 1972–74* (Dublin: Poolbeg, 1996). Bell repeats the allegations that the Dublin and Monaghan bombs were inspired and assisted by the British army but offers no convincing evidence to over-rule the repeated claims by the UVF that it and it alone was responsible. For a compendium of such claims see R. Murray, *The SAS in Ireland* (Cork: Mercier Press, 1990).

8 M. L. R. Smith, *Fighting for Ireland? The Military Strategy of the Irish Republican Movement* (London: Routledge, 1995).

9 K. Boyle, T. Hadden and P. Hillyard, *Ten Years On in Northern Ireland: the Legal Control of Political Violence* (London: Cobden Trust, 1980), p. 22.

10 H. McCallion, 'Locking up the Mad Dog', *Independent*, Section Two, 14 September 1995, p. 4.

11 A. Aughey, *Under Siege: Ulster Unionism and the Anglo-Irish Agreement* (Belfast: Blackstaff Press, 1989).

12 B. Parekh, 'Ethnocentricity of the Nationalist Discourse', *Nations and Nationalism*, vol. 1 (1994), pp. 25–52.

13 S. Bruce, *The Edge of the Union: the Ulster Loyalist Political Vision* (Oxford: Oxford University Press, 1994).

14 The UDA faced similar criticism from within its ranks in the run-up to the loyalist cease-fire, and one brigadier – Alex Kerr – who was removed from his position subsequently became very close to Billy Wright, a leading figure in the mid-Ulster UVF. This led to some speculative reports of a new paramilitary organization being created from disaffected members of the UDA and UVF. In August 1996, the UVF and UDA issued a joint statement instructing Wright and Kerr to leave the province or be shot. That Kerr was in police custody, having just been caught setting up a clandestine press conference to announce a new terror group, suggests that his former comrades are determined to prevent such a threat to their control.

15 In addition to the UDA, the UVF and the Red Hand Commandos (a small group which is effectively a sub-set of the UVF), there were in the early days of the Troubles a large number of groups which paraded, adopted some small elements of a uniform, collected a few weapons, prepared for doomsday and engaged in such illegal acts as blocking roads, but did not murder: the Down Orange Welfare, the Ulster Special Constabulary Association, the Vanguard Special Service Corps and the Orange Volunteers. These generally recruited from a more rural and bourgeois base.

Chapter 9

The British state

Sovereignty and identities

Bernard Crick

The concept of 'the state' arose only in the early modern period. Feudal regimes and purely dynastic regimes had no sense of the state. 'Open in the name of the state!' would once have provoked argument about whether 'the state' had power to override the local *parlement* or *seigneur* or whatever, or else would have seemed some strange derogation of the personal or prerogative power claimed or implicit in 'open in the King's name!' Both the concept and the institution are historically contingent. As the late Carl J. Friedrich of Harvard would say in lectures, the state is 'an abstract corporate halo invented to cover the aggregation of naked power'. Even Max Weber's celebrated definition seems too precise to most modern historians: the new states of the sixteenth and seventeenth centuries did not always readily achieve 'a monopoly of the legitimate means of force'.

It becomes reasonably clear that there is a state when there is a central administrative apparatus that continues after a change of dynasty, whether peaceable or not. In the kingdom of England the work of Thomas Cromwell was not in vain. On the death of the Great Queen, the Council could ensure a peaceful transition to rule by an alien from a mutually hostile nation, and a transition that did not threaten either the powers of the English common lawyers to declare the law or the recent recognition that new law should be made only by statute through parliament. So there is an oft-told, if sometimes badly told, tale of a British *Sonderweg* or exceptionalism, that shows how acting in the name of 'the crown' was never quite the same as actions elsewhere 'in the name of the state'. However, exceptionalism may imply that there was a norm. But if students of comparative government would only read comparative history, they would see two things clearly: that every case is different; and that multi-national and multi-ethnic states with different administrative and political institutions were once almost universal, and are still far from uncommon the deeper one digs. This essay will probe one aspect of English and then British exceptionalism, one that has long been intellectually fascinating and, in political terms, has suddenly become acutely contentious.

The doctrine of parliamentary sovereignty has well been called 'the English ideology'. I want to make some suggestions in broad outline about how and why it arose and how it relates to the surprisingly complex problems of national identity and identities in the British Isles, and how they in turn relate to the state.[1]

To put all this in historical context has been possible only in the last decade or so, when significant advances in historiography and actual history have been made.[2] The first chapter of a recent book, *Conquest and Union: Fashioning a British State, 1485–1725*, written by a colloquium of historians from all four nations of the British Isles, begins with a remarkable and proper tribute to one man.

> Our starting point must be the work of John Pocock, whose (published) plea for 'British History: a New Subject' has been the delayed-action inspiration behind most recent developments in the field. In 1975 he called us to a holistic approach to what he has termed 'the Atlantic archipelago', insisting that we must adopt a pluralistic approach which recognizes but does not exaggerate the extent to which such a history must contain 'the increasing dominance of England as a political and cultural entity'. He went on to show how the component parts of these islands 'interacted so as to modify the conditions of one another's existence', and that 'British history denotes the historiography of no single nation but of a problematic and uncompleted experiment in the creation and interaction of several nations'.[3]

But in delineating the vital role in these interactions once played by the doctrine of parliamentary sovereignty, I will reach a conclusion to this 'uncompleted experiment' that is very different from John Pocock's.

This essay will make four claims. The first is rather obvious: that the claim to sovereignty is a specific and peculiar one, involving neither a meaningless concept nor one synonymous with power in general, but rather a claim to be a necessary attribute of every government of an autonomous or independent country.

The second claim is less obvious: that the doctrine of parliamentary sovereignty has a contingent history. It first arose for the specific needs and purposes of the English state at a specific time, and as these needs and purposes have changed the doctrine is withering away, or is turning from a useful theoretical description of the workings of the British polity into the doctrinal battle cry of a party that may have lost its sense of history and has certainly changed its historical nature – the difference between the traditionalist, Burkean, Old Tories and the radical, neo-liberal, New Conservatives.

The third claim will be that the common confusions between the concepts of 'sovereignty', 'power' and 'authority' were once historically useful, but are now politically dangerous. The claim to sovereignty does not always increase or reflect real power, but can sometimes hinder its exercise. Britain, by joining a larger unit, has been able to achieve things it could not have done on its own; and, if it devolves more power internally (to the Scottish parliament, the Welsh and Northern Ireland assemblies – and possibly to the English regions), more citizens will be involved in the exercise of regional and local powers. Centralized power can be pushed so far as to frustrate the effective use of power, and decentralized power could lead (as some of its opponents fear) to more government rather than less, but hopefully more democratic and responsive government. The recent opposition of English Conservatives to the Scotland Bill shows a lack of historical sense: they learned nothing from the loss of American colonies and from the violent rupture of Ireland when the Home Rule Bill of 1886 was defeated and its revival fatally delayed in 1914.

My fourth claim is that the United Kingdom has been, from its origins in 1707, a multi-national state pretending, for the sake of internal peace, to be a unitary state. And that claim leads to some brief reflections on why John Pocock has come to believe that his reading of British history shows that national identity is threatened by even the present degree of union with the European Union.

I

'Sovereignty', said John Adams in the time of American revolt, 'is very tyranny'. No compromise between parliament and the colonies had been possible because British statesmen in all parties and factions believed that without sovereignty there would be anarchy, and that sovereignty was indivisible. The actual phrase 'sovereignty is indivisible' is probably Robespierre's, following Rousseau; but the presupposition was also that of a most untheoretical man, Lord North, who hated 'speculators' even more than did Burke. But, of course, North's prejudice is also the philosophical theory of Thomas Hobbes, who had taught that the right of sovereign power was 'indivisible', and that 'if there had not been an opinion received of the greatest part of England, that these powers were divided ... the people had never been divided and fallen into this Civil War'.[4] By the 1790s, incidentally, Adams was expressing fear that the new American Union could be torn apart by 'state sovereignties and the national sovereignty', neither of which outcomes he thought desirable. The British answer to Adams's perception of sovereignty as 'very tyranny' had been and continued to be, of course, to reassert the 'sovereignty of Parliament' doctrine: how law, order and liberty could be best combined by responsible representation – Whiggery.[5] But the rejoinder to that answer was, of course, either that parliament was not representative of those it sought to tax and control – what became the Jacobin, Jeffersonian and Chartist rhetoric of the sovereignty of the people; or the Whig–Lockean–Aristotelian answer of an Adams or a Madison that parliament's claim to be sovereign itself violated the idea of a balanced and mixed constitution under law. Between these two polar forces civic republicanism was badly torn.

The claim to sovereignty in the sense that angered Adams was indeed a specific and peculiar one, not an empty phrase synony-mous with power in general or a necessary attribute of every government of an independent country. This is my first claim, the obvious one. A classic formulation, well-known to Adams, was found in Blackstone's *Commentaries on the Laws of England* of 1769:

Parliament hath sovereign and uncontrollable authority in making, confirming, enlarging, restraining, abrogating, repeal-ing, reviving, and expounding of laws, concerning all matters of all possible denominations, ecclesiastical or temporal, civil, military, maritime or criminal: this being the place where that absolute despotic power, which must in all governments reside somewhere, is entrusted by the constitution of these kingdoms. All mischiefs and grievances, operations and remedies, that transcend the ordinary course of the laws, are within the reach of this extraordinary tribunal. It can regulate or new model the succession to the crown; as was done in the reigns of king Henry VIII and William III. It can alter the established religion of the land; as was done in a variety of instances, in the reign of king Henry VIII and his three children. It can change and create afresh even the constitution of the kingdom and the parliaments themselves: as was done by the Act of Union, and the several statutes for triennial or septennial elections. It can, in short, do everything that is not naturally impossible; and therefore some have not scrupled to call its power, by a figure rather too bold, the omnipotence of parliament.[6]

Great lawyers of no other state have ever made such a claim on behalf of a representative body, only the Roman lawyers on the power of emperors. Small wonder the doctrine has been called 'the English ideology'. Better had Blackstone spoken of 'predominance' and not 'omnipotence'. Small wonder that that thoughtful but eccentric Blackstonian, Mr Enoch Powell, was wont to name the very day on which our country, like a foolish virgin, gave away its sovereignty and thereby mortgaged and imperilled our very identity; but a greater wonder to the wise that Professor Pocock, while presumably recognizing that the doctrine is an historical phenomenon, and therefore like all of us a creature of time doomed to mortality, yet has come to see it as essential to British identity, and to a British identity which he identifies with the Commonwealth, or perhaps, more accurately and sadly, to one of its two Antipodean parts.

II

The kingdom of England turned into Great Britain on the death of the Great Queen, but it was a dynastic union, not a parliamentary union. James VI of Scotland and I of England styled himself, in a royal proclamation the year after his coronation, 'king of Great Britain', but though the term would soon pass into general usage, neither parliament would endorse it. To each he was sovereign lord or king of two separate kingdoms, each with its own laws, parliament and Church that limited the manner in which the crown's powers could be exercised; and he was also king of an unincorporated, if part-colonized and part-conquered, Ireland. Dual, even multiple, monarchies were not uncommon in Renaissance Europe.

His two loyal parliaments forced him to back down entirely on his publicly and passionately proclaimed policy to create an 'incorporating and perfect union' between the two states and nations.[7] Despite a common Protestantism, or rather two modes of the same that to a marked extent cut across national divisions (as was to figure prominently in the Civil Wars of the mid-century), there was deep distrust and even hatred of the other in both nations.[8] National consciousness was strong, but the concept of a nation state did not exist. The English state delivered itself to James because he had the best claim of inheritance (and even though a sovereign's claim to a property was one hedged around by many religious, customary and practical limitations); and also simply to avoid the risk of war for the succession (what became Hobbes' utilitarian theory, of the linkage between peace and obedience to any sovereign who could enforce them, was already in the hearts of practical men like the Cecils and the English Council). Tyrone's rebellion of 1598 in Ulster had only just ended when James ascended to the triple monarchy, leaving Tyrone without hope; but while he had at least succeeded in creating something like a national consciousness among traditional tribal chieftaincies, yet he had not set himself up as king of Ireland, but offered kingship to Philip of Spain.[9]

National consciousness needs distinguishing from what became in the nineteenth century the distinctive doctrine of nationalism as most people understand it – that for every nation there should be a sovereign state – and the even more draconian belief that every existing state must reconstitute its peoples as a single nation or, if not, break up.[10] Hugh O'Neill, Earl of Tyrone, before he turned in desperation to the king of Spain, had been willing to settle the grievances of his confederates within the framework of the English crown. The rebellion was not for nationalism; it was to defend traditional property rights against seizures and exploitation by English lord-deputies and their agents; but it began to create a national consciousness. Similarly, that an outlandish Scot should ascend the very throne of England raised no patriotic protest in principle. There were then stronger convictions that overrode national objections to an alien ruler: respect for dynastic inheritance as part of the natural order, and the prudential considerations that went with it: fear of civil war, anarchy and disorder.

Just as it is necessary to distinguish, in the early modern period, the consciousness of being a nation from the full-blown political nationalism of a much later period (that can still so insidiously colour so many readings of the past), so also a sovereign's actual power needs distinguishing from the doctrine of Blackstone and the theory of Hobbes – that for the sake of peace obedience is due to whoever can enforce the peace: since we must all die, to hell with bookish legitimacy; whoever rules, it is better to die in bed than with one's boots on. For sure, James I of England and VI of Scotland believed in the divine right of kings, but at the time, as Conrad Russell has sardonically pointed out, nearly everyone else did.[11] And nobody sane, James included, believed that these rights were absolute and universal. They were limited by divine law and by the common law, perhaps even by natural law. Indeed the concept of 'divine right' is misleading if it implies unlimited autocracy; say rather that kingship is a divine institution of rights to govern for the beneficent purposes for which God instituted it. So there was a lot of room for legitimate argument about what went into that bundle of rights and how they were exercised; and about what were the purposes of monarchy and the limits to sovereignty. James in several instances reasoned with and hectored his judges when cases went against his wishes, but he did not over-rule them. The *authority* of the English common lawyers was considerable, and there was a general belief in an ancient constitution of balanced powers and divided functions. James in learned books and interminable stammered speeches pushed well-ordered arguments for royal supremacy very far, but did not push his power and luck too far in policy and practice. It was his son who tested them, proudly and recklessly, to the point of self-destruction. James was skilled politically in that old art of Scottish monarchy in which he was grimly aware his mother had proved so hopeless: survival. Certainly some royalist writers and preachers in the reign of Charles I came close to claiming that the king had absolute sovereign power; but it was mainly rhetoric. Everyone knew that he did not, and that even if he did, he could not.

Claim begat counter-claim. The late Professor Charles McIlwain of Harvard, in his early study 'The High Court of Parliament', selected the afternoon of 27 May 1642 as the first occasion when parliament, Lords and Commons in unison, claimed supremacy and acted upon it.[12] The two Houses declared that parliament was the Great Council of the Realm 'to provide for the necessity... and preserve the public peace and safety of the kingdom ... and what they do therein hath the stamp of royal authority'. Too much can be made of this claim. It was a desperate reaction to a breakdown in royal government and not, as later in the Acts of Settlement after 1688, an ideology of parliamentary sovereignty. At the time it did not stick. Cromwell had to override it to govern England at all, to contain Scotland and to reconquer Ireland. And Charles II in turn inherited the Commonwealth's breakdown. But was sovereignty really at issue in May 1642; and, if so, vitally in what sense?

The king put his name to a famous document *The Answer to the Nineteen Propositions*, the propositions in question being of parliamentary origin. In refusing these propositions the king asserted that the constitution of England was a mixture of absolute monarchy, aristocracy and democracy and that the monarchy was one of the three estates of the realm together with Lords and Commons; so that parliament's claims destroyed this traditional and natural balance. Professor Pocock has called this a 'fatal move', whereas the king should have responded 'with a doctrine of monarchical sovereignty'.[13] Events might seem to have justified such a judgment. Parliamentary government broke down. But so had the king's government – hence the Civil Wars across the three kingdoms. It was a commonplace of received classical political theory that, except in times of emergency, the institution of monarchy depended too much on the character and political prudence of one mortal. The arguments are, in principle, plausible in either direction: that there must be some sovereign source of initiative in all government; or that in a balanced constitution the concept of sovereignty is redundant. But even in a later 'constitution of laws and not of men' the President of the United States had to be given the powers of commander-in-chief. However, Pocock and I may not be talking about entirely the same thing – as is not uncommon in academic disputation. He has a very broad understanding of sovereignty derived from close reading of the discourse of those days, while I have a very precise one, but drawn from a later period and honed more for general explanation than for contextual explication. For in the same context he remarks that 'sovereignty is about power and authority as a coherent and legal singularity'.[14] Leaving aside that 'coherent' which, while devoutly to be wished, could be said to be a red herring begging the question, his definition is far closer to the language and discourse of the time than is my Hobbesian and Blackstonian, say positivist if you like, perception of sovereignty.

This raises, however, a large question for the history of ideas. Granted that we must understand what key concepts meant in the relativity and context of their times, how they related to other concepts and what their force was in public debate; but to explain what happened, why some systems rise, some fall and others totter along in senile longevity because unchallenged, may we not need tighter alternative definitions, often of the same terms, for these 'essentially contestable concepts'? As Ernest Gellner has argued against the functionalists and the excessive relativists in anthropology, we must understand the role of ritual and prayer integral to the Kingfisher God in Dinka society (or whatever), but we must note that as a method of raising rain and promoting irrigation it did not do them much good in the evolutionary stakes. The history of ideas must take some notice of whether systems work or not. Gellner once criticized Winch, saying that we do not understand a society simply by understanding its dominant discourse and concepts, but only by studying how these concepts work in practice and how they respond, or not, to contingencies.[15]

III

To say that 'sovereignty is about power and authority as a coherent and legal singularity' begs the very questions at issue. 'Power' and 'authority' are by no means the same thing; and in any case some systems of government do not give one a very clear jurisprudential rule with which to identify the source of such sovereignty. A British ambassador in the 1870s wrote home that he was damned if he could find out who to deal with in Washington on the north–west boundaries question – certainly not the President. Would that power and authority did always go together and that 'coherent and legal singularity' did not sometimes have to wait on an unresolved case in a Supreme Court or, for Britain, in a European Court. Teachers, writers and thinkers with little or no coercive power can often have remarkable authority, if we think what they are telling us is true and important and if they do not extend that specific authority to things about which they know nothing (how I define and denounce 'authoritarianism'). The point at issue is that those with legal authority or who claim sovereign authority can sometimes have remarkably little real power, and those with power can easily, if they push it too far, lose what little 'brief authority' they have.

Small wonder that Hobbes, while creating a great baroque melodrama of the state as a Leviathan to frighten us all into civil obedience, yet taught the wise that the claim to authority of a sovereign, whether monarch or parliament, rested solely on those operations necessary to minimize our chances of violent death. If the custodian of the state cannot do that, obligation ceases and we should turn to whoever can.

Bertrand Russell once usefully distinguished, in a little pot-boiler of a book called *Power*, two senses of the concept: 'the ability to carry out a premeditated intention' and 'unchallengeability'. He pointed out that the latter claim could sometimes impede the former. A state in modern Europe, for example, might choose to remain a sovereign power, autonomous and unchallenged by any legal superior; but in doing so it might curtail its ability to carry out premeditated intentions – like maintaining the prosperity, welfare and security of its people.[16]

Both these senses of sovereignty and power animated the constitutional settlement that emerged after 1688. The doctrine of parliamentary sovereignty kept them together and was implicit in the Act of Union of 1707, the negotiated ending of the Scottish parliament, and in the suppression of the Irish parliament in 1800 by an Act of the Westminster parliament. None the less, when Great Britain became the United Kingdom it was, in political as well as cultural reality, a union state and not a unitary state as the political-science textbooks of twenty years ago happily asserted. The pressure from the English side to incorporate Scotland came almost entirely from fear that the Scottish parliament might recognize a different heir to the throne of the two kingdoms, hence civil war. The pressure from the Scottish side for what they/we still call the Treaty of Union came from the same fear of a Catholic Jacobite attempt at restoration, hence civil war. But the Scottish commissioners drove a hard bargain. It was not, as in nationalist mythology, a corrupt surrender, though some bribery there was, as ever.[17] The parliament was less important then to Scottish sentiment and identity than were the independence and establishment of the Kirk and the retention of Scots law and legal institutions. But after 1707 parliament became securely the British national institution and its sovereignty was a guarantee to Lowland Scots and Protestant Irish that they would more likely die in bed than by fighting barbaric Highland or wild Irish Gaelic-speaking Catholic tribesman. Parliamentary sovereignty went with the new civility and politeness, specifically the English cult of the gentleman, which began to travel far.[18] But it was a sovereignty that had to know its limits.

The main business of English politics became holding the new United Kingdom together. A curious mixture of affable conciliation and latent threat emerged. There was no attempt to anglicize the Scots, and only spasmodically, half-heartedly and pessimistically the Irish; and Scotland's distinct civil society continued, indeed flourished, in the eighteenth century both in commerce and the arts. The Scottish enlightenment became one of the glories of Europe and the First British Empire. In Ireland the penal laws against Catholics were loosely enforced, and Dublin came near to rivalling Edinburgh in civility. But when the power of the state or the safety of property was threatened, the toleration of the English – that Montesquieu and Voltaire so praised and envied – gave way to stern coercion or penal counter-violence, as in 1745, 1798 and the repression of the Indian Mutiny. Perhaps one is tolerant only when one is not greatly threatened and is secure in one's own identity.

The sovereign parliament of Blackstone's day, however, got Russell's two senses of power badly confused, as did Blackstone himself; and with well-known practical consequences. To be unchallengeable in law did not mean that legislative intentions would always work. The Stamp Act on the American Colonies provoked civil disobedience and could not be enforced. Prudently the Act was repealed, but together with a Declaratory Act asserting in principle that parliament was sovereign and so had the right to tax. Then unwisely a further attempt was made, this time on a narrower front, via the Townsend Duties, creating *inter alia* a seemingly far easier target than printed papers: tea.

Consider this part of Edmund Burke's great speech 'On American Taxation':

> Seek peace and ensure it – leave America, if she has taxable matter in her, to tax herself. I am not here going into distinctions of rights, nor attempting to mark their boundaries. I do not enter into these metaphysical distinctions; I hate the very sound of them. ... Do not burden them by taxes; you were not used to do so from the beginning. Let this be your reason for not taxing. These are the arguments of states and kingdoms. Leave the rest to the schools; for there only may they be discussed with safety. But if, intemperately, unwisely, fatally, you sophisticate and poison the very source of government, by urging subtle deductions, and consequences odious to those you govern, from the unlimited and illimitable nature of supreme

sovereignty, you will teach them by these means to call that sovereignty into question. When you drive him hard, the boar will surely turn upon the hunters. If that sovereignty and their freedom cannot be reconciled, which will they take? They will cast your sovereignty in your face. Nobody will be argued into slavery.[19]

And the next year he summed up this advice in one of the great dictums of the Western political tradition: 'The question ... is not whether you have a right to render your people miserable; but whether it is not your interest to make them happy.'[20]

That is true politics, and can 'move my heart like the sound of trumpets'. But the head must note that Burke did not give one inch on what was by then to the colonists the crucial question of whether sovereignty could be made less than 'unlimited and illimitable'. Burke believed, as much as Hobbes, Blackstone and Lord North believed, that sovereignty was not just a matter of definition but was, indeed, 'an absolute power, which must in all governments reside somewhere' – an empirical reality, even though one to be applied prudently, politically, with respect for custom and tradition. Today Scotland is getting a devolved parliament with considerable statutory power. But these powers cannot, as some demanded, be entrenched, be removed from the legal competence of some future parliament. Parliament is, indeed, legally so sovereign that in law it cannot bind its successors.[21]

We should not ignore that even in the 1760s and 1770s there were still other authoritative opinions. William Pitt, Lord Chatham, former Prime Minister and the great impresario of the Seven Years' War, dragged himself to parliament to protest that both the Stamp Act and the Declaratory Act were illegal, were unconstitutional! He believed, as did his former Lord Chancellor, Lord Camden, that the ancient constitution of the realm and our common law had no place for taxation without direct consent.[22] The *New Oxford History of England* calls him a demagogue.[23] Indeed, but demagogues paddle in the warm shallows of popular opinion. Yet it was, in vote after vote, a minority opinion in parliament itself. The English governing class by then really believed in their bones with Blackstone that without sovereignty it was anarchy. Only the young Jeremy Bentham, in his first book (*A Fragment on Government* of 1776), had sarcastically asked Blackstone if he thought that in Dutch provinces or Swiss cantons 'there is no such thing as government'.[24] When an

American federal government appeared to be working, English Tory opinion in the early nineteenth century was sure that it was inherently unstable; and the Establishment grunted, 'told you so' at the time of the War Between the States. And in the latter part of the nineteenth century, and again in the 1950s, the Colonial Office was prodigal in writing federal constitutions for the self-government of former colonies; but that was for the colonials and the indigenous others, not for the native British – except in Gladstone's crazed imagination when he raised the cry of 'Home Rule all round' after the defeat of his Ireland Act in 1886. Crazed or not, this became the official policy of the Liberal Party from Asquith's time to the present – quasi-federalism at least, certainly a pluralistic repudiation of, or at least significant modification of, sovereignty theory. But John Pocock was moved in to tell assembled British and American historians magisterially that the history of political thought showed that 'the language of federation and confederation was profoundly alien to British discourse, and has remained so'.[25] At the time he spoke in 1994 federalism had become the 'F' word of John Major's government, seeing the federal project in Europe as the threat of a 'super-power', not the reassurance of a negotiated division of powers; and they feared that Labour's Scottish project would lead to the break-up of the United Kingdom (what he bizarrely called 'the end of a thousand years of British history'). Like others he believed that the strongest form of state must be a unitary national sovereign state (not noticing that the United Kingdom had never been one). Like so many he confused autonomy with real power; and like his predecessor he often confused English with British, both verbally and, if I may use the term, intellectually.

IV

Now I turn to my fourth and final claim: that Britain is a multi-national state pretending to be a unitary state. Just as the claim to a supreme sovereignty is always a kind of bluff, depending on good political judgment and calculated restraint in exercising power, so also the claim that the concept 'British' denotes a full-blown 'nationality' constitutes a kind of bluff or, as I will suggest, a very interesting half-truth.

Apply a bibliographical test to a cultural matter: look under 'nationalism' in the subject catalogue of any great library. One will find under sub-headings American, Italian, French, German,

Polish, Hungarian and so on and on, certainly Irish, Scottish and Welsh; but until very recently (within this decade) almost nothing under 'English', only a handful of ultra-patriotic books about the defeat of the Spanish Armada in 1588 or the Empire from 1870 to 1914 etc., apparently written for use as school prizes for not very bright boys in private schools. Under 'British' you would have found books on political history or sociology, but on national culture or national character virtually nothing worth taking seriously. Orwell was thought eccentric, as a man of the Left, to write in 1946 *The English People*, a celebration and a democratic-socialist interpretation of the national character. In the original version of 1941, *The Lion and the Unicorn*, his real Englishman had appeared as radical and revolutionary.[26]

Why did so few English writers, novelists apart, address themselves seriously to the question of English identity? Precisely because, I argue, after 1707, when Great Britain had become the United Kingdom as a multi-national state, part of the art of governing it and holding it together for nearly three centuries has been an almost deliberate suppression by the English majority of an explicit English nationalism in case it appeared as provocative triumphalism. There are two sides to this coin. There was what even an anglophile Boston Brahmin like A. L. Lowell once called 'a certain condescension of the English', not merely to foreigners but also to the other nationals of the British Isles, sometimes forgetful of their presence, pride and peculiarities. But there was also a tradition in the old English governing class of statecraft by conciliation and compromise. Lord North was unimpressed by that Irish *arriviste* Edmund Burke's reading of the English genius as one for prudence and prescription, but most nineteenth-century Tories were. William Hazlitt gibed that their only idea of wisdom was saying 'ditto to Mr Burke', but himself said of Burke that in 'unfolding one great error he illuminated a hundred truths'. So the development of an explicit state-cult of English nationalism in the nineteenth century would have been counter-productive, at the very time when nationalism swept through almost everywhere else in Europe: when Mazzini's writings were on the shelves of all liberals in Britain and Garibaldi's bust was next on the mantelpiece to Kossuth's; and when Lincoln pioneered the nationalist rhetoric of 'the Union, above all else, the Union'.

An English nationalism would have frustrated reconciliation with Scotland in the early nineteenth century (after the Civil Wars of the seventeenth century and the later Jacobite risings) and made impossible the attempted conciliation of Ireland (a story not of unrelieved oppression but of oscillation between coercion and conciliation – as Irish historians now relate).[27] The Old Tories understood well that since 1688 the main business of government has been holding the United Kingdom together. For that purpose the English ideology of parliamentary sovereignty arose, and the union was a parliamentary union; but an explicit English nationalism would have been an irritant. The English dominated parliament, but the governing elite was not a closed elite: it was open to the rich and the well-connected, as well as to talented adventurers and social climbers (like Edmund Burke), both from the other three nations and from the other classes. 'Politics', intoned Dr Johnson, 'is but a rising in the world.'

A positive cultural politics was practised: when George IV became the first Hanoverian monarch to visit Scotland, once and briefly, the cabinet commissioned Sir Walter Scott to produce the show. At a state banquet in Edinburgh Castle the king actually wore, to the ribald delight of satirical cartoonists, the kilt (albeit over warm, pink tights).[28] Victoria's children wore the tartan plaid, and the old lady came to like living in Scotland where the young woman had been 'requested' by the Prime Minister, Lord Melbourne, *pour raison d'etat* 'to spend an appreciable part of the year'; and in Ireland the children of viceroys wore the green, just as in India the Old Tories had fought off the ambitions of the Benthamite radicals employed by John Company to attempt a uniform, rational and secular administration of the whole subcontinent.[29] The Old Tories, to give the devils their due, had some empathy with native cultures. Indirect rule through existing divisions had been practised, until the Stamp Act, in the North American Colonies even before India. 'Divide and rule' was always a half-truth at best: the general political tactic (which de Tocqueville saw as such a startling contrast between the French and the British colonies) was to govern through existing divisions. The Old Tory, unlike the Liberals and his modern successors, had something of a taste for cultural diversity – part romantic, part cynical.

What is he arguing? No English nationalism! Yes, and no. Something bigger and better emerged as a state-cult: imperialism. For imperialism was open to each of the nations of the British Isles at every social level. Scots and Irish younger sons of impoverished gentry families were disproportionately active as empire builders, and exploiters; and Paddys and Jocks disproportionate among the Squaddies. The sense of state was far stronger in the Colonial Office than in the humdrum Home Office. Certainly, there had been a determined attempt to create a sense of British national identity, and certainly that sense exists – but only in a narrow and specific context, seldom understood at home or abroad. It does not describe a general culture in the way that 'France' and 'French' became inextricably bonded after the Revolution. Linda Colley confuses this point in her otherwise brilliant book, widely praised but worthy of serious criticism, *Britons*.[30]

After the Act of Union, Colley says, a sense of British nationalism was invented and propagated precisely to bind English and Scots together (she excludes Ireland from her thesis, since as usual it does not fit). Scots were to became North Britons. Further, she argues, this deliberate propaganda caught on: the new British nationalism was popular. The long wars against France and the popular fear of Catholicism, both identified with tyranny, wooden shoes and autocracy, created among all classes a popular Protestant–British nationalism. That is true, up to a point. But many of us are not convinced that the sense in which she and we are British covers as many aspects of life as does 'English', 'Scottish', 'Welsh' or 'Irish'. Most eighteenth-century Scots did not come to think of themselves as 'Britons' except when singing patriotic theatre songs. Folk songs were Scottish through and through and in braid Scots, as were the poems of Burns and Fergusson, needing glossaries as well as some political and moral expurgation in early London editions. And Burns, of course, could be bilingual when the bread, or an actress, was to be buttered. Most of Linda Colley's fellow historians are not convinced. Her account of the Court party campaign to enhance Britishness broke new ground, and is vivid and accurate; and her account of the circumstances that helped the campaign is suggestive, but as the editors of a symposium conclude:

> one should beware of pushing the argument too far: one should not confuse a patriot rhetoric of Britishness, forged or deployed in wartime, with a pervasive or persistent sense of Britishness as a primary or normative identity. British Unionism worked precisely because it depended not on the creation of a hegemonic British identity but on the availability of institutions and symbols which offered a means of identity with Britain.[31]

Like Sir Walter Scott, most Scots were strong unionists (still are, if the word had not been body-snatched by the Conservative Party), were loyal to the dynasty and the state, but had no doubt whatever that they were Scottish and proud of it and strongly protective towards uniquely Scottish institutions (institutions, moreover, entrenched, so they believed, in the Act or Treaty of Union). Patriotic loyalty was and is given to the British state but not to a British national culture or national identity, unless that culture or identity is seen – here is the half-truth in Colley – in much narrower terms than is usually meant by 'nation' and 'nationalism'.

'British' to me implies the union itself, the laws, the crown and parliament. But there is a lot of society and human life beyond those pillars of the state. The crown is still a very important element in the unity and identity of the United Kingdom, if only because, unlike in most other systems of representative government, there is no constitution to respect or worship – parliament by itself is too partisan and too prone to the kind of disrespect that even an actual royal family can well earn. Scottish loyalty to the union state was real, but it was highly and sensibly tempered and utilitarian, not emotionally nationalistic. The union and the sovereignty of parliament guaranteed peace, Protestantism, law and order and free trade. The head was British but the heart remained guid Scots.

Most Scots today live reasonably happily with a sense of dual nationality, as do most Welsh; and they express it as being Scottish/Welsh *and* British. Similarly with the large numbers of Irish settled in mainland Britain. Only in Northern Ireland is there a bitter split of primary identification. But when Loyalists insist that they are British and not Irish, they are making a very clear political and legal identification, not claiming, far from it, in the least to be English in culture – everything that Hegel called *Sittlichkeit*, Montesquieu called *moeurs* or the American sociologist Giddings called 'folkways and mores'. Indeed Loyalist activists distrust the English intensely and often use the same Australian expletive as nationalists, 'Brits' (often with a strengthening adjective). So linguistically that word is not self-referential to Loyalists but is a term of art including Scots as well as English, or even Welsh when Plaid Cymru is unwise enough to say anything about 'the damnable question', which shrewdly they rarely do.

It is significant that fellow citizens from the new Commonwealth call themselves (and are being called) 'Black Britons' or 'Black British', but rarely if ever 'Black English', 'Black Welsh' or 'Black

Scots'. The new Britons have a clearer sense than most of the English that being a British citizen does not and need not imply assimilation to a common English culture, but only a common allegiance and a pragmatic, utilitarian sense of obligation to a British culture of civil rights and duties, of protection and obligation, something that is not a culture in the full nationalistic and sociological senses. There has never been a positive movement to 'anglicize the immigrant', just as there never was to anglicize the Scots or, in modern times, the Welsh, but only a negative and mean-minded foot-dragging by recent Conservative ministers against multi-cultural education in the common schools.

Perhaps the theory of national sovereignty in its strong historical sense has had its day in the British Isles as elsewhere in Europe, even in the seemingly benign and highly flexible sense of parliamentary sovereignty. Sovereignty theory was a response to a past need when the minimization of the chances of violent death depended on a central enforcement of peace in the three kingdoms whose economies and peoples were, and still are, inextricably intermingled, and where different senses of national identity existed in a tension that was not always 'creative'. Gross political blunders led to the constitutional severance of what became the Republic of Ireland, not any ethnic inevitability of 'Ireland one Island' or Parnell's quasi-Hegelian 'march of a nation' – except, of course, that people who thought of themselves as Irish came to want it so; and those same blunders made partition so bloody: the manner of which is to be faulted rather than, as supported by large majorities in all three countries or regions at the time, its expediency.

For the Scots and the Welsh the sovereign power of parliament could be tolerated or enjoyed not by virtue of any great enthusiasm for the constitutionless constitution, but by what Burke had vainly urged as policy on the American question: the former 'wise and salutary neglect', the restraint of potential power. Perhaps more than that. To repeat, the Old Tories had a sense of history and a traditional knowledge that the main business of British politics was that of holding the four nations peaceably together in the (or as a) United Kingdom, a union, not a unitary state, in political fact if not in law. Critics have turned Colley on her head. 'The British state was able to function without Britishness ever having been a necessary primary identity'.[32] But the New (suburban) Conservatives have little sense of history, only of something Neal Ascherson shrewdly identified as 'heritage'; so in the general election of 1997 they lost all their Scottish seats by the pig-headed integrity of pretending or believing that a subsidiary Scottish parliament threatens the union and plays into the hands of separatists (which is possibly what they themselves were doing). Consider the astonishing xenophobia that still then raged among many Conservative MPs and ministers towards Europe. Perhaps we are paying the price of the old suppression of a legitimate concern with a reasonable clarity about English national consciousness; so that now it can express itself in negative terms only. It is the English who find it hard to distinguish clearly between 'British' and 'English'.[33] Only in Northern Ireland did the Conservatives pursue their old pragmatic flexibility and show little respect for the over-priced antique shibboleth of sovereignty.

Consider the terms of the Northern Ireland Constitution Act, 1973 – repeated in the so-called Anglo-Irish Agreement of November 1985:

> It is hereby declared that Northern Ireland remains part of Her Majesty's dominions and the United Kingdom, and it is hereby affirmed that in no event will Northern Ireland or any part of it cease to be part of Her Majesty's dominions and of the United Kingdom without the consent of a majority of the people of Northern Ireland voting in a poll held for the purpose of this section and in accordance with Schedule 1 of this Act.

Small wonder that British Irish are a wee bit touchy at times. By statute and an international agreement they are not a normal or integral part of the United Kingdom; they are only a conditional part. They feel betrayed. But did they really believe that sovereignty was inalienable, that the sovereign body, which is not the nation but parliament, might not modify the terms of its sovereignty as in the Anglo-Irish Agreement and as in the Europe Act?

V

Professor Pocock has seen these matters not as political flexibility but as indicators of the near collapse of British identity. He has cast doubt that the very concept of Europe was meaningful, or – in a notable article three years ago entitled 'History and Sovereignty' – constant enough to be lived with honourably. He said that his native New Zealand's identity lay in a reciprocal relationship with Britain and Britishness, and that Britain by her decision to withdraw from it unilaterally to become a European state 'left it clear that those who took it did not respect us and at least doubtful what room they had left for respecting themselves'.[34] To speak personally, I do not lose self-respect by feeling somewhat European, as well as British, English and, by residence and political conviction, Scottish, with half-Welsh children. We can both compound and coexist with, indeed enjoy, many identities.[35] Certainly I cannot extend much respect for those of my fellow English who pretended to belong to an imperial power too long after most of the former empire wanted it, and long after our economic power either warranted or wanted it. Nostalgia in politics corrupts good judgment and often turns nasty. On the contrary, we should have been in Europe from the beginning. So I could not in honesty let pass Pocock's remark about 'respect', even though I respect him greatly as a scholar.

But as a scholar my interest is less in our differences of political judgment and allegiance than in explicating the very broad account of sovereignty on which John Pocock bases this complaint against the Brits. The assumption to be made is that national historiography is the meaning of the state; for it defines the national community in terms of its sovereignty, its history and the problematics of that sovereignty, and the individual in terms of his or her participation in, subjection to or aspiration after that sovereignty and its history. The question to be asked is: what becomes of such a historiography, and the identity it offers the individual, when sovereignty is to be modified, fragmented or abandoned?[36] I am much puzzled. The common-sense answer to these two questions seems to me fairly obvious. History has to change to follow events, and identities do not necessarily depend on either historiography or state formations: nationalists claim far too much. I had thought that John Pocock's demand, with which I began, for a British not an English history, was a demand, which I hope to follow, to write British history as the interrelations of four nations, not the history of an imagined single sovereign state called 'Britain'.

I find my identity in those interrelations – how they modify but never destroy, how they build upon my own Englishness. But, of course, I recognize that the proportions of the mix will vary in us all, and I believe that anyone who does not recognize some mix in his or her make-up is either insensitive and ignorant, or perhaps as cleverly perverse as only a great scholar can be. Britishness is not a full cultural identity: it is qualified loyalty – as all political loyalties should be among free men and women – to a set of political and legal arrangements. Even when sovereignty is completely abandoned (as by the Scots in 1707), national identity can continue.[37] But all this fortifies the suspicion that the whole theory of sovereignty is reaching the end of its useful shelf-life in the very Europe that begat it in the seventeenth century. It no longer describes or explains political reality. Pocock's important and praiseworthy demand that there should be a British history of relationships, not four separate national histories or, worst of all (as was so common, and as is still not rare), an Anglocentric one, has become prescriptive in his recent writings and, as such, is dangerously close to a new comprehensive British historiographical hegemony tied to an old-fashioned and loosely defined sovereignty theory; and tied also to a concept of Britishness, born in the imperial era, that now makes only historical and (for New Zealand especially) cultural sense.[38]

One last but important cadenza: national identities even in Northern Ireland are not merely politically divided, but divide most individuals. Northern Ireland inevitably faces both ways, and inwards to itself. There is no possible solution at all if two states and rival armed movements adhere rigidly to conventional sovereignty theory as the only stable and legitimate form of government. Dublin and London understand this better than do the IRA and UDA in Belfast, and are moving towards some kind of bi-communal government and joint authority even though they still speak the language and rhetoric of sovereignty.[39] Sovereignty theory may be dwindling in some regions of the world, notably our own, into a lament for an irrecoverable past that hinders our ability to live decently in the present while wearing clothes that still fit. Perhaps, after all, the young Harold Laski was right when he argued, against Hobbesian, Blackstonian, Leninist, Fabian and – by implication – most nationalist traditions, that 'all power is federal'. If that conclusion is still too theoretical for some historians, let me at least assert that the sovereignty claimed by the parliamentary union state has proved so flexible as to be almost unbelievable. Political compromise is ever the driving force.

Notes

1   This essay began life in a slender form as a lecture, 'Sovereignty and Identity in the British Isles', given in December 1995, at the Woodrow Wilson Center, Washington DC, and issued as No. 10 in their Historical, Cultural and Literary Studies series. I am indebted to the centre for

a year's fellowship to work on a larger study of the interrelations of the four nations of the British Isles.

2 J. G. A. Pocock set the ball rolling in two key articles: 'British History: a Plea for a New Subject', *Journal of Modern History* (1975), pp. 601–28; and 'The Limits and Divisions of British History' (1975), *American Historical Review* (1982), pp. 311–36. Others were thinking on the same lines, notably Hugh F. Kearney in his *The British Isles: a History of Four Nations* (Cambridge: CUP, 1989), although he objected to the title Cambridge University Press put upon his work because, he says, 'four nations' is for most of the whole period of historical knowledge a gross and misleading modern nationalist anachronism. Subsequently much work has appeared on this integrative theme. An especially good gathering is R. A. Mason (ed.) *Scots and Britons: Scottish Political Thought and the Union of 1603* (Cambridge: CUP, 1994). Something of the same kind was attempted for contemporary politics, with mixed results, in B. Crick (ed.) *National Identities: the Constitution of the United Kingdom* (Oxford: Blackwell, 1991). In 1994 the Anglo-American conference at the Institute of Historical Research for the first time ever astoundingly stayed in plenary session for the whole conference to consider the theme 'The Making of the United Kingdom'. From that came a book, A. Grant and K. J. Stringer (eds) *Uniting the Kingdom: the Making of British History* (London: Routledge, 1995), which was just beaten into print by S. G. Ellis and S. Barber (eds) *Conquest and Union: Fashioning a British State, 1485–1725* (London: Longman, 1995), original essays by leading historians, but also showing that a textbook publisher for students and schools sees all this as more than a fashion likely to fade. A variation on the theme, less even in quality than the last two books but interesting that it happened there and at all, is R. G. Asch (ed.), *Three Nations: A Common History? England, Scotland, Ireland and British History c. 1660–1920* (Bochum: Brockmeyer, 1993); and just published as I revise this is L. Brockliss and D. Eastwood (eds) *A Union of Multiple Identities: the British Isles, c.1750–c.1850* (Manchester: MUP, 1997).

3 J. Morrill, 'The Fashioning of Britain', in Ellis and Barber (eds) *Conquest and Union*, p. 9.

4 T. Hobbes, *Leviathan*, ed. Richard Tuck (Cambridge: CUP, 1991 edn), Ch. 18, p. 127.

5 As had been done in the Declaratory Act of 1766 following the backing down from actual use of power in the repeal of the Stamp Act; and as recently in the White Paper *Scotland's Parliament*, Cm 3658 (1997), which roundly declares that 'the UK Parliament is and will remain sovereign', as it gives away or devolves more power to the new parliament than any of the American states or German Länder possess in legally federal systems.

6 G. Jones (ed.) *The Sovereignty of the Law: Selections from Blackstone's Commentaries on the Laws of England* (London: Macmillan, 1973), pp. 71–2.

7 B. P. Levack, *The Formation of the British State* (Oxford: Clarendon Press, 1987).

8 J. Wormald, 'The Union of 1603' in Mason (ed.) *Scots and Britons*.

9 H. Morgan, *Tyrone's Rebellion: the Outbreak of the Nine Years War in Tudor Ireland* (Belfast: Boydell Press, 1993).

10 The late Elie Kedourie, in his *Nationalism* (London: Praeger, 1961 edn), may still be closer to what nationalists think of as nationalism than are several more recent sociological accounts of its origins, as in Ernest Gellner and Anthony Smith, and he never confuses national consciousness with nationalism. E. Hobsbawm, *Nations and Nationalism Since 1780* (Cambridge: CUP, 1992), is more illuminating on the invention and manipulation of nationalism for purposes of rule.

11 C. Russell, *The Causes of the English Civil War*.

12 Quoted in G. Marshall, *Parliamentary Sovereignty and the Commonwealth* (Oxford: Clarendon Press, 1957), pp. 47–8.

13 J. Pocock and G. J. Schochet, 'Interregnum and Restoration', in J. Pocock (ed.), *The Varieties of British Political Thought, 1500–1800* (Cambridge: CUP, 1993), p. 149.

14 Ibid., pp. 150–1.

15 E. Gellner, *Cause and Meaning in the Social Sciences* (London: Routledge, 1971), on P. Winch, *The Idea of a Social Science and its Relation to Philosophy* (London: Routledge, 1967).

16 B. Russell, *Power: a New Social Analysis* (London: Routledge, 1938).

17 See J. Robertson (ed.) *A Union for Empire: Political Thought and the Union of 1707* (Cambridge: CUP, 1995), especially the editor's 'Empire and Union: Two Concepts of the Early Modern European Order', pp. 3–36, and his 'An Elusive Sovereignty: the Course of the Union Debate in Scotland, 1698–1707', pp. 198–227.

18 Remarkably little of any depth has been written on the English cult of the gentleman despite its obvious role in assimilating 'others' to an existing elite, the political entailments of its values, and its relation to ideas of 'Englishness'. I offer some speculations in my 'The Sense of Identity of the Indigenous British', *New Community*, 21, 2 (1995), pp. 176–9.

19 From the speech 'On American Taxation' of 19 April 1774, as in M. Beloff (ed.) *The Debate on the American Revolution* (London: A. & C. Black, 1960 edn), pp. 218–19.

20 Ibid., p. 224.

21 B. Crick, 'The Sovereignty of Parliament and the Scottish Question', in N. Lewis (ed.) *Happy and Glorious: the Constitution in Transition* (Milton Keynes: Open University Press, 1990); and his 'The Scotland Act 1998' in *Political Quarterly* (October 1995), pp. 237–49.

22 Beloff, *Debate on the American Revolution*, pp. 120–1 and 190–3.

23 P. Langford, *A Polite and Commercial People: England, 1727–1783* (Oxford: Clarendon Press, 1989), p. 339.

24 J. Bentham, *A Fragment on Government*, ed. F. C. Montague (Oxford: OUP, 1931 edn), p. 70.

25 'Contingency, Identity, Sovereignty', the closing address to the IHR Conference and the last chapter in Grant and Stringer (eds.) *Uniting the Kingdom*, p. 294.

26 G. Orwell, *The Lion and the Unicorn* (London: Secker & Warburg, 1941). See also E. P. Thompson's 'The Peculiarities of the English' in his *The Poverty of Theory and Other Essays* (London: Merlin, 1978).

27 As in Roy Foster's masterly *Modern Ireland, 1600–1972* (London: Allen Lane, 1988).

28 J. Prebble, *The King's Jaunt: George IV in Scotland, 1822* (London: Fontana, 1989). This was no small matter since the kilt had been proscribed after the '45 rebellion. Scott reinvented and standardized it with vigorous imagination: the very symbol of rebellion, lawlessness and barbarism became patriotic Lowlanders' 'party dress', and they all became Celts at a touch of his romantic wand.

29 E. Stokes, *The English Utilitarians and India* (Oxford: Clarendon Press, 1959).

30 L. Colley, *Britons: Forging the Nation, 1707–1837* (New Haven, CT, and London: Yale University Press, 1992).

31 See 'Conclusion' in Brockliss and Eastwood (eds.) *A Union of Multiple Identities*; also B. Crick, 'Essay on Britishness', *Scottish Affairs*, vol. 2 (Winter 1993), pp. 71–83, mainly a review of Colley.

32 Brockliss and Eastwood (eds.) *A Union of Multiple Identities*, p. 196.

33 B. Crick, 'The English and the British', in Crick (ed.) *National Identities*.

34 J. Pocock, 'Some Europes in Their History', lecture given at the Woodrow Wilson Center, September 1995 (from which copies are obtainable).

35 As so lucidly and firmly argued by the historian of Scotland T. C. Smout, in 'Perspectives on the Scottish Identity', *Scottish Affairs*, vol. 6 (Winter 1994), pp. 101–13, including a diagram of seven concentric loyalties, each of which can be cross-cut by eight 'social characteristic loyalties'.

36 J. Pocock, 'History and Sovereignty: the Historiographical Response to Europeanization in Two British Cultures', *Journal of British Studies*, vol. 31 (1992), pp. 358–89; and see also his concluding essay to Grant and Stringer (eds.) *Uniting the Kingdom*.

37 As convincingly argued by L. Paterson in his *The Autonomy of Modern Scotland* (Edinburgh: EUP, 1994). The survival of Scottish national consciousness does not depend on having a parliament. Paterson has supported the devolution or home-rule movement strongly, but primarily for democratic rather than nationalist reasons.

38 Asch (ed.) *Three Nations* includes 'A Sceptical Comment' by Scottish historian Keith Brown, pp. 117–28, who invokes some Irish support to resist being swallowed by a 'Pocockian monster', however nice it is, he says, for the 'Anglo-American historical establishment' at last to take Irish, Scottish and Welsh history seriously. There is a middle position. One can welcome Pocock's historiographical prescription, while resisting strongly the unexpected political use he puts it to, and also doubt that historiography is always as determinate as he makes it in shaping national identities. Also several voices from 'the periphery' pointed out at the IHR Conference that his prescription works better for political and economic history than for social history.

39 See B. Crick, 'Why the Northern Ireland Peace Process Must Take So Long', *American Foreign Policy Interests*, 18, 3 (June 1996), pp. 9–16, a lecture delivered at Ireland House, New York University, to the National Committee on American Foreign Policy.

Chapter 10

Nations, states and religions[1]

Ernest Gellner

When I first wrote on nationalism, in a book which had one chapter devoted to that topic, it was reviewed in the *Irish Times*. The reviewer made two comments on the book. One was: 'This man has struck a gallant blow for freedom from English grammar.' The other was: 'This man has had the presumption to write about nationalism without mentioning Ireland.' I quote these remarks from memory. Well, I will not try here to remedy the first of these defects, but I will try to remedy the second. I will not refer directly to Ireland, but I will talk about other things which are selected for parallels or for contrasts with Ireland.

I begin by summarizing as briefly as I can what I think nationalism is about. Nationalism is concerned with the transition from an earlier condition of mankind, when high culture was a speciality and a privilege, to a new condition when high culture becomes universalized and pervades entire societies. I hope I need not stress that when I say 'high' and 'low' in this context I am not in any way evaluating or offering a value assessment; the terms are used in a technical sense. Low culture is something transmitted in the course of life from generation to generation, simply by inserting a person into the society in which he thereafter lives and letting him acclimatize to it. High culture is high in the sense that it is linked to writing, is formally coded and is transmitted by specialists. This distinction between low and high culture is pervasive in what might be called the more advanced agrarian societies, and it leads to a situation of tension in which there is a differentiation between the small, leading, aristocratic or clerical or administrative stratum which is privileged with high culture, and the rest of society which does not have that privilege.

Now something funny happens on the way to modern society, where suddenly a high culture becomes universalized, when universal literacy and education become the political norm, a moral imperative which is not only preached, but is actually *practised*. It is unique among liberal and humane values in that it is widely respected both by authorities and by populations, unlike the other norms which are often asserted and frequently violated. But education is *genuinely* respected. Now I think there are very deep reasons for this, which have nothing to do with the rhetoric according to which education makes one a more complete person, but have a great deal to do with the way modern society actually functions: namely, through semantic, non-physical, work. First, work is communication with anonymous interlocutors, with innumerable anonymous partners, and it is no longer the application of brawn to matter. Second, because it is based upon economic growth, modern society is committed to occupational instability, and to having its members eligible for *any* post, because they are indeed liable to be moved. They are no longer locked into tiny stabilized sub-communities. These two things between them – occupational instability and the semanticization of work – require people to be socialized into a standard and codified idiom so that they can understand each other's messages, and replace one another in any given slot. End of argument.

The implications are that literacy, and the capacity to understand and emit complex messages, are no longer privileges, but preconditions of all the other privileges and, indeed, of participation itself. In consequence, an individual's most important investment and possession is mastery of, and acceptability to, a given high culture. What really matters for all of us is that the society in which we live, which has one standard idiom, should work in the same idiom as the one we have mastered; and that one should possess the general characteristics which make one acceptable within that particular cultural pool. Those two conditions satisfied, life can be quite reasonable. Those two conditions unsatisfied, the most one can hope for is some kind of subordinate and unprestigious position at the bottom of the social ladder – and probably a life of humiliation. *Ergo*, if for some reason there is no convergence between one's own culture and the culture which surrounds one, then one has every reason to try to set it right, and there are a number of ways of doing this – there is assimilation, if one is allowed to do so; there is migration; or there is the option of becoming a nationalist, and trying to change the political boundaries of the unit in which you live. So much by way of summary.

I have reformulated my argument in a way which stresses the changing role of high culture. To put it another way, in traditional agrarian society the main requirement of culture is that it be differentiated, and that it marks, confirms, externalizes and internalizes status. The main requirement of advanced society is that it be homogeneous, and that it mark the boundary of a total political unit, rather than mark nuances of status within it. There is a puzzle at this point; and here I am simply sharing bewilderment because I do not have a very clear answer to it. Why, if I am right in singling out this as the main undercurrent of the passage to modern society, does it manifest itself as nationalism in Europe and some other regions, and as fundamentalism in the world of Islam, and possibly some other regions too? It can have either of these two expressions. The transitions have the same logic. What I do not understand is why it should go one way in one place and another way elsewhere.

What is the difference between fundamentalism and nationalism? Well, both of them, on my account, involve transition to the dominance of a high culture, but the transition takes different forms. In the case of nationalism the culture is a vernacular, which becomes codified, and becomes used by a pervasive democracy. What had been a vernacular becomes a codified high culture, but is dissociated from any particular religious doctrine. By contrast, with fundamentalism the very opposite happens: the old reason for valuing a high culture is maintained (its link to a revealed and authoritative doctrine being underscored), while the link to a specific ethnic group is not emphasized.

Now the major transformation under the impact of the same processes in the Muslim world over the last 100 years has been a shift from low to high culture. Islam, a century ago, was, for an urban elite of scholars, a sober, unitarian, scriptural faith, codified in doctrine and linked to certain prescriptions. But for the mass of believers who identified enthusiastically with the faith, but who had no access to literacy and little taste for sober scriptural study, Islam was a set of rituals, questionably orthodox, linked to worship of saints. Basically it meant the use of saintly mediators who were revered and worshipped, and the heightening of consciousness through participation in ritual. The astonishing transformation of Islam in the last 100 years, which the West only began to notice with the Iranian Revolution, is really this phenomenon: the shift from a low culture of religious practice to a high-culture variant. Underneath that shift, there are basically the same changes: the erosion of closed local groups, and the creation of a more extensive market; political and economic centralization; the incorporation of erstwhile members of local groups in extensive units, politically and economically centralized. This, as far as I can see, has propelled Muslims from folk Islam to high Islam, and turned them in that fundamentalist direction which is the major cultural feature of that world, and which makes Islam a striking exception to the otherwise more or less valid secularization thesis, which asserts that under modern conditions religion loses much of its political clout.

Now in Europe this has not happened. There is obviously some kind of link between the puritanical elements of scripturalism and nationalism. One person who treated this issue was Bernard Shaw. He depicts Joan as condemned to be burnt as a Protestant by the Church and as a nationalist by the English. The interesting question is, why have the two not stayed together? I am not very clear why the same process – mobilizing the population, atomization, creating the conditions for a standard and codified culture – should lead to secular nationalism, on the whole, in Europe, and elsewhere to a fundamentalism, which may indeed have nationalistic overtones, but where the fundamentalism predominates. I have no clear answer to that question. A purely historical answer, in terms of timing, I do not find very satisfactory.

And then, if you accept this general diagnosis – that modern conditions make for cultural homogenization – there is a parting of the ways. A country may be fortunate and, under modern conditions, develop a territorial nationalism: an enthusiastic identification with a geographic and historic unit where the defining conditions of membership are neither language nor religion but simply habitation of that territory. It does not happen often, but it does happen: we then see territorial nationalism which ignores internal differentiation. Examples would include Switzerland, Finland or indeed Scotland, where territorial identity is sufficient. There are other areas where the aspiration for a territorial nationalism was present, but failed.

For one of my case studies I will take a society which both resembles and is interestingly contrasted with Ireland, namely Bohemia. Now there the path from a legalistically pluralist society to its present conditions was complex and tortuous. I will offer a sketch. Any sketch of Czech history tends to face the difficulty that it is almost impossible to separate the two elements – what actually happened, and the way in which it is alleged to have happened – *subsequently* used in the process of nation-building, and in the creation of a homogeneous unit. For the earlier period it is very difficult to separate these elements. It begins as a Catholic country, which suffered from civil and religious turbulence. This occurred during the Hussite period, under the influence of the English theologian Wycliffe, and in conditions of internal tension which are connected with an early manifestation of nationalism. Here of course begins the dispute about what was happening. Was it some kind of proto-Reformation or, even better, some kind of proto-modern egalitarianism, of democracy, even some kind of proto-Enlightenment; or was it, on the contrary, a movement sunk deep in some kind of medieval spirituality? However, turbulence there was, culminating in a movement, primarily religious, the extreme wing of which certainly contained a messianic egalitarianism. In due course, it made a transition from moderate egalitarianism and successful self-defence, to a later stage of inward-looking pacifism and the total rejection of hierarchy – whether worldly or religious, it was seen by some as the work of the devil.

There followed two centuries of political instability, culminating in what can best be described as a Czech version of the Battle of the Boyne, except, of course, that it went the other way. This was followed by a curious non-resistance to the Catholic victory – curious if you accept later nationalist interpretations of the period. During the Czech Battle of the Boyne in 1620 there were still another twenty-eight years of the Thirty Years' War to go, with frequent incursions and temporary occupations by Protestant forces (notably by the Swedes); so that had there been the kind of resistance to that victory which later nationalist propaganda required, there were plenty of opportunities to mobilize and activate it. This did not in fact happen. The one major attempt at re-establishing Bohemian independence was done in the name neither of liberty nor of religion, but simply in the name of personal ambition and opportunism by a successful war-lord. There followed a period of what you might call post-Westphalian peace, with the acceptance of the *cuius regio eius religio* principle. This had curious consequences.

The long period of turbulence and the bloodbath of the Thirty Years' War seem to have eliminated a large part of the gentry, so that what remained was a peasantry without a gentry leadership. Hence the Czechs, when they emerged, with the Industrial Revolution, into modern Europe were not hampered, as were their neighbours the Magyars and the Poles, by an obsession with the values of the gentry. They were sober, hard-working, thrifty and curiously free of panache or display. The bigger estates went to the helpers of the victors in the religious wars, a mixed gang of international soldiers, opportunists, financiers and others who, because of their number and lack of local roots, rapidly became a kind of entrepreneurial aristocracy. They turned to estate management, so that the eventual success of Bohemia in the period of industrialization seems to have had good social roots: an entrepreneurial, opportunist aristocracy and a thrifty peasantry, who believed in work rather than in display – very much unlike their neighbours.

Then came the rebirth. It began towards the start of the eighteenth century in reaction to centralization and bureaucratization under the wave of enlightened centralism of Maria Theresa and Joseph II, which replaced Latin with German as the bureaucratic language, thereby making language and ethnicity relevant to a political and administrative career. The Church and the nascent local nationals were allies, so that contrary to subsequent accounts the national rebirth began in alliance with Catholicism, and with a rather different logic: we do not want centralization, we do not want the use of German; we want the local institutions maintained, and we want to restore our reputation; we want to restore our position in the world, and we want to restore it as good Catholics, rather than as heretics and Protestant rebels.

This picture does not fit with the developed self-image of the nationalists, but has been recently revived. However, this was replaced in the nineteenth century with what has become the classic Czech national self-image – the rediscovery of the Hussite rebels of the early fifteenth century: the central ruler is a Catholic, therefore we had better be something else. We were expressing egalitarian religious principles, so we were proto-social democrats as well as proto-Protestants, and this gives us our identity. So, under the impact of the rediscovery of this Hussite past, a new version of nationalism has emerged which dissociated itself from Catholicism, and which then finally got its expression and its political implementation in the work – both in the thought and the political activism – of Masaryk.

Now Masaryk has an interesting, not to say unique, place in the history of nationalism. There was nothing, absolutely nothing, Sinn Feinish about him – no self-sufficiency. On the contrary, he was very eager to justify his activity of recreating the historic Czech state in terms of a philosophy of world history, a world history which was to be universalistic, and which was to be pan-human, rather than in any nasty way chauvinistic. He clearly felt that there should be no state creation without philosophical justification. In that respect he certainly resembled the authors of the American Declaration of Independence. Seven years after he created the state, he published a book called, curiously enough, *World Revolution* – published in Czech in 1925. It had a different title in its English translation. The title was not a good one, in the sense of giving a good guide to the contents of the book. The book describes, in fact, how he went about the establishment of the new state during the First World War.

In a deeper sense, however, it was a very good title, because what he was really arguing was that his actions had not been undertaken capriciously. World history has a pattern. It is a shift from authoritarian and theocratic regimes to democratic and liberal ones. The new world was to be *intellectually* liberal, individualistic and universalistic, and *politically* liberal, democratic and participatory. We must join it, he reasoned, not because we are chauvinists, but because the Hapsburgs were not willing to go that way. He had some difficulty explaining why he had to raise his hand against the regime in which he had participated for so long and in which he had been a member of parliament – a regime which in many ways he knew not to be restrictive. He seized the opportunity without ever really getting the full support of his compatriots. The outstanding historian Pekar described in an obituary to Masaryk – he greatly respected him although as a historian he disagreed with him – how in 1916 he, Pekar, still took part in the ritual commemorating the death of Franz Joseph, and how all the teachers of Charles University of Prague were present – with two exceptions, two who were otherwise engaged. They were Masaryk and Benes, both abroad, engaged in high treason to Austria.

Masaryk established a national state, based on an anachronistic endorsement of the Hussite tradition as a kind of early Protestantism, which led to modern liberalism. The Hussite gentry of Bohemia had in fact actually strengthened its position and embarked on a resubjugation of the peasantry, to Masaryk's retrospective embarrassment. The fifteenth-century Bohemian gentry do not pass muster as good social democrats. They were not. Masaryk tried to reconstruct the past in such a way as to show that, first, there had been a major movement of mankind towards an individualist and rational order. The Czech nation had been an early harbinger of this movement, but was then deprived of its place, and he himself had finally restored proper order in 1918. In other words, in the end he came down on the side of a nationalism that was both linguistic and religious, but he did so in a subtle way which invoked universalist values.

Masaryk had his critics. The policy of the Republic established by Masaryk was basically that of an ethnically biased political unit which reproduced a state with minorities, and this of course would prove to be its weakness come the age of the terrible dictators. Masaryk, alas, had been wrong in his overall reading of world history. It was not an irreversible march to greater democracy, to rationality and enlightenment. It seemed, rather, to be going the other way, and the state he created, come the storm of Hitler and Stalin, was in no position to resist. Of course, two things happened: one was that, having lost the loyalty of its German citizens – this was very effectively used in its destruction by Hitler – there was nothing much he could have done which would have made any difference. But he also contributed, most unwittingly, to the victory of the second dictator who arrived in 1948. The syllogism which Masaryk had inculcated in an attempt to provide a deep philosophical justification for the creation of the Czech state ran as follows. History is a rational process in which right is might (not might is right: right actually manifests itself through might). Western democracy is right, but it is also very powerful – look at the events of 1918: the French army and the British navy dominate the world. So, not only are they right in their political values, they are also the strongest, so that if we behave like them (and the Czech Republic did in its institutions), then we shall also be strong and, above all, we shall be protected by them. So the major premise was: history is a rational process. The minor premise: the practitioners of the right values, namely those liberal democrats, the West, are strong and will protect those who join them. Therefore, we are safe.

Well, that syllogism received a dreadful drubbing in 1938 and 1940. In 1938 at Munich, it was very firmly demonstrated that the Western liberal democrats would *not* look after their own when it looked like being expensive. Munich was felt as a great betrayal.

They were interested in allies against the Germans, but only, it seemed, when allied action paid off. When it did not pay off the allies were unsupported. In 1940, when France collapsed with humiliating ease, it was demonstrated that not only were Western democrats and liberals treacherous, but they were weak. Yet the whole syllogism had been deeply internalized. By 1945 there was a new minor premise available to replace the old minor premise about Western democratic loyalty and strength. History could still be a rational process – there was a philosophy called Marxism which said as much, with great emphasis. But there was somebody else who was strong – witness the astonishing victory of the Red Army over the German machine, which, after all, had initially controlled the whole Continent of Europe, with the active support of a large number of countries, and the passive support of others. Nevertheless, Stalin and not Hitler had won in 1945. So the syllogism was still valid, only the minor premise had been got slightly wrong by Masaryk. A number of other things happened: 1945 offered a marvellous opportunity for solving at long last the tension between territorial nationalism and an ethno-linguistic one by expelling the Germans, which was done because Stalin endorsed it. There was no question of a nation which had expelled 3 million Germans, and was deeply frightened of Germans, and which at the same time vividly remembered Munich, resisting the communist coup of 1948. It was not resisted.

The rest of the story is this: by the late 1980s it looked as if a variant of the Masarykian philosophy of history was sound after all. The Marxist belief in the inevitability of communism was thoroughly undermined by the double defeat of communism in the Cold War, defeat both in the arms race and in the consumer race, and by the demonstration coming from the other end of the Eurasian Continent that Western capitalism could indeed be overtaken, not by Marxists but by another set of people. When the system collapsed from inside, another bloodless transition took place, and we end up with Czech capitalism, a reconversion to liberal values but more under the law of affluence – and, incidentally, a return to a baroque late-eighteenth-century Catholicism. Ethnic nationalism prevails. It had the opportunity to practise ethnic cleansing, and so you end up with an almost completely ethnically homogeneous population.

Let me take another country where the parallels are different and striking, namely Algeria, in some ways the most interesting and most symptomatic of Muslim countries. Let us take as our baseline 1830, and the almost accidental French conquest of that country. Algeria in 1830 was nominally part of the Ottoman Empire, meaning that a small number of Turks (second- or third-generation putative or real Turks) ruled, acting as overlords in the territory, a large part of which was self-administered by local mutual-assurance, mutual-assistance, groups normally known in the literature as tribes. The Turks were effective sovereigns, but in practice they did not interfere in the internal life of the greater part of the population. The state apparatus was astonishingly small. The French landed in 1830 and won the ensuing battle. The Turkish mamluks offered their services. The offer was declined, and they were shipped off to Istanbul. This small, effective, superimposed machinery worked on the basis of letting local communities run themselves. Some of them had to pay taxes, and some of them, more strategically located in the hills, did not. And the religion, in fact a kind of enthusiastic identification with Islam, was in effect a kind of paganism: saint worship, adherence to religious cults, recourse to ecstatic experience rather than scripturalism. If there were some 'proper' Muslims, educated urbanites, they constituted a very small proportion of the population, and their proportion was diminished by the French conquest.

The conquest had a superb commentator in the person of Alexis de Tocqueville, whose comments on Algeria are as perceptive as his comments on France and the United States. It leads to a curious reversal of the generalization about the difference between East and West. There is a striking contrast between the views of Machiavelli and the views of de Tocqueville. Both of them were right, yet they were diametrically opposed. Machiavelli's observation was that because the Eastern state is centralized it is difficult to conquer, because you are facing a very centralized force. But if you beat that centralized force in one battle, you then become the undisputed master and successor to power. It is quite different with the Western state, with its barons and local potentates, many of whom are discontented or in conflict with the crown. You can easily find allies among them, so some kind of entry is comparatively easy to achieve. But even if you win you will not get anywhere, because you still have a pluralist society to contend with. Tocqueville says exactly the opposite about Algeria. He was impressed by the fact that when the Turks left, the local dervish Abd el Kader emerged as the leader of the tribes against the French, and Tocqueville firmly warned that there was no point in expecting a decisive battle. There is no single battle you can win, and there is no single place you can occupy. You are facing a segmented society, which in defeat disintegrates in the victor's hands. You are dealing with a fragmented and pluralist society.

Well, both visions are true. Both Machiavelli and Tocqueville are right. It is just that they are looking at different aspects of Muslim society. Now Algeria was heavily segmented and less urbanized and less centralized than most other Muslim societies. The French conquest led to plantations and the eventual imposition of 1 million Europeans, counting the French, Italians, Spanish and Maltese: a pluralist society, with a fragmented and basically atomized, subdued, exploited and oppressed rural proletariat, with no national identity initially. It was slightly different in the hills where there are no settlers. But in most of the areas you have an atomized, oppressed, identity-lacking, rural proletariat, sharing what? The Islam they had known in the past was the Islam of saint worship, of saints associated with individual tribes, but the tribes had been eroded. They were no longer in existence. By the beginning of this century a reform movement begins which transforms this quasi-pagan, saint-worshipping, ecstatic Islam into a puritanical, scripturalist Islam. It gives this population, which has as yet no nationality, an identity – an identity based on religion, and based in particular on a puritanical religion. Without the reform movement, which really got going between the wars, and which totally changed the climate of the country, the subsequent Algerian revolution would not have been possible. For there was really no identity and the religion which did give them an identity was a highly localized religion. By shifting from high Islam, which could not be politically viable and effective in the modem world, it could acquire an identity for the atomized, mobile population. So an oppressed peasantry found its identity in a religion which differentiated it from its oppressors, but which in order to perform that function had to reform itself, and present itself in rather puritanical form.

After the victory of the nationalist movement, the new regime reproduced the kind of system which was common in the Middle East, and had been present in Algeria before the French conquest: there was a division of power between a small ruling class of janissaries and mamluks, now technocrats, who control the big things (state, gas, oil), and who leave religion, legitimacy and culture to the newly created petit bourgeoisie which had replaced the

French in the towns along the coast. Here, as in Bohemia, the war ends with ethnic cleansing. In Bohemia it had resulted from a political decision. In Algeria, the extremists on either side in the conflict committed enough atrocities, no doubt knowing what they were doing, to ensure that the other side was provoked into doing the same. And so there was no compromise possible. As in Bohemia, and as in Ireland too, there were formal attempts to create in Algeria a non-territorial, non-ethnic, non-religious nationality. The official policy of the liberation movement during the war was that after the war all ethnic groups should be given a secure place. How sincerely intended it was is not clear: it had to be the official policy in those circumstances. But the extremists in the liberation movement ensured that this would not be put into practice. So there, as in Bohemia (Bohemia in 1945, Algeria in 1962), ethnic cleansing occurred.

Now the rest of the story is curious, and presents a contrast to Ireland. The re-establishment of the old kind of system where military technocrats and official administrators rule and leave religion and petty trade to others, does not work any more. In the past, just as in Iran, religious movements ultimately had to make do with monarchy, however much the logic of the religion might imply a republic: they still needed a monarch with a tribal backing. It had been a kind of compromise between the prevailing religious absolutism and the realities of power. Under modern conditions, and with modern technology, you no longer need the tribal base. In Algeria, the mamluks did take over. At first, according to the climate of the times, one found leftist developmental ideology, and aspirations to a leadership position in the Third World. The revolutionary and radical tendencies made it an object of left-wing pilgrimages, but left-wing pilgrims tended to be a bit disappointed. There was a curious compromise in Algeria between a Third-Worldist, leftist, developmental ideology of the early years, and a respect for a religion which had forged the nation and which could not be ignored. Under modern conditions, the situation is different: at the moment the fundamentalists, those who identify with a high religious culture, are clearly winning. They won the elections, and they would be in power had the mamluks not used force to suppress them; and how long they will succeed in doing so is anyone's guess.

Here you have two societies, each pluralist in the beginning, each having to undergo the brutalities of ethnic cleansing, and each using religion in a complicated and tortuous way to redefine the nation. The parallels and the contrasts are striking.

Note

1   This is a version of a lecture given at Queen's University, Belfast on 7 March 1994.

Index